ACT® Mastery Math

Teacher Manual – Part 1

4th Edition

MasteryPrep

Inquiries concerning this publication should be mailed to:

MasteryPrep
7117 Florida Blvd.
Baton Rouge, LA 70806

MasteryPrep is a trade name and/or trademark of Ring Publications LLC.

10 9 8 7 6 5 4 3 2 1

ISBN-13: 978-1-948846-10-3

Table of Contents

ACT® Mastery Math

Through the ACT Mastery Math curriculum, students have the opportunity to review the skills that they struggle with most, thus preparing them for any challenges they may encounter on the ACT math test. The course includes lessons carefully constructed around only the math topics that appear most frequently on the test. If your students can master these skills, they are well on their way to increasing their ACT scores.

ACT Math Subtest Overview

Number of questions: 60 questions
Amount of time given: 60 minutes
Score range: 1–36

The math subtest is designed to measure a student's ability to understand a broad range of mathematical topics. There are six types of items on the math test.

Pre-Algebra: 14 out of 60 questions are pre-algebra. These are word problems that require students to perform basic mathematical tasks. Students might need to add, subtract, multiply, or divide, find a percent, or work out an average.

Elementary Algebra: 10 out of 60 questions are elementary algebra. These basic algebra problems can be solved by using the FOIL method, by factoring, or by setting up an equation with variables.

Plane Geometry: 14 out of 60 questions are plane geometry. These problems ask students to solve problems involving area, perimeter, volume, angles, triangles, and other shapes.

Trigonometry: 4 out of 60 questions are trigonometry. These problems require students to use trig functions. 2 out of the 4 questions are basic trig problems that require students to know how to use sine, cosine, and tangent.

Intermediate Algebra: 9 out of 60 questions are intermediate algebra. These problems involve complex inequalities, complex numbers, systems of equations, and matrices.

Coordinate Geometry: 9 out of 60 questions are coordinate geometry. These problems involve coordinate planes, slopes, *y*-intercepts, and coordinates.

Pacing: There is an inherent order of difficulty on the math test. As a result, students are best advised to move quickly—but accurately—through the first 30 questions and to spend more time on the last 30.

Students should attempt the sections in order, from beginning to end, working questions as they go. They should be prepared to make educated guesses on questions they find difficult, even early on in the test. Students should be especially prepared to have difficulty working the last 10 questions, though they should still find time to attempt them and leave nothing blank, no matter the circumstance. Students should not spend more than 2 minutes on any question, averaging 60 seconds per question.

Chapter Anatomy

Entrance Ticket
Role: The entrance ticket is designed for three purposes. First, it serves as a way to begin the class. Second, the activity provides a method for informal assessment. Third, it primes the students for the lesson content by exposing the skills and material they have not yet mastered.

Implementation: Direct students to complete the entrance ticket as they come into class each day. Have the question displayed on the slide so that students can begin as soon as they enter the classroom, even if the bell has not yet rung. Give them 2-5 minutes to complete the entrance ticket, depending on the activity. Review the activity together as a class before moving to the learning targets and self-assessment.

Learning Targets
Role: The learning targets are designed to give students a goal for each lesson. They also serve as guideposts for the teacher as the lesson is taught.

Implementation: Review the learning targets at the beginning of each lesson. Refer to the learning targets as the lesson is taught to give the students a sense of progression. Be sure to review them one last time before the class ends.

Self-Assessment

Role: The self-assessment serves as a moment of reflection for the students. It allows them to consider their incoming knowledge and encourages them to set a daily learning goal. It also functions as informal assessment of the students prior to the lesson, which can help guide the teaching depth.

Implementation: Have students rate their knowledge of the material on the self-assessment page after reviewing the learning targets. Instruct the students to reassess themselves after the completion of the exit ticket to chart their daily progress.

Quick Check

Role: The quick check is designed to briefly review important material that is prerequisite knowledge for the lesson. Students should be familiar with this content. If they are not, the teacher will need to integrate the quick check into the lesson content. The quick check also contains a review of vocabulary pertinent to the lesson.

Implementation: Review the quick check material after the students have assessed themselves. Spend no more than 5 minutes on the quick check, and focus on informally assessing students as they respond to the prompts. If students struggle during this portion, spend additional time reviewing the content during the lesson content.

Lesson Elements

Role: The lesson elements contain the bulk of instructional time during any given lesson. They are designed to address the content of the ACT in ways that are approachable by students of all skill levels. The lesson elements contain enough content and flexibility to support differentiation in the class based on previous data and the informal assessments carried out at the start of class time during the entrance ticket, self-assessment, and quick check.

Implementation: Each lesson element has its own particular implementation, but in general, the lessons vary from teacher-led instruction or discussions to group activities or individual work. Each lesson element contains material designed to build up to the ACT practice sets contained at the end of the lesson.

Practice Sets

Role: The practice sets are authentic recreations of ACT practice questions based on MasteryPrep's research. They are designed to build subject mastery on the ACT. Each lesson contains five practice sets, which each contain three questions. Be sure to emphasize that these questions are at the ACT's level of difficulty.

Implementation: The practice sets can be used in various ways. Primarily, the sets should be implemented throughout the lesson so that students can begin to measure their progress in a tangible, ACT-centric way. For example, after a lesson element is completed, have the students try a practice set. This will help them realize their progress and reveal any further skills needed that will be covered in the next lesson topic. You can also skip straight to the practice sets during the lesson should students exhibit mastery of the lesson content.

Each practice set should be timed for 3 minutes. Ultimately, no additional time should be given so that students can develop pacing skills in addition to content skills. If pacing is a major issue, though, students can be given extended time, gradually working up to ACT pacing. To ensure good pacing practice, be sure to monitor the time for each set and do not allow students to work on the next set.

Exit Ticket

Role: The exit tickets are to be used as formal assessments of student progress. They can be scored and analyzed to assess overall student proficiency of each family of ACT questions, which allows teachers to adjust the class accordingly.

Implementation: After completing the lesson, students complete the exit ticket individually. Each ticket should be timed for 3 minutes. No additional time should be given in order to produce the most accurate results. Review the correct answers and demonstrate how to solve for them. After completing the questions, students should trade papers and grade each other's answers as you provide the answers and explanations.

Cover Art Caption

Role: The cover art is intended to provide a creative depiction of the topic at hand. It serves to introduce students to challenging content in a way that is approachable and not intimidating.

Implementation: After completing the lesson and exit ticket, close the lesson by instructing the students to return to the cover art. Have them write a caption for the lesson in the space provided.

The caption should be a one-sentence summary of the lesson, a main rule or tip they want to remember, or an explanation of how the picture relates to the lesson topic. Students will get the most out of this exercise if the rule they select as the caption is the most essential to success on the ACT practice questions and the exit ticket they just completed. If there is additional time, students can share and compare their captions with the class. On review days, students can return to the captions from all of the lessons to remind themselves of the most important points they want to remember.

Glossary

Role: The glossary contains all of the vocabulary words necessary for the lessons and the ACT math test. Students will review different definitions throughout the lessons and will see multiple iterations of the definitions in order to produce the strongest understanding. The glossary represents the definitive definitions, so students can continue to review vocabulary throughout the course.

Implementation: The glossary exists primarily as an additional resource for students, but it can also be used to emphasize vocabulary in each class. If there is sufficient time, ask students to recall prior definitions and have them check their answers against the definitions in the glossary to ensure that they are on point.

Linear Equations

This lesson will show how to solve linear equations with one variable and review concepts such as distribution and isolating single variables.

ACT Standards:

A 202. Solve equations in the form $x + a = b$, where a and b are whole numbers or decimals

A 302. Solve one-step equations to get integer or decimal answers

A 403. Solve routine first-degree equations

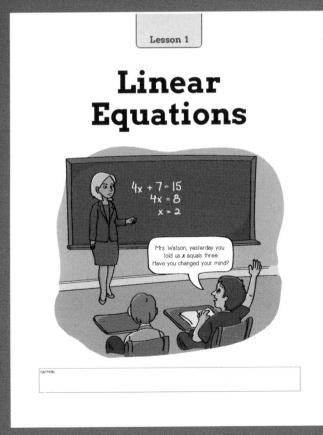

Student Page 7

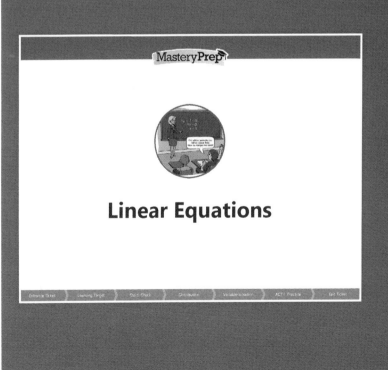

1.1 Entrance Ticket

▶ Have students try the following three ACT practice questions. Students should work independently. Once the entrance ticket has been completed, review the questions with the students and have them share their answers. Give students the correct answers to the questions, as well as a step-by-step demonstration of how to solve the problems, but do not go into detailed explanation. This will serve as an introduction to the lesson content but is not intended to be the main lesson.

1. **The correct answer is E.** Solve for x by isolating it.

$$-3x + 7 = -17$$

$$-3x = -24$$

$$x = 8$$

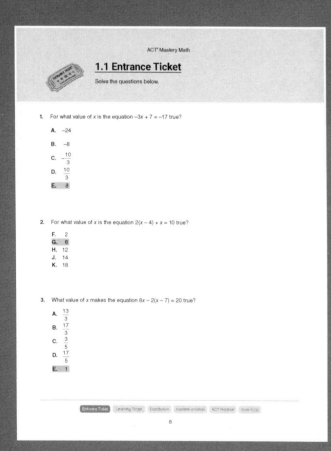

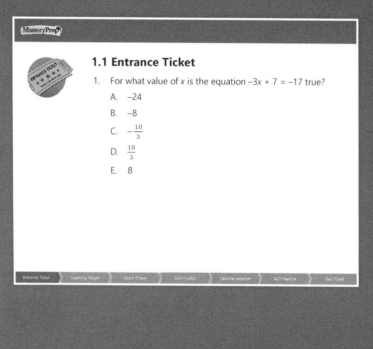

Student Page 8

1.1 Entrance Ticket

2. **The correct answer is G.** Solve for x by isolating it.

    $2(x - 4) + x = 10$

    $2x - 8 + x = 10$

    $3x - 8 = 10$

    $3x = 18$

    $x = 6$

MasteryPrep

1.1 Entrance Ticket

2. For what value of x is the equation $2(x - 4) + x = 10$ true?

    F.   2

    G.   6

    H.   12

    J.   14

    K.   18

| Entrance Ticket | Learning Target | Quick Check | Distribution | Variable Isolation | ACT Practice | Exit Ticket |

1.1 Entrance Ticket

3. **The correct answer is E.** Solve for x by isolating it.

   $8x - 2(x - 7) = 20$

   $8x - 2x + 14 = 20$

   $6x = 6$

   $x = 1$

MasteryPrep

1.1 Entrance Ticket

3. What value of x makes the equation $8x - 2(x - 7) = 20$ true?

   A. $\dfrac{13}{3}$

   B. $\dfrac{17}{3}$

   C. $\dfrac{3}{5}$

   D. $\dfrac{17}{5}$

   E. 1

Entrance Ticket · Learning Target · Quick Check · Distribution · Variable Isolation · ACT Practice · Exit Ticket

1.2 Learning Target

► Review the learning target with your students, displayed on the slide and in their workbooks.

► After reviewing the learning target, ask students to assess their knowledge and confidence level on this target. They should rate themselves on a scale of 1 to 4, with 1 being not confident or uncertain, and 4 being completely confident or certain. They should circle this number in the designated section of their workbooks.

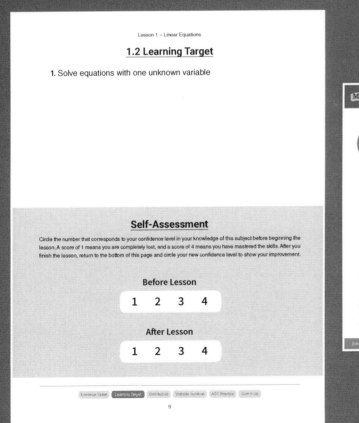

Student Page 9

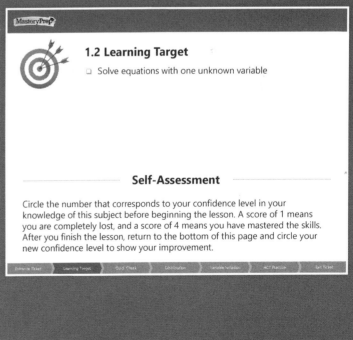

1.2 Quick Check

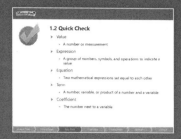

▶ Teacher Dialogue: **Define *value*.**

   Value: A number or measurement

▶ Teacher Dialogue: **Define *expression*.**

   Expression: A group of numbers, symbols, and operations to indicate a value

▶ Teacher Dialogue: **Define *equation*.**

   Equation: Two mathematical expressions set equal to each other

▶ Teacher Dialogue: **Define *term*.**

   Term: A number, variable, or product of a number and a variable

▶ Teacher Dialogue: **Define *coefficient*.**

   Coefficient: The number next to a variable

▶ Show students the illustration of the Lone Variable on the slide.

▶ Teacher Dialogue: **When the ACT asks you to find the value of a single variable inside an equation, you should think of it as the Lone Variable. No matter what is going on in the equation, the Lone Variable stands alone.**

▶ Go through the following questions with students, giving them a few chances to offer their guesses before revealing the answer.

▶ Teacher Dialogue: **What do you think it means to call the variable the *Lone Variable*?**

   It means that you need to isolate the variable in an equation.

▶ Teacher Dialogue: **What are some of the ways you can get the variable all alone?**

   Dividing coefficients, subtracting or adding other terms, or multiplying by reciprocals.

▶ Teacher Dialogue: **Are there any steps that need to come before trying to isolate the variable?**

   Yes, steps like combining like terms or distributing.

1.2 Quick Check

▶ Write the following example on the board. Ask students to provide feedback on each step in solving the equation.

$3(x + 2) - 4 = x + 6$

$3x + 6 - 4 = x + 6$

$2x + 2 = 6$

$2x = 4$

$x = 2$

▶ Teacher Dialogue: **What are some general rules you can come up with when solving these types of equations?**

1. Distribute anything possible.

2. Combine like terms on each side of the equation.

3. Move all of the terms with a variable to the left side of the equation.

4. Move all of the terms without a variable to the right side of the equation.

5. Divide on both sides by the coefficient of the variable.

1.3.1 Distribution

▶ Teacher Dialogue: **As you can all see, the first step in isolating the variable is to distribute. That means the ACT is going to complicate the distribution as much as possible. There are a few ways the test can do this, but let's first talk about the rules for distribution.**

▶ Show the students the following expression:

$$4(2x + 3)$$

▶ Teacher Dialogue: **What step is involved in the distribution of this problem?**

Multiply the two terms inside the parentheses by 4.

▶ Students write down the step needed and show their work in the first blank space in their workbook.

Student Page 10

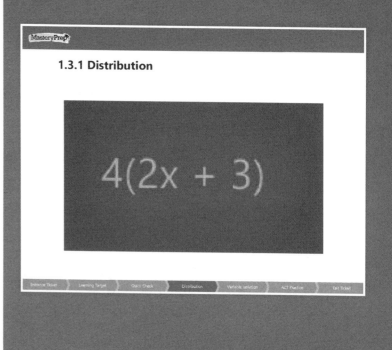

1.3.1 Distribution

▸ Show the students the following expression:

$$\frac{(3x + 6)}{3}$$

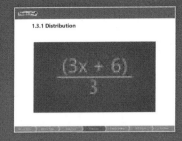

▸ Teacher Dialogue: **What step is involved in distribution in this problem?**

Divide both terms inside the parentheses by 3 OR multiply all terms by $\frac{1}{3}$.

▸ Students write down the step needed and show their work in the second blank space in their workbooks.

▸ Show the students the following expression:

$$\frac{-2(3x - 6)}{-6}$$

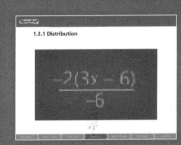

▸ Teacher Dialogue: **What steps are involved in distribution in this problem?**

First, distribute the −2 across the two terms inside the parentheses and then distribute the $-\frac{1}{6}$ across the two resulting terms, or multiply all terms by $\frac{2}{6}$.

▸ Students write down the steps needed and show their work in the third blank space in their workbooks.

> **Two Wrongs Make a Right:** Two negatives are the same as a positive. Look out for negative signs and treat them with extra precaution. Many careless errors are made when negative signs are overlooked.

▸ Teacher Dialogue: **Remember to always show your work, and you'll be less likely to miss negative signs. The ACT is specifically designed to trick you into making errors. Showing your work and looking out for negative signs are incredibly important in solving linear equations problems.**

> Two Wrongs Make a Right and Show Your Work. These two tips go hand in hand. You will be less likely to miss negative signs if you show your work. These methods help with any question that requires a lot of manipulation, but they are incredibly important for linear equations.

1.3.2 Variable Isolation

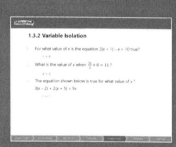

Student Page 11

▶ Show students the following problems on the slide for them to work through.

1. For what value of x is the equation $2(x + 1) - x = 10$ true?

    $2x + 2 - x = 10$

    $x + 2 = 10$

    $x = 8$

2. What is the value of x when $\dfrac{3x}{2} + 8 = 11$?

    $\dfrac{3x}{2} = 3$

    $3x = 6$

    $x = 2$

3. The equation shown below is true for what value of x ?

    $3(x - 2) + 2(x + 5) = 9x$

    $3x - 6 + 2x + 10 = 9x$

    $5x + 4 = 9x$

    $4 = 4x$

    $x = 1$

> **Spotting Linear Equations:** If the question asks for the value of the only variable in the equation and there are no exponents, you know you're dealing with a linear equation question and need to isolate the variable.

1.3.2 Variable Isolation

► Teacher Dialogue: **Put away your pencils and close your book. You will now have two minutes to solve the following equation without using pencils, paper, or any other way to show your work.**

$$\frac{-5(2x - 4)}{2} = 2(2x - 1) - 6x + 3$$

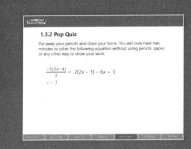

$$\frac{-10x + 20}{2} = 4x - 2 - 6x + 3$$

$-5x + 10 = 4x - 2 - 6x + 3$

$10 + 2 - 3 = 5x + 4x - 6x$

$9 = 3x$

$3 = x$

This example gives students an idea of how much easier these problems are when you show your work.

> **Show Your Work:** Always show your work when isolating the variable. This will help you make fewer calculation errors. It is especially important to rewrite the entire equation before taking any of the steps for isolation.

1.4 ACT Practice

▶ Have students work on questions from the ACT practice sets here. Pacing should be 3 minutes per practice set or 60 seconds per question.

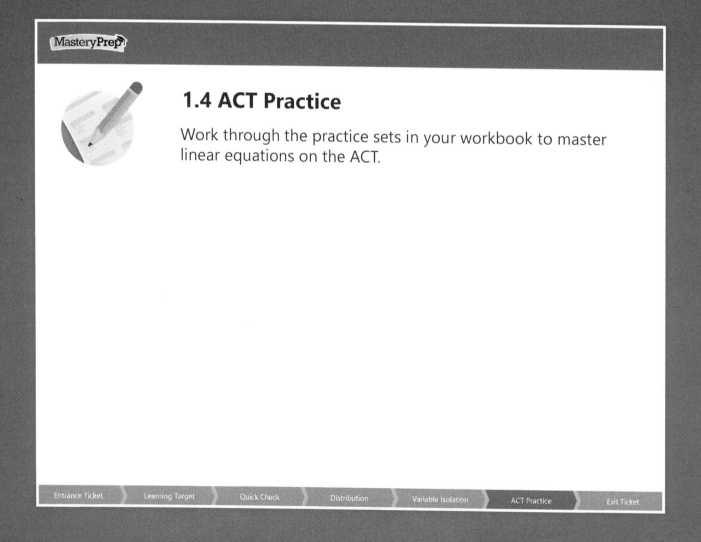

1.4.1 Set One

1. For what value of x is the equation $3(x + 2) - 2x = 12$ true?

   A. 6
   B. 10
   C. 12
   D. 14
   E. 18

1. **The correct answer is A.** Solve by isolating x.

$$3(x + 2) - 2x = 12$$
$$3x + 6 - 2x = 12$$
$$x = 6$$

2. If $5(x - 6) = -8$, then $x = ?$

   F. $-\dfrac{38}{5}$

   G. $-\dfrac{8}{5}$

   H. $-\dfrac{2}{5}$

   J. $\dfrac{2}{5}$

   K. $\dfrac{22}{5}$

2. **The correct answer is K.** Solve by isolating x.

$$5(x - 6) = -8$$
$$5x - 30 = -8$$
$$5x = 22$$
$$x = \frac{22}{5}$$

3. If $3(x - 7) = -22$, then $x = ?$

   A. $-\dfrac{43}{3}$

   B. -5

   C. $-\dfrac{1}{3}$

   D. $\dfrac{1}{3}$

   E. 5

3. **The correct answer is C.** Solve by isolating x.

$$3(x - 7) = -22$$
$$3x - 21 = -22$$
$$3x = -1$$
$$x = -\frac{1}{3}$$

1.4.2 Set Two

4. The equation shown below is true for what value of x?

$$2(x - 3) - 4(x - 6) = 7x$$

F. $-\dfrac{18}{5}$

G. -2

H. $\;2$

J. $\dfrac{18}{5}$

K. $\dfrac{11}{2}$

4. **The correct answer is H.** Solve by isolating x.

$2(x - 3) - 4(x - 6) = 7x$

$2x - 6 - 4x + 24 = 7x$

$-2x + 18 = 7x$

$18 = 9x$

$x = 2$

---

5. What is the solution to the equation $5x - (x + 4) = 2$?

A. $-\dfrac{1}{2}$

B. $\dfrac{1}{2}$

C. $\;1$

D. $\;\dfrac{3}{2}$

E. $\;3$

5. The correct answer is D. Solve by isolating x.

$5x - (x + 4) = 2$

$5x - x - 4 = 2$

$4x = 6$

$x = \dfrac{6}{4} = \dfrac{3}{2}$

---

6. What value of x makes the equation $6x - (5x + 7) = 10$ true?

F. $\dfrac{4}{11}$

G. $\dfrac{17}{11}$

H. $\;3$

J. $\;4$

K. $\;17$

6. **The correct answer is K.** Solve by isolating x.

$6x - 1(5x + 7) = 10$

$6x - 5x - 7 = 10$

$x = 17$

Student Page 13

1.4.3 Set Three

7. What is the value of x when $\dfrac{2x}{3}+12=8$?
   A. −6
   B. −2
   C. 2
   D. 6
   E. 30

7. **The correct answer is A.** Solve by isolating x.

$$\frac{2x}{3} + 12 = 8$$

$$\frac{2x}{3} = -4$$

$$2x = -12$$

$$x = -6$$

8. If $\dfrac{5x}{2}+3=18$, then $x=$?

   F. $\dfrac{15}{2}$

   G. $\dfrac{75}{2}$

   H. 3

   J. 6

   K. 15

8. **The correct answer is J.** Solve by isolating x.

$$\frac{5x}{2} + 3 = 18$$

$$\frac{5x}{2} = 15$$

$$5x = 30$$

$$x = 6$$

9. If $6x + 4 = 20 - 2x$, then $x =$?
   A. 2
   B. 6
   C. 8
   D. 16
   E. 24

9. **The correct answer is A.** Solve by isolating x.

$$6x + 4 = 20 - 2x$$

$$8x = 16$$

$$x = 2$$

1.4.4 Set Four

10. If $3x - 1 = 11$, then $2x = ?$

   F. $\dfrac{20}{3}$

   G. 2

   H. 4

   J. 8

   K. 72

10. The correct answer is J. Solve by isolating x and then multiplying by 2.

$3x - 1 = 11$

$3x = 12$

$x = 4$

$2x = 8$

11. If $5x + 2 = 27$, then $3x = ?$

   A. 3
   B. 5
   C. 15
   D. 45
   E. 75

11. The correct answer is C. Solve by isolating x and then multiplying by 3.

$5x + 2 = 27$

$5x = 25$

$x = 5$

$3x = 15$

12. If $2x - 18 = -5$, then $2x = ?$

   F. -23

   G. $-\dfrac{23}{2}$

   H. $\dfrac{13}{4}$

   J. $\dfrac{13}{2}$

   K. 13

12. The correct answer is K. Solve by isolating x and then multiplying by 2.

$2x - 18 = -5$

$2x = 13$

$x = \dfrac{13}{2}$

$2x = 13$

1.4.5 Set Five

13. For what value of x is $11x - 5 = 7x + 19$ true?

   A. $\dfrac{7}{9}$

   B. $\dfrac{7}{2}$

   C. 6

   D. 24

   E. 96

13. **The correct answer is C.** Solve by isolating x.

$$11x - 5 = 7x + 19$$
$$4x = 24$$
$$x = 6$$

---

14. What is the solution of the equation $-4x = -6(8 + x)$?

   F. -24

   G. $-\dfrac{24}{5}$

   H. $\dfrac{24}{5}$

   J. $\dfrac{48}{5}$

   K. 24

14. **The correct answer is F.** Solve by isolating x.

$$-4x = -6(8 + x)$$
$$-4x = -48 + -6x$$
$$2x = -48$$
$$x = -24$$

---

15. If $\dfrac{2x}{3} + \dfrac{x}{2} = \dfrac{1}{6}$, then $x = $?

   A. $\dfrac{1}{30}$

   B. $\dfrac{1}{15}$

   C. $\dfrac{1}{7}$

   D. $\dfrac{1}{5}$

   E. $\dfrac{1}{3}$

15. **The correct answer is C.** Solve by isolating x.

$$\dfrac{2x}{3} + \dfrac{x}{2} = \dfrac{1}{6}$$
$$4x + 3x = 1$$
$$7x = 1$$
$$x = \dfrac{1}{7}$$

Lesson 1 – Linear Equations

Sum It Up

Linear Equations

Rules for Isolation

1. Distribute everything possible.
2. Combine like terms on each side of the equation.
3. Move all of the terms with a variable to the left-hand side of the equation.
4. Move all of the terms without a variable to the right-hand side of the equation.
5. Divide both sides by the coefficient of the variable.

Tips and Techniques

Two Wrongs Make a Right: Two negatives are the same as a positive. Look out for negative signs and treat them with extra precaution. Many careless errors are made when negative signs are overlooked.

Spotting Linear Equations: If the question asks for the value of the only variable in the equation and there are no exponents, you know you're dealing with a linear equation question and need to isolate the variable.

Show Your Work: Always show your work when isolating the variable. This will help you make fewer calculation errors. It is especially important to rewrite the entire equation before taking any of the steps for isolation.

Entrance Ticket   Learning Target   Distribution   Variable Isolation   ACT Practice   Sum It Up

1.5 Exit Ticket

► Students complete the three questions on their exit ticket.

Students are timed 3 minutes for the three questions (60 seconds per question). There is no break between questions.

Lesson 1 – Linear Equations

Name _____   Date _____

Exit Ticket

1. For what value of x is the equation $2(x + 7) = 3(x + 11)$ true?

   A. 19
   B. −4
   C. 18
   D. 19
   E. 47

   DO YOUR FIGURING HERE.

2. What is the value of x that satisfies the equation $3(x − 2) = 6x + 5$?

   F. $\frac{11}{3}$

   G. $-\frac{7}{3}$

   H. −1

   J. 1

   K. $\frac{7}{3}$

3. If $5(x − 3) + 11 = 6$, what is the value of x ?

   A. $-\frac{2}{5}$

   B. $\frac{32}{5}$

   C. −4

   D. 2

   E. 4

   Answered Correctly
   ____ / 3

MasteryPrep

1.5 Exit Ticket

Solve the questions on your exit ticket.

Entrance Ticket Learning Target Quiz Check Distribution Variable Isolation ACT Practice Exit Ticket

1.5 Exit Ticket Review

▶ Students work the first question.

1. **The correct answer is A.** Solve by isolating x.

    $2(x + 7) = 3(x + 11)$

    $2x + 14 = 3x + 33$

    $-19 = x$

1.5 Exit Ticket Review

1. For what value of x is the equation
    $2(x + 7) = 3(x + 11)$ true?

    A. -19

    B. -4

    C. 18

    D. 19

    E. 47

Entrance Ticket　Learning Target　Quick Check　Distribution　Variable Isolation　ACT Practice　Exit Ticket

1.5 Exit Ticket Review

▶ Students work the second question.

2. **The correct answer is F.** Solve by isolating x.

$3(x - 2) = 6x + 5$

$3x - 6 = 6x + 5$

$-11 = 3x$

$\dfrac{-11}{3} = x$

MasteryPrep

1.5 Exit Ticket Review

2. What is the value of x that satisfies the equation $3(x - 2) = 6x + 5$?

F. $-\dfrac{11}{3}$

G. $-\dfrac{7}{3}$

H. -1

J. 1

K. $\dfrac{7}{3}$

Entrance Ticket Learning Target Quick Check Distribution Variable Isolation ACT Practice Exit Ticket

1.5 Exit Ticket Review

▶ Students work the third question.

3. **The correct answer is D.** Solve by isolating x.

$5(x - 3) + 11 = 6$

$5x - 15 + 11 = 6$

$5x - 4 = 6$

$5x = 10$

$x = 2$

▶ After all three questions are completed, students exchange papers. Solve the three exit items step by step on the board. Students grade using their red pens and then return papers to their classmates.

▶ After solving the three exit items, revisit the learning target slide. Students again assess their knowledge and confidence on the same 1 to 4 scale that they used at the beginning of the lesson. Students write this number in the designated area at the start of the lesson in their workbooks, along with any comments or questions they might have.

▶ Finally, to close the lesson, have students return to the cover page of the lesson and write a caption for the picture there. The caption should be a one-sentence summary of the lesson, a main rule or tip they want to remember, or an explanation of how the picture relates to the topic. If there is additional time, students can share and compare their captions with the class.

Systems of Equations

This lesson will cover how to solve systems of equations. Students will learn techniques such as substitution, addition of equations, and how to manipulate equations into new forms.

ACT Standards:

A 604. Solve systems of two linear equations

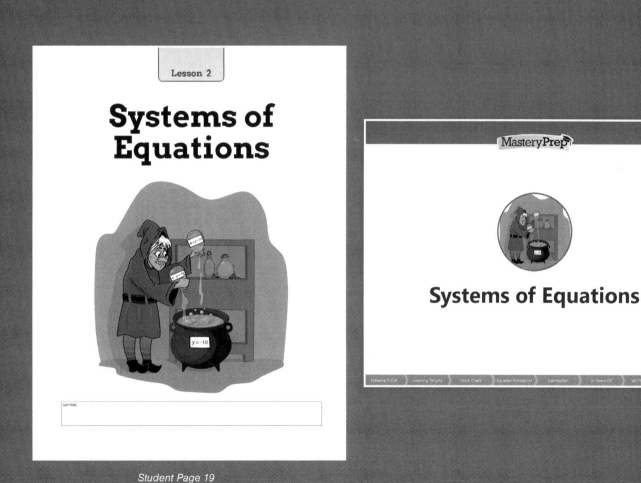

Student Page 19

2.1 Entrance Ticket

Student Page 20

► Have the students consider the statements on the slide and write a paragraph explaining what condition is necessary in order for all three of the statements to make sense and why.

1. When I study hard, I pass my tests.

2. When I study hard at the last minute, I have to stay up late.

3. When I study hard but don't get enough sleep, I don't always do well on the test the next day.

► After the exit ticket is completed, call on a few students to offer their answers and lead a class discussion.

Sometimes in life there will be two or more situations that all share some required condition to be true. In order for each of the above statements to be true, the required condition that must be present is that the person must be studying hard. Each part of each statement could be thought of as a variable since it can either be true or false.

► Have the class consider the middle statement, "When I study hard at the last minute, I have to stay up late."

► Teacher Dialogue: **What would the variables of this statement be?**

The variables of the statement would be "Am I studying hard?" and "Is it the last minute?" since these are the conditions that determine whether you must stay up late.

► Teacher Dialogue: **A system of mathematical equations is the same way; in order for multiple equations to be simultaneously true, x will equal the same thing in each equation.**

2.2 Learning Targets

▶ Review learning targets with your students, displayed on the slide and in their workbooks.

▶ After reviewing the learning targets, ask students to assess their knowledge and confidence level on these targets. They should rate themselves on a scale of 1 to 4, with 1 being not confident or uncertain, and 4 being completely confident or certain. They should circle this number in the designated section of their workbooks.

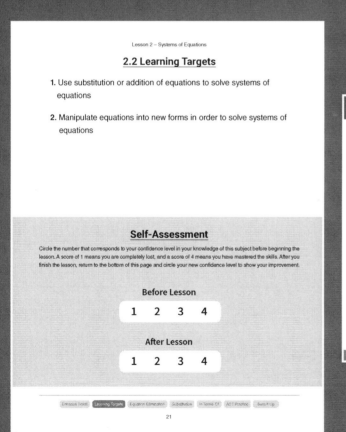

Student Page 21

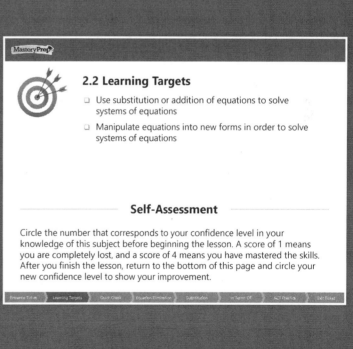

2.2 Quick Check

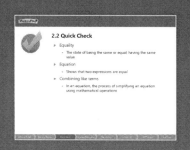

▶ Teacher Dialogue: **Define *equality*.**

Equality: The state of being the same or equal; having the same value

▶ Teacher Dialogue: **Define *equation*.**

Equation: Shows that two expressions are equal

▶ Teacher Dialogue: **Define *combining like terms*.**

Combining like terms: In an equation, the process of simplifying an equation using mathematical operations

When combining like terms, numbers can only be combined with numbers, and variable quantities must have the same variable, including any exponent the variable may have.

▶ Try a couple of examples. Write the equation on the board and have the students do their work on their whiteboards.

▶ Teacher Dialogue: **Combine $7 + 4 + 3x + 5x$.**

$7 + 4 = 11$

$3x + 5x = 8x$

The expression simplifies to $11 + 8x$.

▶ Teacher Dialogue: **Combine $3x + 2x + 2x^2$.**

$3x + 2x = 5x$

$2x^2$ does not have any like terms.

The expression simplifies to $5x + 2x^2$.

2.2 Quick Check

▶ Teacher Dialogue: **In many questions on the ACT, you will be required to work with and combine multiple equations. When multiple equations are being worked with at the same time, it is known as a *system of equations*.**

▶ Teacher Dialogue: **The ACT will ask you for a certain value and require that you use *both* equations presented to get the answer. How do you approach solving algebraic equations versus solving systems of equations? What is the difference?**

When working with algebraic equations, such as if you are trying to determine the value of x in the equation $15 = x + 3$, you would subtract 3 from both sides in order to isolate the variable on one side of the equation. For a system of equations, however, it will be necessary to solve for x (or other variables) in multiple equations. The good news is that these systems of equations are solved in pretty much the same way, by isolating the variable on one side of each equation.

▶ Teacher Dialogue: **What are the two ways of solving a system of equations for a particular value?**

The first is to add the two equations together, and the second is to use a technique called substitution. In each method, the point is to get the desired variable by itself in order to determine its value.

2.3.1 Equation Elimination

▶ The first technique to review with the class will be addition/subtraction of equations. Begin by showing the following two equations on the slide. Have students copy them into the example section of their workbook.

$$4x + y = 14$$
$$x - y = 16$$

▶ Teacher Dialogue: **What do you notice about the y values in the equations?**

They have the same coefficient (1) and opposite signs.

▶ Teacher Dialogue: **What would happen if you added the y values together?**

They would equal zero.

▶ Teacher Dialogue: **The objective is to get one of the variables by itself. If you were to add the two equations together, the variable y in each equation would be cancelled out and you would be left with only one variable, for which you are then able to easily solve.**

$$4x + y = 14$$
$$+\ \underline{x\ \ \ y - 16}$$
$$5x + 0 = 30 \text{ or } 5x = 30 \text{ then } x = 6$$

▶ Students should copy the example with the work into their workbooks.

▶ Teacher Dialogue: **If you then want to know what value of y makes both of the equations true, what do you need to do?**

Students just need to plug x into either of the equations and solve it for y.

Let the class know that it should not matter which equation they use; they should get the same value from both. This can be used as a means of checking their work. If the equations do not equal the same value, they know they have made an error.

$4(6) + y = 14$	OR	$(6) - y = 16$
$24 + y = 14$		$6 = 16 + y$
$y = 14 - 24$		$6 - 16 = y$
$y = -10$		$y = -10$

On the ACT, some questions will only ask for one of the variables, while others will ask the value of all of the variables.

▶ Students should copy the example and the work into their workbooks.

▶ Teacher Dialogue: **Why are you able to add the equations? Why does this strategy work?**

Because you can always add the same amount to both sides of an equation.

2.3.1 Equation Elimination

► Have the students try the following examples in their workbooks, solving each example for both variables.

1. $-2x + y = 14$

   $2x + 8y = 4$

   Add the equations together to get $9y = 18$. Then, divide both sides by 9 to solve for $y = 2$. Plug the value of y into either equation and solve for x:

   $-2x + 2 = 14$

   $-2x = 12$

   $x = -6$

   Solution: $(-6,2)$

2. $2x + y \quad = 14$

   $3x - y + 4 = 15$

   Even though one of the equations has an extra term ($+ 4$), you are still able to add the equations and solve them as normal. Adding the equations gives you $5x + 4 = 29$. Subtracting 4 from both sides gives $5x = 25$, and then dividing both sides by 5 gives $x = 5$. Plug $x = 5$ back in to either equation to solve for y:

   $2(5) + y = 14$

   $10 + y = 14$

   $y = 4$

   Solution: $(5,4)$

3. $9 - 2x = y$

   $3x - y = 16$

   Before you're able to add these two equations together, they must be rearranged so that both are in the same format. Rearrange the bottom equation by subtracting $3x$ from both sides. Then rewrite the first equation so that it begins with y. The equations then become the following:

   $y = 9 - 2x$

   $-y = 16 - 3x$

   Adding the equations gives $0 = 25 - 5x$ or $5x = 25$. Divide each side by 5 to get $x = 5$. Plug $x = 5$ into either equation to solve for y:

   $y = 9 - 2(5)$

   $y = 9 - 10$

   $y = -1$

   Solution: $(5,-1)$

► Once the class has worked through the examples above, let them know it's time to increase the level of difficulty.

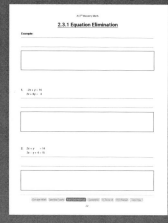

Student Page 22

2.3.1 Equation Elimination

▶ Teacher Dialogue: **Not every system of equations has a variable with opposite signs that will conveniently cancel out when the equations are added together, as *y* did in the examples we just worked through. When this is the case, you have to *make* them cancel out by changing the numbers in some way. Sometimes one or more of the equations needs to be multiplied by a constant before adding to allow one of the variables to be cancelled.**

▶ Work through the fourth example with the class by writing the solution on the board.

▶ Teacher Dialogue: **Even though each equation has an *x* term, they will not cancel since both are positive. We can change that by multiplying every term in one of the equations by −1. Remember, any operation you perform on one side of the equation (such as multiplying by −1) must be done on *both* sides of the equation in order for the equation to remain true.**

$$-1(x - 2y) = -1(-9) \rightarrow -x + 2y = 9$$

$$\text{So} \quad -x + 2y = 9$$
$$+ \ \underline{x + 3y = 16}$$
$$5y = 25 \quad y = 5$$

▶ Teacher Dialogue: **Once you have solved for *y*, you need to plug it back into either of the original equations, and then solve that equation to find *x*, just like in the first set of examples.**

$$x + 3(5) = 16 \qquad x + 15 = 16 \qquad x = 1$$

Solution: $(1,5)$

▶ Work through the fifth example with the class by writing the solution on the board:

▶ Teacher Dialogue: **Solve this system of equations by eliminating *y* first. In order to do this, you could either divide the top equation by 2, or multiply the bottom equation by 2, since the sign on *y* is already opposite and only the coefficient is different. Here, multiply the bottom equation, since it will generally save time, to avoid working with fractions (and the ACT is a timed test).**

$$2(x + y) = 2(7) \rightarrow 2x + 2y = 14$$

$$\text{So} \quad x - 2y = 1$$
$$+ \ \underline{2x + 2y = 14}$$
$$3x + 0 = 15 \qquad \text{which means } x = 5.$$

Once the value of *x* is known, we can once again plug *x* in to either equation and solve for *y*.

$$5 + y = 7 \rightarrow y = 2$$

Solution: $(5,2)$

Student Page 23

2.3.1 Equation Elimination

▶ Work through the sixth and final example on the board with the class, which will involve multiplying each equation by a different value. Remind the class that they can multiply or divide an equation by any number they choose that will make the problem easier to solve, as long as they perform the same operation on *both* sides of the equation.

$$3x - 2y = -9$$
$$x + 3y = -3$$

Student Page 24

▶ Teacher Dialogue: **What would you need to do if you first wanted to eliminate y from each equation?**

First find a number divisible by 2 and 3 so that when they scale both equations, the coefficient of y is equal, and y will cancel when the scaled equations are added together.

An easy way to find a suitable number is to multiply the coefficients of y. 2 times 3 is 6, so we would like to try to make 6 the coefficient of y in each equation.

For the top equation, multiply by 3:

$$3(3x - 2y) = 3(-9) \rightarrow 9x - 6y = -27$$

For the bottom equation, multiply by 2:

$$2(x + 3y) = 2(-3) \rightarrow 2x + 6y = -6$$

▶ Teacher Dialogue: **Combine the two equations.**

We are now able to add the equations together and cancel y from the system of equations.

$$9x - 6y = -27$$
$$+\ \underline{2x + 6y = -6}$$
$$11x + 0 = -33 \qquad \text{so } x = -3$$

▶ Teacher Dialogue: **What should we now do in order to solve for y?**

Plug $x = -3$ into one of the original equations, and then solve that equation to find y.

$$-3 + 3y = -3$$
$$3y = 0$$
$$y = 0$$

Solution: $(-3, 0)$

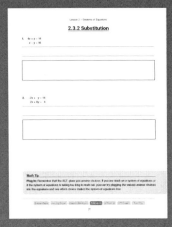

Student Page 25

2.3.2 Substitution

▶ Teacher Dialogue: **Sometimes problems don't have simple equations that can easily be scaled and added to cancel a variable. If a problem looks like it would involve too much multiplying of equations or other algebraic manipulations, substitution is a good method to try. All substitution requires is solving one equation for one of the variables, then plugging this value into the second equation and solving for the remaining variable.**

▶ To illustrate this, work through the same examples already covered when you practiced adding equations that can also be solved using substitution.

1. Solve the first equation for y.

    $4x + y = 14 \rightarrow y = 14 - 4x$

    Now, plug this new value in for y in the second equation.

    $x - y = 16 \rightarrow x - (14 - 4x) = 16$

    Then solve for x.

    $x - (14 - 4x) = 16$

    $x - 14 + 4x = 16$

    $5x - 14 = 16$

    $5x = 30$

    $x = 6$

    Once they have solved for x, have them plug the value back into either of the original equations to find the value of y.

    $4x + y = 14$

    $4(6) + y = 14$

    $24 + y = 14$

    $y = -10$

    Solution: $(6, -10)$

2.3.2 Substitution

2. Solve the first equation for y.

$-2x + y = 14 \rightarrow y = 14 + 2x$

Plug this new value for y into y in the second equation.

$2x + 8(14 + 2x) = 4$

$2x + 112 + 16x = 4$

$18x = -108$

$x = -6$

Then, plug x into either equation and solve for y.

$2(-6) + 8y = 4$

$-12 + 8y = 4$

$8y = 16$

$y = 2$

Solution: $(-6,2)$

▶ Then have the class go back to pages 4 and 5 of their workbook and rework the rest of the problems using the substitution method.

Plug It In: Remember that the ACT gives you answer choices. If you're stuck on a system of equations or if the system of equations is taking too long to work out, you can try plugging the various answer choices into the equations and see which one makes the system of equations true.

2.3.3 In Terms Of

▶ Show the students the following sentences.

▶ Teacher Dialogue: **Which one is the sentence *thank you very much* in terms of Spanish?**

  Thank you very much = Muchas gracias

▶ Teacher Dialogue: **Which one is the sentence *thank you very much* in terms of Greek?**

  Thank you very much = Ευχαριστώ πολύ

▶ Teacher Dialogue: **Which one is the sentence *thank you very much* in terms of French?**

  Thank you very much = Merci beaucoup

▶ Teacher Dialogue: **Is there ever any French on both sides of the equal sign? What about Spanish or Greek?**

  No.

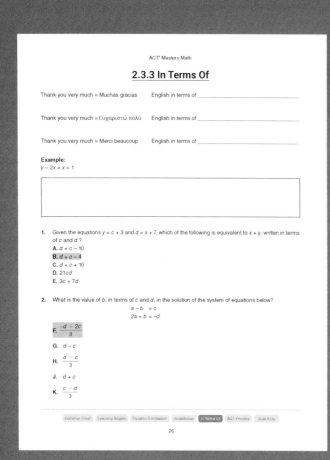

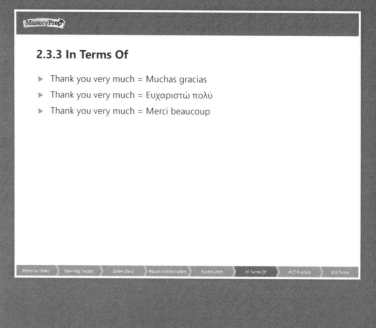

Student Page 26

2.3.3 In Terms Of

▶ Explain to students that in each "equation," all of the French/Spanish/Greek is isolated to only one side of the equation, and all of the English that is being translated is isolated on the other side. That is to say, none of the sentences look like this:

Thank you beaucoup = Merci very much

▶ Show the class an equation on the slide and ask them if they are able to put y in terms of x just like how in the language examples above, the sentence is put in terms of French (or Spanish or Greek).

$y - 2x = x + 1$

▶ Teacher Dialogue: **You can think about it as if *y* is the sentence in English and *x* is the language you would like to translate it to, so that all of *x* language is on one side of the equation, and the sentence we are translating, *y*, is by itself on the other side of the equation.**

To put y in terms of x, students just need to add $2x$ to both sides, giving $y = 3x + 1$.

▶ Students should write this in their workbooks.

2.3.3 In Terms Of

▶ Teacher Dialogue: **On many ACT questions about systems of equations, a problem will have many different variables and ask you to solve the system *in terms of* only one of the variables.**

▶ Work through the first problem with the students.

1. Given the equations $y = c + 3$ and $d = x + 7$, which of the following is equivalent to $x + y$, written in terms of c and d ?

   The correct answer is B. Translate x into terms of c and d since y is already in terms of c. Then add x and y.

   $d = x + 7$

   $x = d - 7$

   $x + y$

   $(d - 7) + (c + 3) = d + c - 4$

▶ Show them the following problem and ask them if they have an idea about how to approach it. Have them think about what "translation" they need to perform in order to get these in the correct language. Then, work through the problem on the board with them and show them the steps of translating for b in terms of the other variables.

2. What is the value of b, in terms of c and d, in the solution of the system of equations below?

   $a - b = c$

   $2a + b = -d$

   The correct answer is F. Though it may be easier to add the equations and eliminate b, the question asks for the value of b. So it's better to eliminate a and then solve for b.

   $a - b = c \rightarrow -2(a - b) = -2(c) \rightarrow -2a + 2b = -2c$

   So $2a + b = -d$

   $+ \ \underline{-2a + 2b = -2c}$

   $\qquad 3b = -d - 2c$

   $b = \dfrac{-d - 2c}{3}$

▶ Have the students try working through the next two problems independently in their workbooks.

3. If $q = 3t - 7$ and $r = 4 - t$, which of the following expresses r in terms of q ?

   The correct answer is A. Add the equations to eliminate t and then solve for r.

   $r = 4 - t \rightarrow 3(r) = 3(4 - t) \rightarrow 3r = 12 - 3t \rightarrow 3r = -3t + 12$

   So $q = 3t - 7$

   $+ \ \underline{3r = -3t + 12}$

   $\qquad q + 3r = 5$

   $r = \dfrac{5 - q}{3}$

Student Page 27

2.3.3 In Terms Of
Complete the activity in your workbook.

2.3.3 In Terms Of

4. If $a = b - 2$ and $c = a^2 + 4a - 10$, which of the following expresses c in terms of b?

The correct answer is G. Use substitution and plug in the expression that a equals for a in the second equation. Then solve for c.

$a = b - 2$

$c = a^2 + 4a - 10$

$c = (b - 2)^2 + 4(b - 2) - 10$

$c = b^2 - 4b + 4 + 4b - 8 - 10$

$c = b^2 - 14$

Negatives: Beware of negative signs. When performing lots of algebraic manipulations to equations, it is easy to lose track of a minus sign and make a careless error. Be *very* careful about keeping track of negative signs, as it could be the difference between solving a simple question in 45 seconds and accidentally spending 10 minutes on it.

2.4 ACT Practice

▶ Have students work on questions from the ACT practice sets here. Pacing should be 3 minutes per practice set or 60 seconds per question.

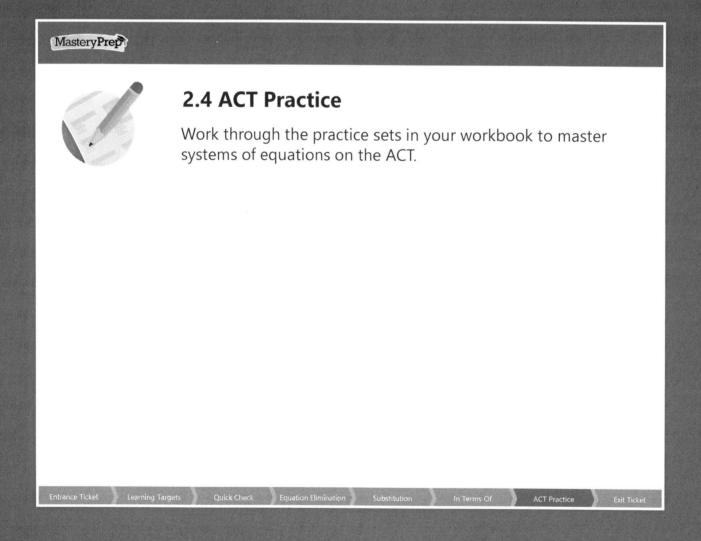

MasteryPrep

2.4 ACT Practice

Work through the practice sets in your workbook to master systems of equations on the ACT.

Entrance Ticket Learning Targets Quick Check Equation Elimination Substitution In Terms Of ACT Practice Exit Ticket

2.4.1 Set One

1. If $p + q = 36$, and $p - q = 20$, then $q = ?$
   A. –8
   B. 8
   C. 16
   D. 28
   E. 56

1. **The correct answer is B.** Combine the two equations to solve for p, then plug it back in to solve for q.

   $2p = 56$

   $p = 28$

   $p + q = 36$

   $28 + q = 36$

   $q = 8$

2. Which of the following (a,b) pairs is the solution for the system of equations $2a + b = 3$ and $a - 3b = 5$?

   F. $(-2, 7)$

   G. $(0, 3)$

   H. $(\frac{3}{4}, \frac{6}{4})$

   J. $(2, -1)$

   K. $(3, -3)$

2. **The correct answer is J.** Combine the two equations to solve for one variable, then plug it back in to find the other.

   $a - 3b = 5 \rightarrow -2(a - 3b) = -2(5) \rightarrow -2a + 6b = -10$

   $-2a + 6b = -10$

   $+ \underline{2a + b = 3}$

   $7b = -7$

   $b = -1$

   $2a + (-1) = 3$

   $2a = 4$

   $a = 2$

   So the solution is $(2, -1)$.

3. What is the value of y in the solution to the following system of equations?
   $$x - 4y - 8 = 20$$
   $$2x + y = 20$$

   A. –4
   B. –1.8
   C. 8
   D. 10
   E. 14

3. **The correct answer is A.** Combine the equations and solve for y.

   $x - 4y - 8 = 20 \rightarrow x - 4y = 28 \rightarrow -2(x - 4y) = -2(28)$

   $\rightarrow -2x + 8y = -56$

   $-2x + 8y = -56$

   $+ \underline{2x + y = 20}$

   $9y = -36$

   $y = -4$

2.4.2 Set Two

4. If $a + b = 28$ and $a - b = 10$, then $b = ?$

   F. −18
   G.   9
   H. 18
   J.   19
   K. 38

4. **The correct answer is G.** Combine the two equations and solve for a, then plug back in to solve for b.

$$a + b = 28$$
$$+\ \underline{a - b = 10}$$
$$2a = 38$$
$$a = 19$$
$$19 + b = 28$$
$$b = 9$$

---

5. What is the solution to the following system of equations?

$$3x + 7y = 34$$
$$x + 7y = 30$$

          x y
   A. −1   1
   B.   1   −1
   C.   2   4
   D.   4   2
   E. 32   6

5. **The correct answer is C.** Combine the two equations and solve for one variable, then plug back in to find the other.

$$x + 7y = 30 \rightarrow -1(x + 7y) = -1(30) \rightarrow -x - 7y = -30$$
$$-x - 7y = -30$$
$$+\ \underline{3x + 7y = 34}$$
$$2x = 4$$
$$x = 2$$
$$3(2) + 7y = 34$$
$$7y = 28$$
$$y = 4$$

So, $x = 2$ and $y = 4$.

---

6. Let $3a + 4b = 18$ and $5a + 3b = 19$. What is the value of $7a + 2b$?

   F. −16
   G.   −4
   H.   8
   J.   20
   K. 24

6. **The correct answer is J.** Solve for a and b by combining the two equations and then plug in the answers to $7a + 2b$ to find the value of that expression.

$$3a + 4b = 18 \rightarrow -5(3a + 4b) = -5(18) \rightarrow -15a - 20b = -90$$
$$5a + 3b = 19 \rightarrow 3(5a + 3b) = 3(19) \rightarrow 15a + 9b = 57$$
$$-15a - 20b = -90$$
$$+\ \underline{15a + 9b = 57}$$
$$-11b = -33$$
$$b = 3$$
$$3a + 4(3) = 18$$
$$3a = 6$$
$$a = 2$$

Now solve for $7a + 2b$.

$$7(2) + 2(3)$$
$$14 + 6$$
$$20$$

2.4.3 Set Three

7. If $a = 3b + 4$ and $b = 7$, what is the value of a ?

    A. 11
    B. 14
    C. 17
    D. 25
    E. 84

7. **The correct answer is D.** Plug in 7 for b and solve for a.

$a = 3b + 4$

$b = 7$

$a = 3(7) + 4$

$a = 21 + 4 = 25$

---

8. If $y = 5x - 2$ and $x = 4b + 3$, then y is equivalent to which of the following?

    F. $b + 1$
    G. $20b + 1$
    H. $20b + 13$
    J. $20bx + 1$
    K. $5x + 4b + 1$

8. **The correct answer is H.** Substitute $4b + 3$ for x in the first equation.

$y = 5(4b + 3) - 2$

$y = 20b + 15 - 2$

$y = 20b + 13$

---

9. For what value of b is $y = 4$ a solution to the equation $y + 2 = by + 8$?

    A. -2
    B. -0.5
    C. 1
    D. 0.5
    E. 2

9. **The correct answer is B.** Plug in 4 for y and solve for b.

$4 + 2 = 4b + 8$

$6 = 4b + 8$

$-2 = 4b$

$-0.5 = b$

2.4.4 Set Four

10. Given the equations $Q = x + 6$ and $y = R - 3$, which of the following expressions is equivalent to $Q + R$ written in terms of x and y ?

F. $x + y + 3$
G. $x + y + 9$
H. $x - y - 3$
J. $18xy$
K. $6x + 3y$

10. The correct answer is G. First find R in terms of y.

$y = R - 3$

$R = y + 3$

Now, express $Q + R$ in terms of x and y.

$Q + R = x + 6 + y + 3$

$Q + R = x + y + 9$

11. If $x = 7 - p$ and $y = 3p + 4$, which of the following expresses y in terms of x ?

A. $17 - x$
B. $25 - x$
C. $17 - 3x$
D. $25 - 3x$
E. $25 + 3x$

11. The correct answer is D. First find p in terms of x.

$x = 7 - p$

$p = 7 - x$

Now, substitute $7 - x$ for p in the second equation and simplify.

$y = 3(7 - x) + 4$

$y = 21 - 3x + 4$

$y = 25 - 3x$

12. Given the equations $A = c + 7$ and $d = B - 4$, which of the following expressions is equivalent to $A - B$ written in terms of c and d ?

F. $c - d + 3$
G. $c - d + 11$
H. $c + d + 3$
J. $c + d + 11$
K. $7c + 4b$

12. The correct answer is F. First find B in terms of d.

$d = B - 4$

$B = d + 4$

Now, express $A + B$ in terms of c and d.

$A - B = c + 7 - (d + 4)$

$A - B = c + 7 - d - 4$

$A - B = c - d + 3$

2.4.5 Set Five

---

13. If the following system has a solution, what is the *x*-coordinate of the solution?

$$4x + 8y = 60$$
$$x + 8y = 30$$

A. 6
B. 10
C. 18
D. 30
E. The system has no solution.

13. The correct answer is B. Combine the equations and solve for *x*.

$x + 8y = 30 \rightarrow -1(x + 8y) = -1(30) \rightarrow -x - 8y = -30$

${-x - 8y = -30}$

$+\ \underline{4x + 8y = 60}$

$3x = 30$

$x = 10$

---

14. What is the value of *y* in the solution to the system of equations below?

$$5x - 5y = 25$$
$$x + 4y = -10$$

F. −22
G. −3
H. −1
J. 3
K. 5

14. The correct answer is G. Combine the equations and solve for *y*.

$x + 4y = -10 \rightarrow -5(x + 4y) = 5(-10) \rightarrow -5x - 20y = 50$

${-5x - 20y = 50}$

$+\ \underline{5x - 5y = 25}$

${-25y = 75}$

$y = -3$

---

15. If $x = 12 - s$ and $y = 5s + 6$, which of the following expresses *y* in terms of *x* ?

A. 66 − 5*x*
B. 66 − *x*
C. 60 + 5*x*
D. 66 + *x*
E. 66 + 5*x*

15. The correct answer is D. First find *s* in terms of *x*.

$x = 12 - s$

$s = 12 - x$

Now, substitute 12 − *x* for *s* in the second equation and simplify.

$y = 5(12 - x) + 6$

$y = 60 - 5x + 6$

$y = 66 - 5x$

Lesson 2 – Systems of Equations

Sum It Up

Systems of Equations

Equality
The state of being the same or equal; having the same value

Equation
Shows that two expressions are equal

Tips and Techniques

Plug In: Plug in answer choices if you are stuck or running out of time on a system of equations problem.

Negatives: Watch out for negatives. Any time they show up in a problem, be careful about keeping track of them.

2.5 Exit Ticket

► Students complete the three questions on their exit ticket.

Students are timed 3 minutes for the three questions (60 seconds per question). There is no break between questions.

Lesson 2 – Systems of Equations

Name _____   Date _____

Exit Ticket

1. When $4a - 9b = 22$ and $b = -2$, what is the value of a ?

   A. $-\frac{10}{3}$

   B. $\frac{14}{9}$

   C. 1

   D. 4

   E. 10

   DO YOUR FIGURING HERE.

2. What is the solution to the following system of equations?

   $f + 3g = 15$
   $f - g = 7$

	f	g
F.	-9	16
G.	-2	5
H.	3	1.5
J.	9	2
K.	18	11

3. If $a = 3t - 10$ and $b = 8 - t$, which of the following expresses b in terms of a ?

   A. $b = \frac{14 - a}{3}$

   B. $b = \frac{34 - a}{3}$

   C. $b = 18 - 3a$

   D. $b = 8 - a$

   E. $b = 14 - a$

Answered Correctly
___ / 3

55

2.5 Exit Ticket Review

Students work the first question.

1. **The correct answer is C.** Plug in −2 for *b* and solve for *a*.

   $4a − 9(−2) = 22$

   $4a + 18 = 22$

   $4a = 4$

   $a = 1$

MasteryPrep

2.5 Exit Ticket Review

1. When $4a − 9b = 22$ and $b = −2$, what is the value of *a* ?

   A. $-\dfrac{10}{3}$

   B. $-\dfrac{14}{9}$

   C. 1

   D. 4

   E. 10

Entrance Ticket | Learning Targets | Quick Check | Equation Elimination | Substitution | In Terms Of | ACT Practice | Exit Ticket

2.5 Exit Ticket Review

Students work the second question.

2. **The correct answer is J.** Combine the equations and solve for one variable. Then plug it back in to determine the other.

$f - g = 7 \rightarrow 3(f - g) = 3(7) \rightarrow 3f - 3g = 21$

$3f - 3g = 21$

$+\underline{\ f + 3g = 15}$

$4f = 36$

$f = 9$

$9 + 3g = 15$

$3g = 6$

$g = 2$

MasteryPrep

2.5 Exit Ticket Review

2. What is the solution to the following system of equations?

$$f + 3g = 15$$
$$f - \ g = \ 7$$

	f	g
F.	−9	16
G.	−2	5
H.	2	1.5
J.	9	2
K.	18	11

Entrance Ticket　Learning Targets　Quick Check　Equation Elimination　Substitution　In Terms Of　ACT Practice　Exit Ticket

2.5 Exit Ticket Review

▸ Students work the third question.

3. **The correct answer is A.** Isolate t and then use the two expressions to solve for b in terms of a.

$a = 3t - 10 \rightarrow a + 10 = 3t$

$a + 10 = 3t$

$b = 8 - t \rightarrow 3(b) = 3(8 - t) \rightarrow 3b = 24 - 3t \rightarrow 3b - 24 = -3t$

$$a + 10 = 3t$$
$$+ \ \underline{3b - 24 = -3t}$$
$$a + 3b - 14 = 0$$
$$3b = 14 - a$$
$$b = \frac{14 - a}{3}$$

▸ After all three questions are completed, students exchange papers. Solve the three exit items step by step on the board. Students grade using their red pens and then return papers to their classmates.

▸ After solving the three exit items, revisit the learning targets slide. Students again assess their knowledge and confidence on the same 1 to 4 scale that they used at the beginning of the lesson. Students write this number in the designated area at the start of the lesson in their workbooks, along with any comments or questions they might have.

▸ Finally, to close the lesson, have students return to the cover page of the lesson and write a caption for the picture there. The caption should be a one-sentence summary of the lesson, a main rule or tip they want to remember, or an explanation of how the picture relates to the topic. If there is additional time, students can share and compare their captions with the class.

Solving Equations: Word Problems

This lesson will cover how to translate word problems into mathematical expressions and how to solve systems of equations word problems.

ACT Standards:

A 202. Solve equations in the form $x + a = b$, where a and b are whole numbers or decimals

A 302. Solve one-step equations to get integer or decimal answers

A 403. Solve routine first-degree equations

A 502. Solve real-world problems by using first-degree equations

A 604. Solve systems of two linear equations

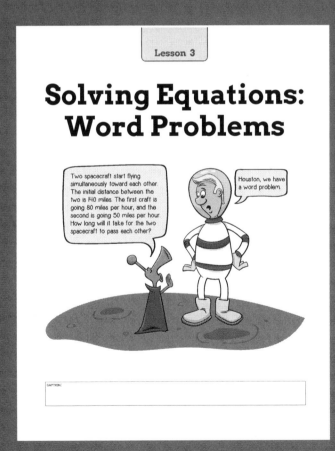

Student Page 35

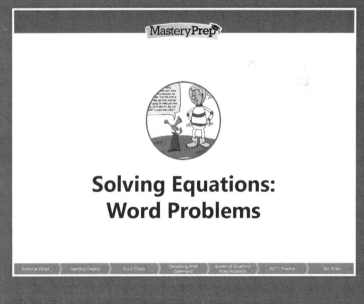

3.1 Entrance Ticket

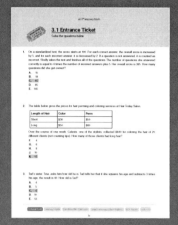

Student Page 36

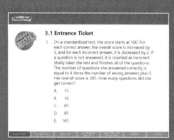

▶ Have students try the following three ACT practice questions. Students should work independently. Once the entrance ticket has been completed, review the questions with the students and have them share their answers. Give students the correct answers to the questions, as well as a step-by-step demonstration of how to solve the problems, but do not go into detailed explanation. This will serve as an introduction to the lesson content but is not intended to be the main lesson.

1. **The correct answer is C.** Translate the word problem into a system of equations, where x represents the number of correct answers, and y represents the number of incorrect answers and solve.

   $395 = 100 + 5x - 2y$

   $295 = 5x - 2y$

   $x = 4y + 5$

   $295 = 5(4y + 5) - 2y$

   $295 = 20y + 25 - 2y$

   $270 = 18y$

   $15 = y$

   $x = 4(15) + 5$

   $x = 60 + 5 = 65$

   She answered 65 questions correctly.

3.1 Entrance Ticket

2. **The correct answer is K.** Translate the word problem into a system of equations and solve.

$30s + 50l = 840$

$s + l = 20$

$s = 20 - l$

$30(20 - l) + 50l = 840$

$600 - 30l + 50l = 840$

$20l = 240$

$l = 12$

12 clients had long hair.

3.1 Entrance Ticket

2. The table below gives the prices for hair perming and coloring services at Hair Today Salon.

Length of Hair	Color	Perm
Short	$30	$50
Long	$50	$80

    Over the course of one week, Celeste, one of the stylists, collected $840 for coloring the hair of 20 different clients (not counting tips). How many of those clients had long hair?

    F. 4

    G. 6

    H. 8

    J. 10

    K. 12

3.1 Entrance Ticket

3. **The correct answer is C.** Translate the word problem into a mathematical expression and solve.

$40 = x^2 - 3x$

$0 = x^2 - 3x - 40$

$0 = (x - 8)(x + 5)$

$x = 8, -5$

Tad cannot be a negative age, so he is 8 years old.

MasteryPrep

3.1 Entrance Ticket

3. Tad's sister, Tina, asks him how old he is. Tad tells her that if she squares his age and subtracts 3 times his age, the result is 40. How old is Tad?

    A.   4

    B.   5

    C.   8

    D.   10

    E.   13

Entrance Ticket | Learning Targets | Quick Check | Translating Math Statements | System of Equations Word Problems | ACT Practice | Exit Ticket

3.2 Learning Targets

▶ Review learning targets with your students, displayed on the slide and in their workbooks.

▶ After reviewing the learning targets, ask students to assess their knowledge and confidence level on these targets. They should rate themselves on a scale of 1 to 4, with 1 being not confident or uncertain, and 4 being completely confident or certain. They should circle this number in the designated section of their workbooks.

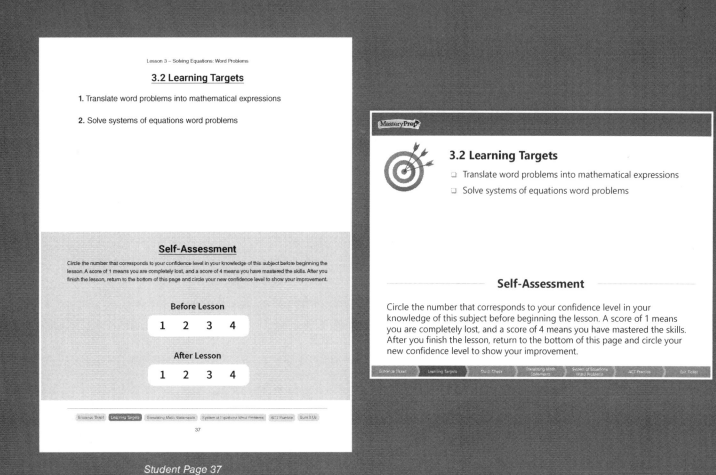

Student Page 37

3.2 Quick Check

► Review the following definitions with the students.

► Teacher Dialogue: **Define *value*.**

Value: A number or measurement

► Teacher Dialogue: **Define *expression*.**

Expression: A group of numbers, symbols, and operations to indicate a value

► Teacher Dialogue: **Define *equation*.**

Equation: Two mathematical expressions set equal to each other

► Teacher Dialogue: **Define *coefficient*.**

Coefficient: The number next to a variable

► Teacher Dialogue: **Define *combining like terms*.**

Combining like terms: In an equation, the process of simplifying the equation using mathematical operations

3.2 Quick Check

► Value

 ‑ A number or measurement

► Expression

 ‑ A group of numbers, symbols, and operations to indicate a value

► Equation

 ‑ Two mathematical expressions set equal to each other

► Coefficient

 ‑ The number next to a variable

► Combining Like Terms

 ‑ In an equation, the process of simplifying the equation using mathematical operations

Entrance Ticket | Learning Targets | Quick Check | Translating Math Statements | System of Equations Word Problems | ACT Practice | Exit Ticket

3.3.1 Translating Math Statements

▶ Ask students the following questions.

▶ Teacher Dialogue: **What math operations do you think words such as together, and, combined, both translate to?**

Answer: Addition

▶ Teacher Dialogue: **What math operations do you think words such as minus, without, less, difference, change translate to?**

Answer: Subtraction

▶ Teacher Dialogue: **What math operations do you think words such as times, product, each, per, of translate to?**

Answer: Multiplication

▶ Teacher Dialogue: **What math operations do you think words such as divided into, split between or among, doled out, divvyed up translate to?**

Answer: Division

▶ Teacher Dialogue: **What symbol do the words equal to, is, is the same as translate to?**

Answer: Equals sign

▶ Teacher Dialogue: **What do the words what, unknown, a number translate to?**

Answer: A variable

▶ Have the students "translate" the examples in the workbook. They do not need to solve the problems. The focus here is the translation.

Student Page 38

3.3.1 Translating Math Statements

▶ Review the answers on the slide.

MasteryPrep

3.3.1 Translating Math Statements

▶ What is the sum of 2 and 5?

　➤ $x = 2 + 5$

▶ Together, 2 hamburgers and 1 drink cost $15.

　➤ $2h + d = 15$

▶ What is 15% of 100?

　➤ $x = 0.15 \cdot 100$

▶ The sum of 2 numbers is 20.

　➤ $x + y = 20$

▶ The difference of 2 numbers is 5.

　➤ $x - y = 5$

| Entrance Ticket | Learning Targets | Quick Check | Translating Math Statements | System of Equations Word Problems | ACT Practice | Exit Ticket |

3.3.1 Translating Math Statements

▸ Have the students translate the ACT questions into equations and then solve them.

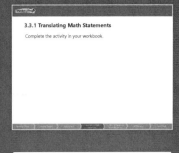

1. A certain positive number is multiplied by 4, and then the result is subtracted from the original number. The result is 21 less than 0. What is the number?

   Translated Equation: $x - 4x = -21$

   $-3x = -21$

   $x = 7$

2. When asked her age, Susan replied, "If you take my age and square it and then subtract 22 times my age, the result is 75." How old is she?

   Translated Equation: $x^2 - 22x = 75$

   $x^2 - 22x - 75 = 0$

   $(x - 25)(x + 3) = 0$

   $x = 25, -3$

   Since her age must be positive, Susan is 25.

Students may not be familiar or particularly strong with factoring quadratic equations. Remind them that the focus is learning to translate word problems into the appropriate equations. If they do not remember how to factor, they can always plug in answer choices once they have determined the initial equation from the problem.

Student Page 39

3. Jack got a rough start in science class this year. He got a 68 on his first test and a 72 on his second. After that, he studied very hard and scored a 100 on each remaining test. At the end of the semester, his total test score average was 88, with each test having equal weight. How many tests, in total, did Jack take in science class this semester?

   Translated Equation: $\dfrac{68 + 72 + 100x}{x + 2} = 88$

   $\dfrac{140 + 100x}{x + 2} = 88$

   $88x + 176 = 140 + 100x$

   $36 = 12x$

   $3 = x$

   Jack took $3 + 2 = 5$ tests this semester.

The translation of this question is not quite as straightforward. Students must recognize that this question implies using the formula to find an average. Students are given the average and must work backward to solve for the unknown. Part of the translation skill is not only determining the necessary formula, but also identifying which part of the word problem needs to be represented by the variable.

If you are given a word problem with math language and no variables in the answer choices, your best strategy is to translate the word problem into an equation and solve.

ACT® Mastery Math

3.3.2 System of Equations Word Problems

1. The cost of 2 tacos and a drink is $3.07. The cost of 3 tacos and a drink is $3.86. How much does a drink cost?

   Translated Equations:

2. Josh bought 800 plastic whistles to give away to the kids at a street fair. Some of the whistles were small and cost $0.50 each. The larger whistles cost $0.75. In total, he spent $550 on the whistles. How many of the small whistles did he buy?

   Translated Equations:

3. Sherry bought 20 apples at the grocery store. The Braeburn apples were $0.80 each, and the Granny Smith apples were $0.65 each. All together, the apples cost $14.95. How many Granny Smith apples did she buy?

   Translated Equations:

Entrance Ticket · Learning Targets · Translating Math Statements · System of Equations Word Problems · ACT Practice · Sum It Up

40

Student Page 40

68

3.3.2 System of Equations Word Problems

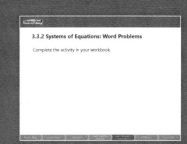

► Tell students to translate the first problem into math language but don't solve it.

1. Students may come up with different answers. If so, that's because they can get more than one equation out of this information:

$2t + d = 3.07$

$3t + d = 3.86$

We don't know the price of tacos or a drink, so these are unknowns and, therefore, are represented by a variable.

► Teacher Dialogue: **If you are getting more than one equation out of a word problem, you are dealing with a system of equations problem. Translate the given information in a word problem into multiple equations (usually two), then solve like a regular system of equations problem.**

► Have the students translate the next two questions in their workbook into equations. These are systems of equations problems, so students will get more than one equation translated out of each question. Students do not need to solve. This is just translation practice.

2. Translate into a system of equations.

$s + l = 800$

$0.50s + 0.75l = 550$

3. Translate into a system of equations.

$b + g = 20$

$0.80b + 0.65g = 14.95$

3.3.2 System of Equations Word Problems

Student Page 41

▶ Now bring students up to ACT level by letting them solve the three problems just translated, using substitution or addition of equations. After students have completed the problems, write the solutions on the board or allow students who got correct answers to show their work at the board and give a class explanation.

1. **The correct answer is C.**

   $2t + d = 3.07 \rightarrow d = 3.07 - 2t$

   $3t + d = 3.86$
   $3t + (3.07 - 2t) = 3.86$
   $t = 0.79$

   $d = 3.07 - 2(0.79)$
   $d = 3.07 - 1.58$
   $d = 1.49$
   A drink costs $1.49.

2. **The correct answer is F.**

   $s + l = 800 \rightarrow l = 800 - s$

   $0.50s + 0.75l = 550$
   $0.50s + 0.75(800 - s) = 550$
   $0.50s + 600 - 0.75s = 550$
   $-0.25s = -50$
   $s = 200$
   He bought 200 small whistles.

3. **The correct answer is A.**

   $b + g = 20 \rightarrow b = 20 - g$
   $0.80b + 0.65g = 14.95$

   $0.80(20 - g) + 0.65g = 14.95$
   $16 - 0.80g + 0.65g = 14.95$
   $-0.15g = -1.05$
   $g = 7$
   Sherry bought 7 Granny Smith apples.

ACT® Mastery Math

3.3.2 System of Equations Word Problems

1. Kelly bought 4 shirts and 3 skirts for her doll and paid $11.40 total. After she did a doll fashion show for her best friend, Caitlyn wanted to know how much one of the skirts cost. Kelly remembered that each skirt cost $0.30 more than each shirt. How much did one skirt cost?

Translated Equations:

```
┌──────────────────────────┐     ┌──────────────────────────┐
│                          │     │                          │
│                          │     │                          │
└──────────────────────────┘     └──────────────────────────┘
```

   A. $1.50
   B. $1.60
   C. $1.65
   D. $1.75
   E. $1.80

2. Bobby opened a bag of candy and counted how many pieces were in the bag. There were 68 pieces of orange, lime, and cherry candies in total. He separated them by flavor and found that there were 2 more orange than lime and 4 more cherry than orange. How many cherry candies were in the bag?

Translated Equations:

```
┌──────────────────────────┐     ┌──────────────────────────┐
│                          │     │                          │
│                          │     │                          │
└──────────────────────────┘     └──────────────────────────┘
```

   F. 20
   G. 22
   H. 24
   J. 26
   K. 28

3.3.2 System of Equations Word Problems

▶ Now have students try two questions that are a little more difficult. Review the answers with the class. Work the problem on the board when explaining the correct answer.

1. **The correct answer is E.** Set up a system of equations and solve.

    Let h be the cost of a shirt and k be the cost of a skirt.

    $k = h + 0.30$

    $4h + 3k = 11.40$

    $4h + 3(h + 0.30) = 11.40$

    $4h + 3h + 0.90 = 11.40$

    $7h = 10.50$

    $h = 1.50$

    $k = h + 0.30$

    $k = 1.50 + 0.30$

    $k = 1.80$

    The cost of one skirt is $1.80.

2. **The correct answer is J.** Set up a system of equations and solve. You can reduce the number of variables using substitution.

    $o + l + c = 68$

    $o = l + 2$

    $c = o + 4$

    $c = o + 4 \rightarrow c = (l + 2) + 4$

    $o + l + c = 68 \rightarrow (l + 2) + l + [(l + 2) + 4] = 68 \rightarrow l + 2 + l + l + 2 + 4 = 68$

    $3l + 8 = 68$

    $3l = 60$

    $l = 20$

    $o = 20 + 2 = 22$

    $c = 22 + 4 = 26$

    There are 26 cherry candies in the bag.

If you get more than one equation from a question, treat it like a system of equations problem.

3.4 ACT Practice

▶ Have students work on questions from the ACT practice sets here. Pacing should be 3 minutes per practice set or 60 seconds per question.

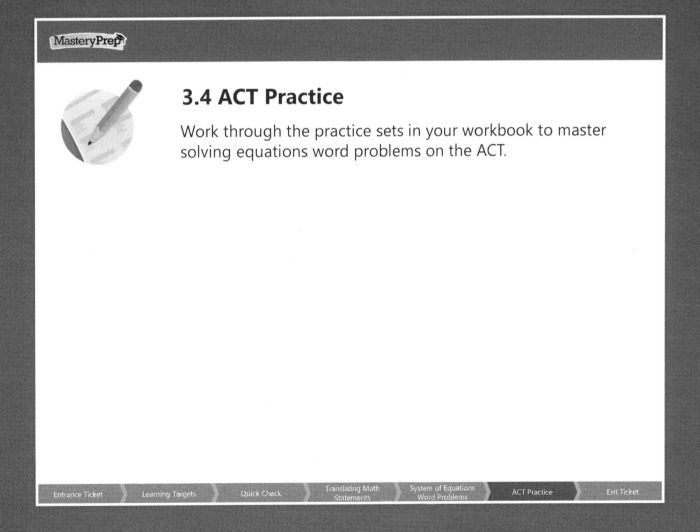

3.4.1 Set One

1. The sum of the real numbers x and y is 15. Their difference is 3. What is the value of xy ?
   A. 3
   B. 6
   C. 9
   D. 15
   E. 54

1. **The correct answer is E.** Translate the word problem into a system of equations and solve.

   $x + y = 15$

   $x - y = 3$

   $x - y = 3 \rightarrow x = 3 + y$

   $x + y = 15 \rightarrow (3 + y) + y = 15$

   $2y = 12$

   $y = 6$

   $x + y = 15 \rightarrow x + 6 = 15$

   $x = 9$

   $xy = (6)(9) = 54$

2. Lilly and Laura pooled their money to purchase their brother, Liam, a video game for his birthday. The video game cost a total of $45. If Laura was only able to contribute $\frac{2}{3}$ of what Lilly did, how much did Laura put toward the present?
   F. $18
   G. $21
   H. $24
   J. $27
   K. $30

2. **The correct answer is F.** Translate the word problem into an equation and solve.

   $45 = y + \frac{2}{3}y$

   $45 = \frac{5}{3}y$

   $27 = y$

   Lilly contributed $27, meaning that Laura contributed $\frac{2}{3}$ of this, or $18.

3. A rectangular field is 3 times as long as it is wide, and it has an area of 192 square yards. How many yards long is it?
   A. 8
   B. 24
   C. 48
   D. 72
   E. 96

3. **The correct answer is B.** Translate the word problem into a system of equations and solve.

   $3w = l$

   $wl = 192$

   $wl = 192 \rightarrow w(3w) = 192$

   $3w^2 = 192$

   $w^2 = 64$

   $w = 8$

   $3w = l \rightarrow 3(8) = l$

   $l = 24$

3.4.2 Set Two

4. The sum of the real numbers x and y is 25. Their difference is 13. What is the value of xy ?

    F. 19
    G. 100
    H. 104
    J. 114
    K. 124

4. **The correct answer is J.** Translate the word problem into a system of equations and solve.

$x + y = 25$

$x - y = 13$

$x + y = 25 \rightarrow x = 25 - y$

$x - y = 13 \rightarrow (25 - y) - y = 13$

$25 - 2y = 13$

$-2y = -12$

$y = 6$

$x + y = 25 \rightarrow x + 6 = 25 \rightarrow x = 19$

$xy = (19)(6) = 114$

5. Theresa decides to donate money to cancer research each year. Her brother, Tony, also decides to contribute. Together, they donate $1,000 per year to cancer research. If Tony is able to donate $1\frac{1}{2}$ times the amount that Theresa is able to donate, what is the amount in dollars that Tony will donate after 5 years, assuming the amount and proportions remain the same each year?

    A. $2,000
    B. $2,100
    C. $2,450
    D. $3,000
    E. $3,600

5. **The correct answer is D.** Translate the word problem into an equation and solve.

$d + 1.5d = 1000$

$2.5d = 1000$

$d = 400$

This represents the amount that Theresa donates; Tony donates 1.5 times this amount, or 600. So, after 5 years, he will donate $(600)(5) = \$3,000$.

6. When asked his age, Michael said, "If you square my age, then subtract 12 times my age, the result is 85." How old is he?

    F. 5
    G. 12
    H. 17
    J. 24
    K. 85

6. **The correct answer is H.** Translate the word problem into an equation and solve.

$x^2 - 12x = 85$

$x^2 - 12x - 85 = 0$

$(x - 17)(x + 5) = 0$

$x = -5$ and 17

Since his age must be positive, he is 17 years old.

3.4.3 Set Three

7. The sum of the real numbers x and y is 24. Their difference is 12. What is the value of xy ?

  A. 108
  B. 90
  C. 58
  D. 18
  E. 6

7. **The correct answer is A.** Translate the word problem into a system of equations and solve.

$x + y = 24$

$x - y = 12$

$x + y = 24 \rightarrow x = 24 - y$

$x - y = 12 \rightarrow (24 - y) - y = 12 \rightarrow 24 - 2y = 12$

$12 = 2y$

$6 = y$

$x + y = 24 \rightarrow x + (6) = 24 \rightarrow x = 18$

$xy = (18)(6) = 108$

---

8. A vending machine sells chips for $0.50 and candy bars for $1.00. If Jim spent $5.50 on snacks in the machine over the course of a week, how many candy bars did he buy?

  F. 1
  G. 2
  H. 3
  J. 4
  K. Cannot be determined from the given information

8. **The correct answer is K.** You need two equations to relate the variables in order to solve the system. Here, you only know that Jim spent $5.50 on snacks, and you know the cost of the two snacks ($0.50 and $1.00). You would need to know how many snacks total he bought in order to solve this problem, so you do not have enough information.

---

9. A school held a kiddie carnival to raise money for the PTA. Admission for adults was $8, and admission for children was $5. In the end, 87 people attended the carnival, and they raised $468. How many adults attended the carnival?

  A. 6
  B. 11
  C. 23
  D. 64
  E. 76

9. **The correct answer is B.** Translate the word problem into a system of equations and solve.

$a + c = 87$

$8a + 5c = 468$

$a + c = 87 \rightarrow c = 87 - a$

$8a + 5c = 468 \rightarrow 8a + 5(87 - a) = 468$

$8a + 435 - 5a = 468$

$3a = 33$

$a = 11$

There were 11 adults who attended the carnival.

3.4.4 Set Four

10. A group of 10 people go to see a movie. The tickets cost $11.95 for adults and $7.50 for children. If the total cost for tickets was $101.70 for the group, how many adults were in the group?

    F. 4
    G. 5
    H. 6
    J. 7
    K. 8

10. **The correct answer is H.** Translate the word problem into a system of equations and solve.

$a + c = 10$

$11.95a + 7.50c = 101.70$

$a + c = 10 \rightarrow c = 10 - a$

$11.95a + 7.50c = 101.70 \rightarrow 11.95a + 7.50(10 - a) = 101.70 \rightarrow 11.95a + 75 - 7.50a = 101.70$

$4.45a = 26.70$

$a = 6$

There were 6 adults in the group.

---

11. A restaurant sells burgers and fries. If two burgers and one order of fries cost $5.10, and one burger and two orders of fries cost $4.80, how much is one burger and one order of fries?

    A. $3.00
    B. $3.30
    C. $3.60
    D. $4.00
    E. $4.95

11. **The correct answer is B.** Translate the word problem into a system of equations and solve.

$2b + f = 5.10$

$b + 2f = 4.80$

$2b + f = 5.10 \rightarrow f = 5.10 - 2b$

$b + 2f = 4.80 \rightarrow b + 2(5.10 - 2b) = 4.80$

$b + 10.20 - 4b = 4.80$

$5.40 = 3b$

$1.80 = b$

$2b + f = 5.10 \rightarrow 2(1.80) + f = 5.10$

$1.60 + f = 5.10$

$f = 1.50$

The cost of 1 burger and 1 order of fries is $1.80 + $1.50 = $3.30.

---

12. Mrs. Jones is handing out candy to trick-or-treaters. She gives out candy bars to kids in costume and small packages of gummies to kids without a costume. The candy bars cost $0.80, and the gummies cost $0.25. At the end of the night, 100 children visited Mrs. Jones's home, and she gave out $69.00 in candy. How many children who visited Mrs. Jones's home were wearing a costume?

    F. 20
    G. 50
    H. 69
    J. 80
    K. 92

12. **The correct answer is J.** Translate the word problem into a system of equations and solve.

$c + g = 100$

$0.80c + 0.25g = 69.00$

$c + g = 100 \rightarrow g = 100 - c$

$0.80c + 0.25g = 69.00 \rightarrow 0.80c + 0.25(100 - c) = 69.00$

$0.80c + 25 - 0.25c = 69.00$

$0.55c = 44.00$

$c = 80$

80 students who visited Mrs. Jones's home were wearing a costume.

3.4.5 Set Five

13. Marco bought pens and pencils with his company's name and website address to give away to people at a festival. He bought a total of 300 pens and pencils together and spent $62.50. If pencils cost $0.15 each and pens cost $0.25 each, how many pens did Marco buy?

A. 175
B. 165
C. 140
D. 130
E. 125

13. The correct answer is A. Translate the word problem into a system of equations and solve.

$p + l = 300$

$0.25p + 0.15l = 62.50$

$p + l = 300 \rightarrow l = 300 - p$

$0.25p + 0.15l = 62.50 \rightarrow 0.25p + 0.15(300 - p) = 62.50$

$0.25p + 45 - 0.15p = 62.50$

$0.10p = 17.50$

$p = 175$

Marco bought 175 pens.

14. In a game, Theodore received a handful of coins (pennies, nickels, dimes, and quarters) as a prize. When he got home, he found that he had managed to get $2.09 in change. He noticed that he had three times as many pennies as dimes, one more nickel than dimes, and twice as many quarters as dimes. How many quarters did Theodore get in his prize?

F. 4
G. 5
H. 6
J. 7
K. 8

14. The correct answer is H. Translate the word problem into a system of equations and solve. Reduce the number of variables by using substitution.

$0.01p + 0.05n + 0.10d + 0.25q = 2.09$

$3d = p$

$d + 1 = n$

$2d = q$

Find the number of pennies and nickels in relation to the number of quarters.

$2d = q \rightarrow d = 0.5q$

$d + 1 = n \rightarrow 0.5q + 1 = n$

$3d = p \rightarrow 3(0.5q) = p$

Substitute all variables to solve for q.

$0.01(3)(0.5)q + 0.05(0.5q + 1) + 0.10(0.5q) + 0.25q = 2.09$

$0.015q + 0.025q + 0.05 + 0.05q + 0.25q = 2.09$

$0.34q = 2.04$

$q = 6$

There are 6 quarters in Theodore's prize.

15. Nathan has 102 solid-colored disks that are red, blue, and green. He lines them up on the floor and finds that there are 3 more red disks than blue and 6 more blue disks than green. How many red disks are there?

   A. 26
   B. 29
   C. 31
   D. 35
   E. 38

15. **The correct answer is E.** Translate the word problem into a system of equations and solve. Reduce the number of variables by using substitution.

$r + b + g = 102$

$3 + b = r$

$6 + g = b$

Find the number of green disks in relation to red disks.

$3 + b = r \rightarrow b = r - 3$

$6 + g = b \rightarrow 6 + g = r - 3 \rightarrow g = r - 9$

Substitute all variables and solve for r.

$r + (r - 3) + (r - 9) = 102$

$3r - 12 = 102$

$3r = 114$

$r = 38$

ACT® Mastery Math

Sum It Up

Solving Equations: Word Problems

Value
A number of measurement

Expression
A group of numbers, symbols, and operations to indicate a value

Equation
Two mathematical expressions set equal to each other

Coefficient
The number next to a variable

Combining Like Terms
In an equation, the process of simplifying the equation using mathematical operations

Tips and Techniques

Decoding: If you are given a word problem with lots of math language and no variables in the answer choices, your best strategy is to translate the word problem into an equation and solve.

3.5 Exit Ticket

▶ Students complete the three questions on their exit ticket.

Students are timed 3 minutes for the three questions (60 seconds per question). There is no break between questions.

Lesson 3 – Solving Equations: Word Problems

Name _____   Date _____

Exit Ticket

1. A parking meter in downtown Seattle takes dollar coins and quarters only. When the machine was last emptied, there were 250 coins in it, with a total value of $137.50. Which of the following systems of equations gives the number of quarters, q, and the number of dollar coins, d ?

   A. $d + q = 250$ and $100d + 25q = 137.50$
   B. $d + q = 250$ and $0.1d + 0.25q = 137.50$
   C. $d + q = 250$ and $d + 0.25q = 137.50$
   D. $d + q = 137.50$ and $d + 0.25q = 250$
   E. $d + q = 137.50$ and $100d + 25q = 250$

   DO YOUR FIGURING HERE.

2. For two consecutive integers, the result of adding double the smaller integer and triple the larger integer is 153. What are the two integers?

   F. 29, 30
   G. 30, 31
   H. 49, 50
   J. 50, 51
   K. 76, 77

3. In a certain triangle, the longest side is twice as long as the shortest side, and the shortest side is 4 inches shorter than the middle side. If the perimeter of the triangle is 52 inches, how long is the longest side?

   A. 10 inches
   B. 12 inches
   C. 16 inches
   D. 20 inches
   E. 24 inches

   Answered Correctly
   ___ / 3

MasteryPrep

3.5 Exit Ticket

Solve the questions on your exit ticket.

Entrance Ticket | Learning Targets | Quick Check | Translating Math Statements | System of Equations Word Problems | ACT Practice | Exit Ticket

3.5 Exit Ticket Review

▶ Students work the first question.

1. **The correct answer is C.** Translate the word problem into a system of equations.

   $d + q = 250$ This is because there are a total of 250 coins and two types of coins.

   $d + 0.25q = 137.50$ This is because the coefficients represent the monetary value of the coin type, and the sum of their values add up to equal a total monetary value of 137.50.

3.5 Exit Ticket Review

1. A parking meter in downtown Seattle takes dollar coins and quarters only. When the machine was last emptied, there were 250 coins in it, with a total value of $137.50. Which of the following systems of equations gives the number of quarters, q, and the number of dollar coins, d ?

   A. $d + q = 250$ and $100d + 25q = 137.50$

   B. $d + q = 250$ and $0.1d + 0.25q = 137.50$

   C. $d + q = 250$ and $d + 0.25q = 137.50$

   D. $d + q = 137.50$ and $d + 0.25q = 250$

   E. $d + q = 137.50$ and $100d + 25q = 250$

Entrance Ticket | Learning Targets | Quick Check | Translating Math Statements | System of Equations Word Problems | ACT Practice | Exit Ticket

3.5 Exit Ticket Review

▶ Students work the second question.

2. **The correct answer is G.** Translate the word problem into an equation and solve.

$2x + 3(x + 1) = 153$

$2x + 3x + 3 = 153$

$5x = 150$

$x = 30$

The two integers are 30 and 31.

MasteryPrep

3.5 Exit Ticket Review

2. For two consecutive integers, the result of adding double the smaller integer and triple the larger integer is 153. What are the two integers?

F. 29, 30

G. 30, 31

H. 49, 50

J. 50, 51

K. 76, 77

3.5 Exit Ticket Review

▶ Students work the third question.

> 3. **The correct answer is E.** Translate the word problem into an equation and solve. Reduce the number of variables using substitution.
>
> $l = 2s$
>
> $s + 4 = m$
>
> $l + s + m = 52$
>
> Find the length of the longest side in relation to the other two.
>
> $l = 2s \rightarrow s = \dfrac{l}{2}$
>
> $s + 4 = m \rightarrow \dfrac{l}{2} + 4 = m$
>
> Substitute all variables and solve for l.
>
> $l + \dfrac{l}{2} + \dfrac{l}{2} + 4 = 52$
>
> $2l = 48$
>
> $l = 24$
>
> The longest side of the triangle is 24 inches.

▶ After all three questions are completed, students exchange papers. Solve the three exit items step by step on the board. Students grade using their red pens and then return papers to their classmates.

▶ After solving the three exit items, revisit the learning targets slide. Students again assess their knowledge and confidence on the same 1 to 4 scale that they used at the beginning of the lesson. Students write this number in the designated area at the start of the lesson in their workbooks, along with any comments or questions they might have.

▶ Finally, to close the lesson, have students return to the cover page of the lesson and write a caption for the picture there. The caption should be a one-sentence summary of the lesson, a main rule or tip they want to remember, or an explanation of how the picture relates to the topic. If there is additional time, students can share and compare their captions with the class.

Percentages

This lesson will cover how to determine the percentage of a number and how to solve word problems that involve percentages.

ACT Standards:

AF 301. Solve routine one-step arithmetic problems using positive rational numbers, such as single-step percentages

AF 401. Solve routine two-step or three-step arithmetic problems involving concepts such as rate and proportion, tax added, percentage off, and estimating by using a given average value in place of actual values

AF 601. Solve word problems containing several rates, proportions, or percentages

AF 701. Solve complex arithmetic problems involving percent of increase or decrease or requiring integration of several concepts (e.g., using several ratios, comparing percentages, or comparing averages)

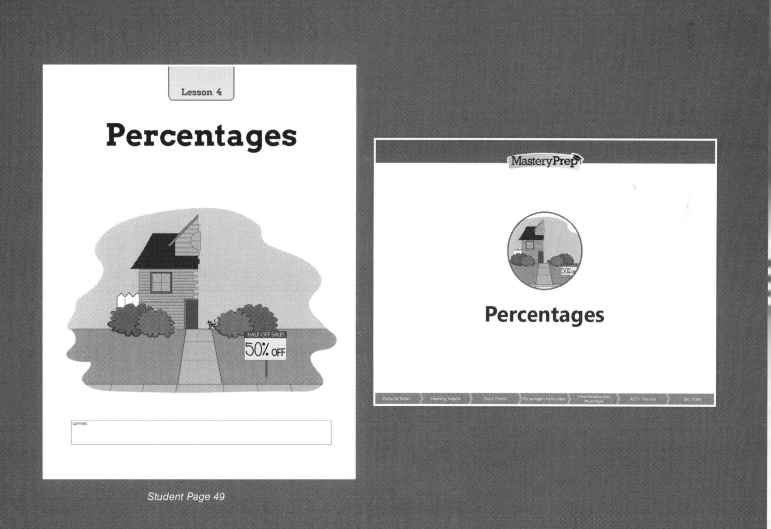

Student Page 49

4.1 Entrance Ticket

Have students try the following three ACT practice questions. Students should work independently. Once the entrance ticket has been completed, review the questions with the students and have them share their answers. Give students the correct answers to the questions, as well as a step-by-step demonstration of how to solve the problems, but do not go into detailed explanation. This will serve as an introduction to the lesson content but is not intended to be the main lesson.

1. **The correct answer is B.** Convert the percentage into a decimal and solve.

   $125\% = 1.25$

   $1.25 \cdot 20 = 25$

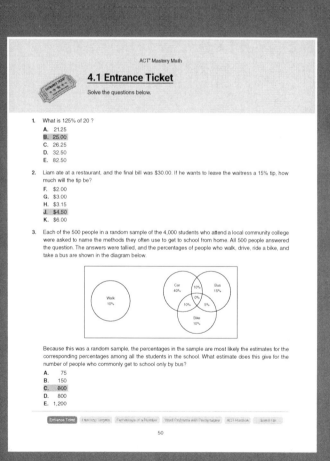

Student Page 50

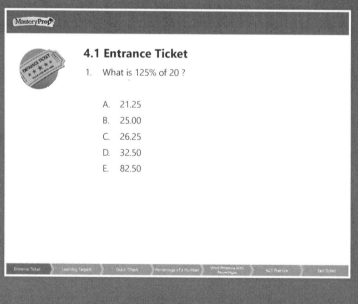

4.1 Entrance Ticket

2. **The correct answer is J.** Convert the percentage into a decimal and solve.

    15% = 0.15

    $30 · 0.15 = $4.50

4.1 Entrance Ticket

2. Liam ate at a restaurant, and the final bill was $30.00. If he wants to leave the waitress a 15% tip, how much will the tip be?

    F. $2.00

    G. $3.00

    H. $3.15

    J. $4.50

    K. $6.00

Entrance Ticket | Learning Targets | Quick Check | Percentage of a Number | Word Problems With Percentages | ACT Practice | Exit Ticket

4.1 Entrance Ticket

3. **The correct answer is C.** Translate into an equation, using the data in the figure, and solve. Use the total number of students in the school, 4,000, since the question notes that the sample is representative of this larger portion and the question asks for this data.

   $15\% \cdot 4{,}000$

   $0.15 \cdot 4{,}000 = 600$

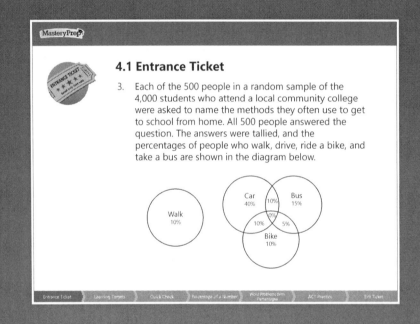

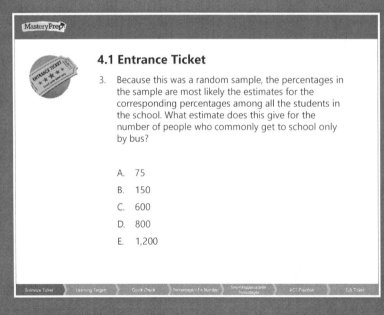

4.2 Learning Targets

▶ Review learning targets with your students, displayed on the slide and in their workbooks.

▶ After reviewing the learning targets, ask students to assess their knowledge and confidence level on these targets. They should rate themselves on a scale of 1 to 4, with 1 being not confident or uncertain, and 4 being completely confident or certain. They should circle this number in the designated section of their workbooks.

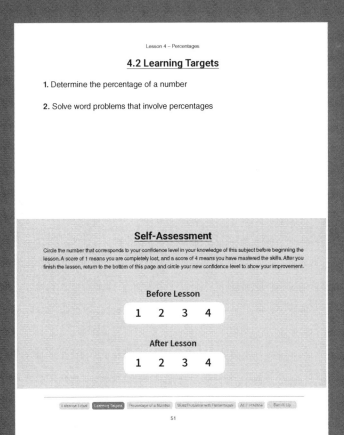

Student Page 51

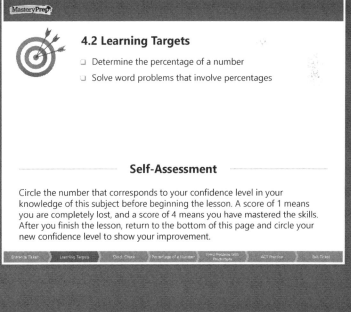

4.2 Quick Check

▶ Teacher Dialogue: **What is a percentage? What does it represent?**

A ratio expressing parts per whole out of 100

▶ Teacher Dialogue: **Fill in the following blank. To convert a percentage to a decimal...**

Move the decimal two places to the left and remove the percentage sign.

Ex: 60% → 0.6

▶ Teacher Dialogue: **Fill in the following blank. To convert a decimal to a percentage...**

Move the decimal two places to the right and add a percentage sign.

Ex: 0.6 → 60%

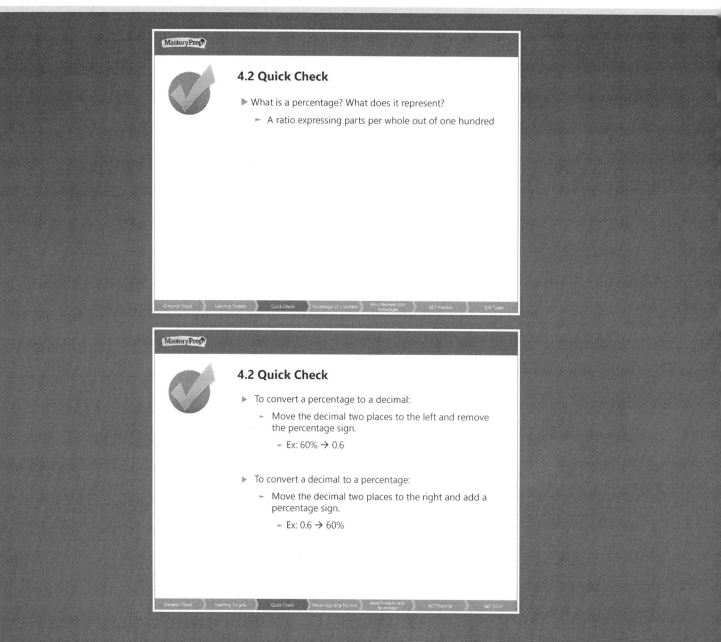

4.2 Quick Check

▶ Next, ask students how they would convert 60% to a fraction. Call on one or two students to offer their suggestions.

▶ Teacher Dialogue: **Fill in the following blank. To convert a percentage to a fraction...**

Set the percentage over 100, remove the percentage sign, and simplify.

Ex: $60\% \rightarrow \dfrac{60}{100} \rightarrow \dfrac{30}{50} \rightarrow \dfrac{15}{25} \rightarrow \dfrac{3}{5}$

▶ Teacher Dialogue: **Fill in the following blank. To convert a fraction to a percentage...**

Convert the fraction to a decimal by dividing the numerator by the denominator, and then move the decimal two places to the right and add a percentage sign.

Ex: $\dfrac{3}{5} \rightarrow 0.6 \rightarrow 60\%$

MasteryPrep

4.2 Quick Check

▶ To convert a percentage to a fraction:

   ▻ Set the percentage over 100, remove the percentage sign, and simply.

      ▻ Ex: $60\% \rightarrow \dfrac{60}{100} \rightarrow \dfrac{30}{50} \rightarrow \dfrac{15}{25} \rightarrow \dfrac{3}{5}$

▶ To convert a fraction to a percentage:

   ▻ Convert the fraction to a decimal by dividing the numerator by the denominator, and then move the decimal two places to the right and add a percentage sign.

      ▻ Ex: $\dfrac{3}{5} \rightarrow 0.6 \rightarrow 60\%$

Entrance Ticket | Learning Targets | Quick Check | Percentage of a Number | Word Problems With Percentages | ACT Practice | Exit Ticket

4.3.1 Percentage of a Number

Show students the following problem on the slide.

> What is 10% of 50?

▶ Teacher Dialogue: **How would you translate this question into an equation?**

Use the variable x to stand in for an unknown quantity.

$x = 0.1 \cdot 50$

▶ Teacher Dialogue: **What is the correct answer?**

5

▶ Next, show students the following problem and translation on the slide. Have them break into pairs to discuss the question before coming together as a class to discuss.

> What is 30% of 100?

$0.3 \cdot x = 100$

▶ Teacher Dialogue: **Is this the correct translation of the equation? If not, what is?**

No, it is incorrect. The correct answer is: $x = 0.3 \cdot 100$

▶ Now show students the next problem and translation on the slide. Have them break into pairs to discuss the question before coming together as a class to discuss.

> What is 85% of 15?

$x = 0.85 \cdot 15$

▶ Teacher Dialogue: **Is this the correct translation of the equation? If not, what is?**

Yes, it is correct.

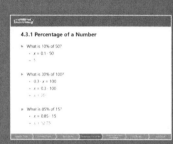

Student Page 52

4.3.1 Percentage of a Number

▶ Now, ask students to come up with a rule to translate these problems into equations, filling in the following blanks:

What: ____

Is: ____

Of: ____

Percent: ____

▶ Randomly call on one student per blank to offer an answer. Students should come up with:

What: x

Is: $=$

Of: $\cdot$

Percent: $\dfrac{p}{100}$

MasteryPrep

4.3.1 Percentage of a Number

What: X

Is: $=$

Of: $\cdot$

Percent: $\dfrac{p}{100}$

4.3.1 Percentage of a Number

Next, have students practice with a series of problems. Tell students that they encounter these sorts of problems in everyday life, such as when certain items on online retail sites are discounted.

▶ Students work on the following five problems, shown on the slide and written in their workbooks. For each problem, they will be told the discount percentage of each book and have to determine how much of a discount is offered.

▶ Give students 5 minutes to work through the problems. Then come together as a class and go over each question. Call on students to write their answers on the board and give explanations.

1. **The correct answer is $6.84.**

   $x = 0.38 \cdot \$17.99$

   $x = 6.8362 \approx \$6.84$

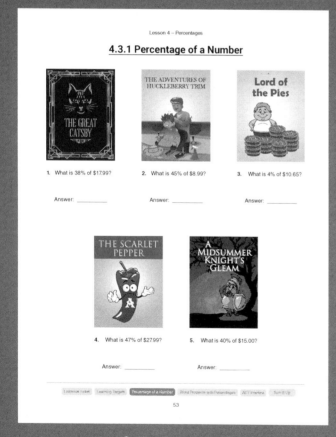

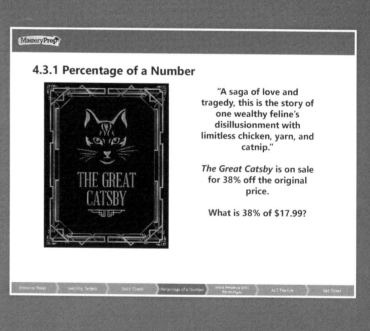

Student Page 53

4.3.1 Percentage of a Number

2. **The correct answer is $4.05.**

   $x = 0.45 \cdot \$8.99$

   $x = 4.0455 \approx \$4.05$

3. **The correct answer is $0.43.**

   $x = 0.04 \cdot \$10.65$

   $x = 0.426 \approx \$0.43$

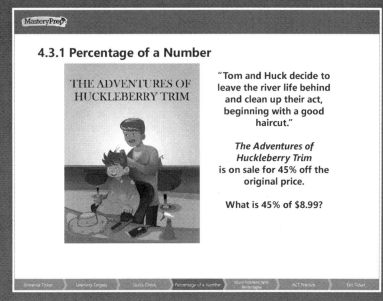

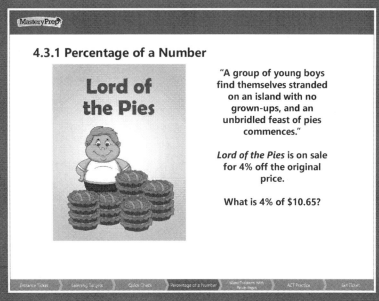

4.3.1 Percentage of a Number

4. The correct answer is $13.16.

$x = 0.47 \cdot \$27.99$

$x = 13.1553 \approx \$13.16$

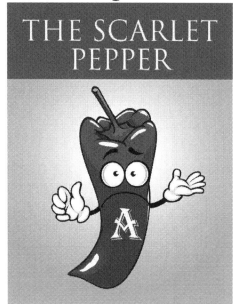

4.3.1 Percentage of a Number

5. The correct answer is $6.00.

$x = 0.40 \cdot \$15.00$

$x = \$6.00$

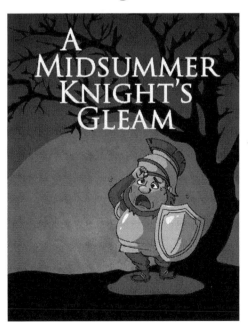

4.3.1 Percentage of a Number

"A sweaty knight finds his armor too warm for the summer heat."

A Midsummer Knight's Gleam is on sale for 40% off the original price.

What is 40% of $15.00?

Entrance Ticket | Learning Targets | Quick Check | Percentage of a Number | Word Problems With Percentages | ACT Practice | Exit Ticket

Student Page 54

4.3.2 Word Problems with Percentages

▸ Show students the first problem on the slide.

▸ Teacher Dialogue: **When solving word problems, you will need to sift through all the information in order to locate the problem you have to solve. All you need to know is the total number of items and either the percentage of what you are trying to find or the number of what you are trying to find.**

▸ Have students break into pairs and discuss which equation they would need to solve to get the answer to the problem in thier workbooks.

▸ Reconvene as a class. Call on one or two pairs to offer their answers and then reveal the answer on the slide. Have students copy down the work in the relevant section of their workbooks.

1. **The correct answer is E.**

   Important information:

   80 total voters

   34 people voted for Chelsea

   $$\frac{34}{80} = 0.425$$

   $0.425 \cdot 100\% = 42.5\%$

Start Easy: Many percentage problems can be overwhelming due to all of the steps involved. Instead of letting the question overwhelm you, do the first thing you know how to do and work from there. The problem will probably become much easier as you go.

4.3.2 Word Problems with Percentages

2. **The correct answer is $3.**

   $x = 25\% \cdot \$12$

   $x = 0.25 \cdot \$12$

   $x = \$3$

4.3.2 Word Problems with Percentages

2. Eliza bought a meal that cost $12. She tipped the waiter 25% of that amount. How much was the tip?

   ▶ $x = 25\% \cdot \$12$

   ▶ $x = 0.25 \cdot \$12$

   ▶ $x = \$3$

| Entrance Ticket | Learning Targets | Quick Check | Percentage of a Number | Word Problems With Percentages | ACT Practice | Exit Ticket |

4.3.2 Word Problems with Percentages

3. The correct answer is $13\frac{1}{3}$%.

$$x = \frac{8}{60} \cdot 100\%$$

$$x = 13\frac{1}{3}\% \text{ or } 13.33\%$$

Lesson 4 – Percentages

4.3.2 Word Problems with Percentages

3. Penny took a poll to find out her classmates' favorite pizza toppings. All 60 of her classmates provided their answers. The results are shown in the table below.

Pizza Toppings	Number of Classmates
Cheese	22
Pepperoni	11
Sausage	19
Peppers	8

What percentage of her classmates chose peppers as their favorite pizza topping?

Answer: _____

4. A florist is told that 40% of the 350 flowers ordered must be red roses. How many red roses must be in the order?

Answer: _____

5. Luis received a discount of $24 on his new phone, which had an original price of $140. By what percentage was the original price discounted?

Answer: _____

Math Tip

Show Your Work: When you encounter a percentage problem, show your work, step by step. If you are over-confident and make mental errors, you will miss out on points. Show your work to prevent yourself from falling into trap answer choices.

55

Student Page 55

MasteryPrep

4.3.2 Word Problems with Percentages

3. Penny took a poll of her classmates' favorite pizza toppings. All 60 of her classmates provided their answers. The results are shown in the table below.

Pizza Toppings	Number of Classmates
Cheese	22
Pepperoni	11
Sausage	19
Peppers	8

What percentage of her classmates chose peppers as their favorite pizza topping?

▶ $x = \frac{8}{60} \cdot 100\%$

▶ $x = 13\frac{1}{3}\%$

4.3.2 Word Problems with Percentages

4. **The correct answer is 140.**

$x = 40\% \cdot 350$

$x = 0.4 \cdot 350$

$x = 140$ red roses

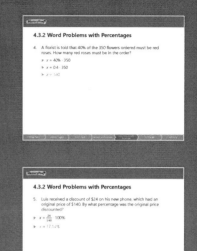

5. **The correct answer is 17.14%.**

$x = \dfrac{24}{140} \cdot 100\%$

$x \approx 17.14\%$

> **Show Your Work:** Most questions that focus on percentages are all about showing your work for every step. The ACT writers expect you to be overconfident and make mental errors. Show your work to prevent yourself from falling into trap answers.

4.4 ACT Practice

▶ Have students work on questions from the ACT practice sets here. Pacing should be 3 minutes per practice set or 60 seconds per question.

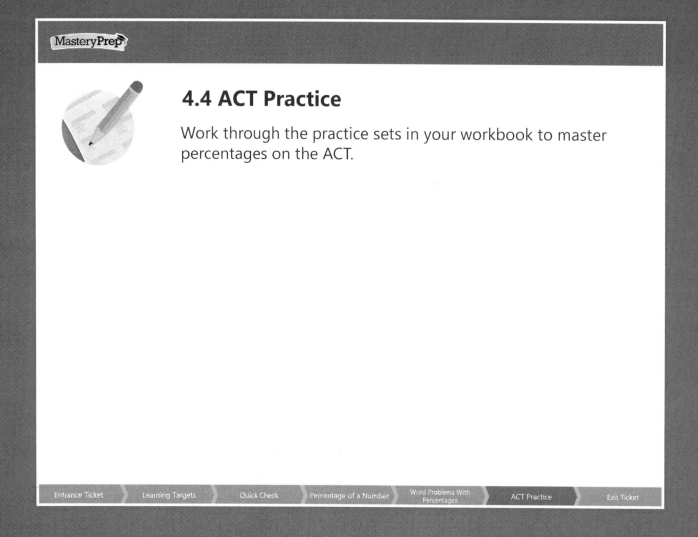

MasteryPrep

4.4 ACT Practice

Work through the practice sets in your workbook to master percentages on the ACT.

Entrance Ticket | Learning Targets | Quick Check | Percentage of a Number | Word Problems With Percentages | ACT Practice | Exit Ticket

4.4.1 Set One

1. What is 15% of 150 ?
   A. 2.25
   B. 3
   C. 10
   D. 15
   E. 22.5

1. **The correct answer is E.** Convert the percentage into a decimal and solve.

   15% · 150

   0.15 · 150 = 22.5

2. If 120% of a number is 720, what is 50% of that same number?
   F. 300
   G. 360
   H. 432
   J. 600
   K. 1,224

2. **The correct answer is F.** Translate the problem into an equation and solve.

   120% · x = 720

   1.2 · x = 720

   x = 600

   50% · 600 = 0.5 · 600 = 300

3. What is 4% of 80 ?
   A. 320
   B. 32
   C. 3.2
   D. 0.32
   E. 0.032

3. **The correct answer is C.** Translate the problem into an equation and solve.

   4% · 80

   0.04 · 80 = 3.2

4.4.2 Set Two

4. What is 4% of 50% of 5 ?
   F. 0.01
   G. 0.05
   H. 0.10
   J. 0.50
   K. 1.00

4. The correct answer is H. Translate the problem into an equation and solve.

$4\% \cdot (50\% \cdot 5)$

$0.04 \cdot (0.50 \cdot 5)$

$0.04 \cdot 2.5 = 0.1$

---

5. What is 150% of 264 ?
   A.   132
   B.   176
   C.   296
   D.   396
   E.   3,960

5. The correct answer is D. Translate the problem into an equation and solve.

$150\% \cdot 264$

$1.5 \cdot 264 = 396$

---

6. What is $\frac{2}{3}$ of 15% of $2,000 ?
   F. $100
   G. $200
   H. $300
   J. $450
   K. $500

6. The correct answer is G. Translate the problem into an equation and solve.

$\frac{2}{3} \cdot (15\% \cdot \$2,000)$

$\frac{2}{3} \cdot (0.15 \cdot \$2,000)$

$\frac{2}{3} \cdot \$300 = \$200$

4.4.3 Set Three

7. The table below shows the distribution of the Cub Scouts throughout Pack 552.

Den	Tigers (6 years old)	Wolves (7 years old)	Bears (8 years old)	Webelos (9 years old)
% of Cub Scouts	19%	36%	17%	28%

What percentage of the Cub Scouts are at least as old as a Bear Scout?
A. 45%
B. 54%
C. 64%
D. 65%
E. 83%

7. **The correct answer is A.** Use the graph to find the number of Cub Scouts at least as old as a Bear Scout. This includes the column labeled *Bears* and the column labeled *Webelos*. Add the two percentages together.

17% + 28% = 45%

8. Of the 80 spaces in the XYZ Industries' parking lot, 5% of them are reserved for handicapped parking. Of the non-handicapped spaces, 16 are reserved for company VIPs. How many spaces that are NOT reserved for handicapped parking are available to non-VIP employees?
F. 76
G. 70
H. 64
J. 60
K. 56

8. **The correct answer is J.** Translate the problem into an equation and solve.

First, calculate the number of handicapped spots.

5% · 80

0.05 · 80 = 4

Of the remaining spots, 80 − 4 = 76 spots are left. Of these spots, 16 are reserved for company VIPS, so the amount left to regular employees is 76 − 16 = 60.

9. Patrick and Cheryl dined at a restaurant, and their bill was $42.68. They would like to leave a tip of approximately 16% of their bill. Which of the following is closest to that amount?
A. $6.40
B. $6.83
C. $7.25
D. $8.11
E. $8.96

9. **The correct answer is B.** Translate the problem into an equation and solve.

$42.68 · 16%

$42.68 · 0.16 = 6.8288, or approximately $6.83

4.4.4 Set Four

10. The pie chart below shows how a sports organization makes its profit. Last year the team made $2,000,000 in profit, and this year it increased its profits to $2,500,000. How much money was made on food sales in both years?

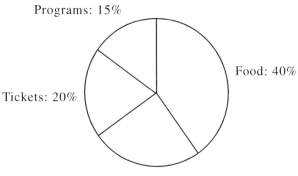

Programs: 15%

Tickets: 20%

Food: 40%

Souvenirs: 25%

F. 1,800,000
G. 1,000,000
H.   900,000
J.   800,000
K.   500,000

10. The correct answer is F. Translate the problem into an equation and solve. 40% of money was made in food sales for both years, so take 40% of both $2,000,000 and $2,500,000 and add.

$2,000,000 · 40%

$2,000,000 · 0.40

$800,000

$2,500,000 · 40%

$2,500,000 · 0.40

$1,000,000

$800,000 + $1,000,000 = $1,800,000

---

11. Stacie had a meal that cost $36.00. If she tipped the waiter 18% of the total bill for the service, how much was the tip?

A. $2.00
B. $3.96
C. $4.68
D. $5.76
E. $6.48

11. The correct answer is E. Translate the problem into an equation and solve.

18% · $36.00

0.18 · $36.00 = $6.48

---

12. While watching television from 8:00–9:00 one morning, Kiera notices that each commercial break is comprised of 3 commercials that are each 40 seconds long, and there are a total of 4 commercial breaks during that time. To the nearest percentage, what percentage of the hour was taken up by commercials?

F.   7%
G.   8%
H. 13%
J. 15%
K. 20%

12. The correct answer is H. Translate the problem into an equation and solve. First calculate the total amount of time that commercials took in that hour.

3 · 40 · 4 = 480 seconds of commercial breaks

1 minute = 60 seconds, so 480 seconds = $\frac{480}{60}$ = 8 minutes

Next, calculate what percentage of 60 minutes this 8 minutes represents.

$\frac{8}{60}$ ≈ 0.1333, or approximately 13%

4.4.5 Set Five

13. Brent has a diagram that he needs to place into a report. It is only 3.5" tall × 4" wide, but it needs to be about twice that big to make the impact he wants. Brent has use of a photocopy machine that can enlarge the height and width of an image by 20%. If he repeatedly uses the machine to enlarge each subsequent image, what is the minimum number of times he will have to make a copy to get the image to at least 7" tall?

   A. 1
   B. 2
   C. 3
   D. 4
   E. 5

13. The correct answer is D. Translate the problem into an equation and solve. Focus on the information asked about in the question: how many times Brent must enlarge the image so that it is at least 7" tall. Since he is starting with a height of 3.5", multiply this by 20% and add to the original 3.5" to see how tall it would be after one enlargement. Repeat until reaching 7".

One enlargement:

$3.5 + (3.5 \cdot 20\%)$

$3.5 + (3.5 \cdot 0.2)$

$3.5 + 0.7$

4.2

Two enlargements:

$4.2 + (4.2 \cdot 20\%)$

$4.2 + (4.2 \cdot 0.2)$

$4.2 + 0.84$

5.04

Three enlargements:

$5.04 + (5.04 \cdot 20\%)$

$5.04 + (5.04 \cdot 0.2)$

$5.04 + 1.008$

6.048

Four enlargements:

$6.048 + (6.048 \cdot 20\%)$

$6.048 + (6.048 \cdot 0.2)$

$6.048 + 1.2096$

7.2576

Four enlargements will be needed to reach 7".

14. Kelly needs to get a minimum of 75% on today's 60-point math test in order to pass the class. What is the least number of points that she must score to achieve this goal?

   F. 15
   G. 35
   H. 40
   J. 45
   K. 50

14. The correct answer is J. Translate the problem into an equation and solve.

$75\% \cdot 60$

$0.75 \cdot 60 = 45$

15. 480 is 8% of what number?

   A.   38.4
   B.   60
   C.   488
   D. 3,840
   E. 6,000

15. The correct answer is E. Translate the problem into an equation and solve.

$$480 = 8\% \cdot x$$

$$480 = 0.08x$$

$$6{,}000 = x$$

Lesson 4 – Percentages

Sum It Up

Percentages

Converting Percentages to Decimals
To convert a percentage to a decimal, move the decimal two places to the left and remove the percent sign.
Ex: 42% = 0.42, 5% = 0.05

Converting Decimals to Percentages
To convert a decimal to a percentage, move the decimal two places to the right and add a percent sign.
Ex: 0.33 = 33%, 0.012 = 1.2%

Converting Percentages to Fractions
To convert a percentage to a fraction, set the percentage over 100, remove the percent sign, and simplify.

Ex: $10\% = \dfrac{10}{100} = \dfrac{1}{10}$

Converting Fractions to Percentages
To convert a fraction to a percentage, convert the fraction to a decimal by dividing the numerator by the denominator, and then move the decimal two places to the right and add a percent sign.

Ex: $\dfrac{3}{4} = 0.75 = 75\%$

Percentage
A ratio expressing parts per 100

Tips and Techniques

Start Easy: Don't let the number of calculations overwhelm you. Start with the first thing you can do and work from there.

Show Your Work: Show your work, especially when working a percentage word problem.

Entrance Ticket   Learning Targets   Percentage of a Number   Word Problems with Percentages   ACT Practice   Sum It Up

61

4.5 Exit Ticket

▶ Students complete the three questions on their exit ticket.

Students are timed 3 minutes for the three questions (60 seconds per question). There is no break between questions.

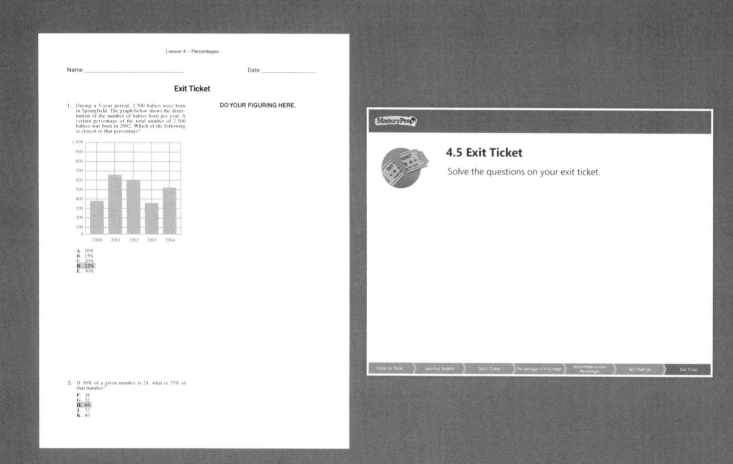

4.5 Exit Ticket Review

▶ Students complete the first question.

1. **The correct answer is D.** According to the graph, 600 babies were born in 2002. Calculate the percentage this represents of the total, 2,500.

   $$\frac{600}{2,500} = 0.24, \text{ or approximately 25\%}$$

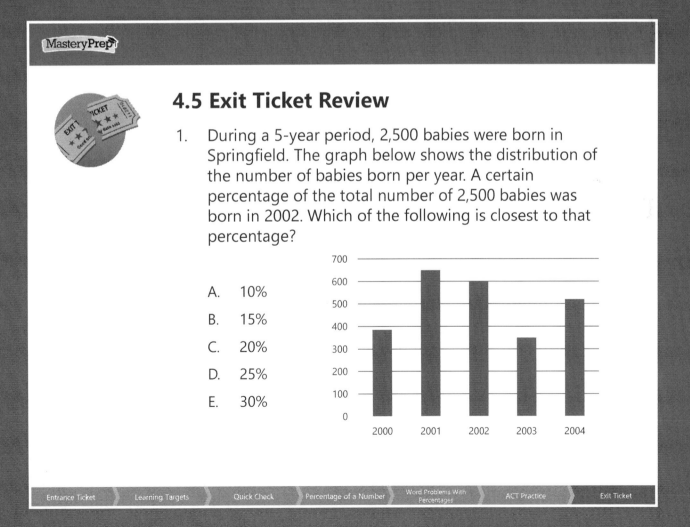

MasteryPrep

4.5 Exit Ticket Review

1. During a 5-year period, 2,500 babies were born in Springfield. The graph below shows the distribution of the number of babies born per year. A certain percentage of the total number of 2,500 babies was born in 2002. Which of the following is closest to that percentage?

   A. 10%

   B. 15%

   C. 20%

   D. 25%

   E. 30%

Entrance Ticket Learning Targets Quick Check Percentage of a Number Word Problems With Percentages ACT Practice Exit Ticket

4.5 Exit Ticket Review

▶ Students work the second question.

2. **The correct answer is H.** Translate the word problem into an equation and solve.

$30\% \cdot x = 24$

$0.3x = 24$

$x = 80$

$75\% \cdot 80$

$0.75 \cdot 80 = 60$

MasteryPrep

4.5 Exit Ticket Review

2. If 30% of a given number is 24, what is 75% of that number?

F. 18

G. 32

H. 60

J. 72

K. 80

4.5 Exit Ticket Review

▶ Students work the third question.

3. **The correct answer is E.** Of the students, 14 chose gym as their favorite subject. Calculate what percentage of 60 this represents.

$$\frac{14}{60} = 0.2333, \text{ or approximately } 23.3\%$$

▶ After all three questions are completed, students exchange papers. Solve the three exit items step by step on the board. Students grade using their red pens and then return papers to their classmates.

▶ After solving the three exit items, revisit the learning targets slide. Students again assess their knowledge and confidence on the same 1 to 4 scale that they used at the beginning of the lesson. Students write this number in the designated area at the start of the lesson in their workbooks, along with any comments or questions they might have.

▶ Finally, to close the lesson, have students return to the cover page of the lesson and write a caption for the picture there. The caption should be a one-sentence summary of the lesson, a main rule or tip they want to remember, or an explanation of how the picture relates to the topic. If there is additional time, students can share and compare their captions with the class.

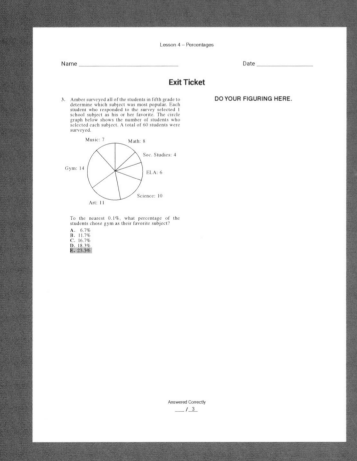

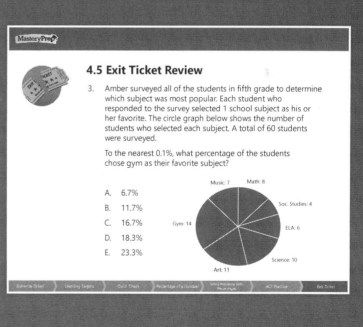

Percent Change

This lesson will cover how to solve problems involving percent increase, percent decrease, and a combination of percent increase and decrease.

ACT Standards:

AF 201. Solve problems in one or two steps using whole numbers and using decimals in the context of money

AF 301. Solve routine one-step arithmetic problems using positive rational numbers, such as single-step percentages

AF 401. Solve routine two-step or three-step arithmetic problems involving concepts such as rate and proportion, tax added, percentage off, and estimating by using a given average value in place of actual values

AF 601. Solve word problems containing several rates, proportions, or percentages

AF 701. Solve complex arithmetic problems involving percent of increase or decrease or requiring integration of several concepts (e.g., using several ratios, comparing percentages, or comparing averages)

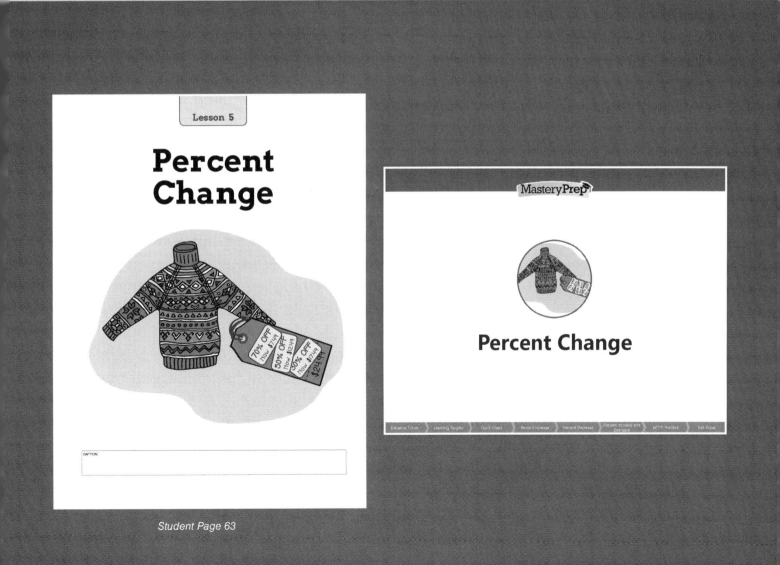

Student Page 63

5.1 Entrance Ticket

▶ Have students try the following three ACT practice questions. Students should work independently. Once the entrance ticket has been completed, review the questions with the students and have them share their answers. Give students the correct answers to the questions, as well as a step-by-step demonstration of how to solve the problems, but do not go into detailed explanation. This will serve as an introduction to the lesson content but is not intended to be the main lesson.

1. **The correct answer is C.** Calculate the discount and subtract this from the original amount.

   $75.82 \cdot 0.35 \approx 26.54$

   $75.82 - 26.54 = 49.28$

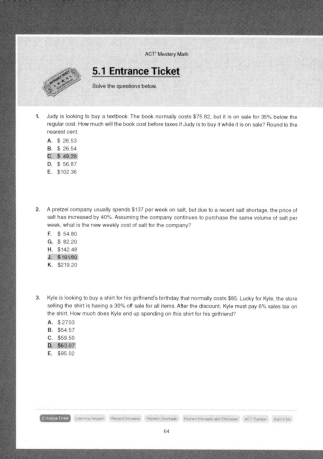

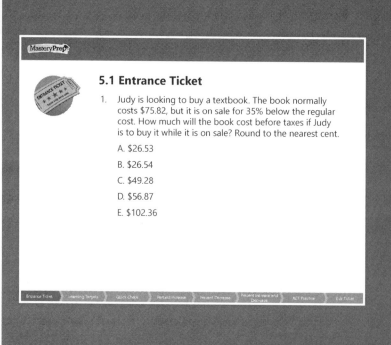

Student Page 64

5.1 Entrance Ticket

2. **The correct answer is J.** Calculate the increase in cost, and add it to the original weekly cost.

$137 · 0.4 = $54.80

$137 + $54.80 = $191.80

MasteryPrep

5.1 Entrance Ticket

2. A pretzel company usually spends $137 per week on salt, but due to a recent salt shortage, the price of salt has increased by 40%. Assuming the company continues to purchase the same volume of salt per week, what is the new weekly cost of salt for the company?

F. $54.80

G. $82.20

H. $142.48

J. $191.80

K. $219.20

| Entrance Ticket | Learning Targets | Quick Check | Percent Increase | Percent Decrease | Percent Increase and Decrease | ACT Practice | Exit Ticket |

5.1 Entrance Ticket

3. The correct answer is D. Calculate the discount and subtract this amount from the original. Then use this new value to calculate the sales tax, and add this to the discounted cost of the shirt to calculate the total cost.

$85 · 0.3 = $25.50

$85 − $25.50 = $59.50

$59.50 · 0.06 = $3.57

$59.50 + $3.57 = $63.07

5.1 Entrance Ticket

3. Kyle is looking to buy a shirt for his girlfriend's birthday that normally costs $85. Lucky for Kyle, the store selling the shirt is having a 30% off sale for all items. After the discount, Kyle must pay 6% sales tax on the shirt. How much does Kyle end up spending on this shirt for his girlfriend?

A. $27.03

B. $54.57

C. $59.50

D. $63.07

E. $95.02

| Entrance Ticket | Learning Targets | Quick Check | Percent Increase | Percent Decrease | Percent Increase and Decrease | ACT Practice | Exit Ticket |

5.2 Learning Targets

▶ Review learning targets with your students, displayed on the slide and in their workbooks.

▶ After reviewing the learning targets, ask students to assess their knowledge and confidence level on these targets. They should rate themselves on a scale of 1 to 4, with 1 being not confident or uncertain, and 4 being completely confident or certain. They should circle this number in the designated section of their workbooks.

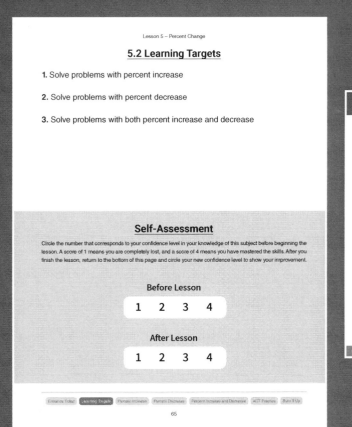

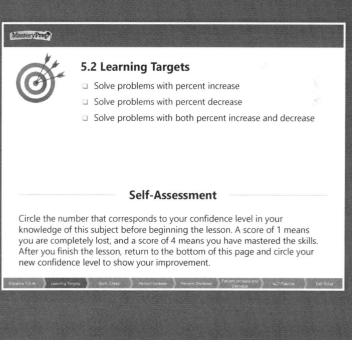

Student Page 65

5.2 Quick Check

▶ Teacher Dialogue: **What does a percentage represent?**

Percent: Parts per 100

▶ Next, have students fill in the following blanks.

When a value **increases** by a certain percentage, the new value will be represented by the original value _(answer: plus)_ the percent increase of the original value.

When a value **decreases** by a certain percentage, the new value will be represented by the original value _(answer: minus)_ the percent decrease of the original value.

5.3.1 Percent Increase

► Show students the following example on the slide, which is also in student workbooks.

You go out to eat, and your bill is $50. You want to tip your waiter 20%. What is the **total amount** you should pay on this bill?

► Give students one minute to discuss how they would approach this problem. Then call on a few students to offer their suggestions. What different steps would they need to take?

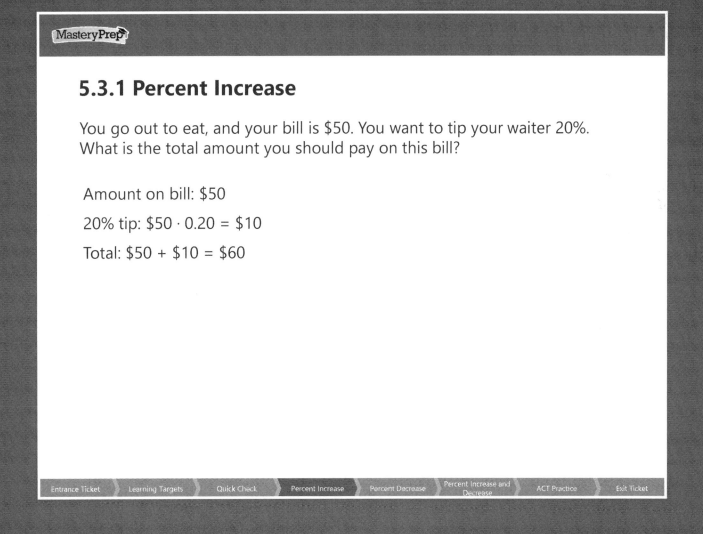

5.3.1 Percent Increase

▶ Review the calculations and solution displayed on the slide. Have students copy it all down into the corresponding portion of their workbooks.

Amount on bill: $50

20% tip: $50 · 0.2 = $10

Total: $50 + $10 = $60

▶ Ask students to come up with a formula for how to solve these types of problems. Give students one minute to work together and write their solutions on their whiteboards.

▶ Students should come up with something similar to:

Initial value + (Initial value)(Percent increase) = Value after increase

▶ Have students copy this formula down in the designated section of their workbooks.

5.3.1 Percent Increase

▶ Next, have students work independently on the following four practice problems in their workbooks. Give students 5 minutes to work through the practice problems on their own.

▶ After, have the students come together as a class and call on one student per question to write their solutions on the board. Go over each answer with the class, correcting any that are wrong.

1. A car rental service recently purchased all new vehicles. To help cover the cost, rental rates have to increase by 26% of the normal rate of $45.00 per day. What should the new rate be?

> **The correct answer is D.** Calculate the increase in rental rate and then add this to the original daily rate.
>
> $45 \cdot 0.26 = $11.70
>
> $45 + $11.70 = $56.70

2. Watermelons at a local stand now sell for $5.00 each. To make a profit, the owner marked up the original cost of the watermelons by 25%. What was the original cost of each watermelon?

> **The correct answer is G.** Work backward to calculate the original price.
>
> $x + 0.25x = $5.00
>
> $1.25x = $5.00
>
> $x = 4$, so the original price was $4.00

3. A computer analyst types at a speed of 80 words per minute. Over the next year, she wants to improve her speed by 20%. How fast does she want to be able to type 1 year from now, in words per minute?

> **The correct answer is D.** Calculate the increase in speed that would be represented by 20% and add this to her original speed.
>
> $80 \cdot 0.2 = 16$
>
> $80 + 16 = 96$

4. This summer, Fat Cow Ice Cream Shoppe increased its prices by 10% to try to make more profit. If an ice cream cone used to cost $3.50, how much does it cost now, after the price increase?

> **The correct answer is H.** Calculate the price increase and add it to the original price.
>
> $3.50 \cdot 0.1 = $0.35
>
> $3.50 + $0.35 = $3.85

> **Process of Elimination:** If the question is asking for a percent increase, you can eliminate any answer choices that are smaller than or equal to the original.

Student Page 66

Student Page 67

5.3.2 Percent Decrease

▶ Show students the following example on the slide, which is also in their workbooks.

You are shopping for a new sweatshirt. The sweatshirt you like is $40, and it has a 15% discount on it. What is the price of the sweatshirt after the discount?

▶ Give students one minute to discuss how they would approach this problem. Call on a few students to offer their suggestions on how to approach the problem. What different steps would they need to take?

5.3.2 Percent Decrease

You are shopping for a new sweatshirt. The sweatshirt you like is $40, and it has a 15% discount on it. What is the price of the sweatshirt after the discount?

Cost of sweatshirt: $40
15% discount: $40 · 0.15 = $6
Total: $40 − $6 = $34

| Entrance Ticket | Learning Targets | Quick Check | Percent Increase | Percent Decrease | Percent Increase and Decrease | ACT Practice | Exit Ticket |

5.3.2 Percent Decrease

► Show the solution on the slide and have students copy it all down into the designated portion of their workbooks.

　Cost of sweatshirt: $40

　15% discount: $40 · 0.15 = $6

　Total: $40 − $6 = $34

► Ask students to come up with a formula for how to solve these types of problems. Give students 1 minute to work together and write their solutions on their whiteboards.

► Students should come up with something similar to:

　Initial value − (Initial value)(Percent decrease) = Value after decrease

► Have students copy this formula down in the designated section of their workbooks.

► Teacher Dialogue:　**The formula is very similar to the formula for percent increase. The only difference is that you are subtracting the percent change from the total instead of adding it to the total.**

5.3.2 Percent Decrease

▶ Next, have students work independently on the following four practice problems in their workbooks. Give students 5 minutes to work through the practice problems on their own.

▶ After, have students come together as a class and call on one student per question to come up and write their solutions on the board. Go over each answer with the class, correcting any that are wrong.

1. Josh works on an assembly line at a local factory and makes $400 per week. However, Josh has to pay 23% of his check as taxes. How much money is Josh actually taking home every week?

   The correct answer is B. Calculate the amount that Josh pays in taxes and then subtract this from the original amount.

   $400 \cdot 0.23 = \$92$

   $400 - 92 = \$308$

2. Jeff is paid $9 an hour at the grocery store he works. He was caught sleeping at work 3 times this past week, so his boss gave him a 15% pay cut. How much does Jeff now earn per hour?

   The correct answer is F. Calculate the pay cut that Jeff was penalized, and then subtract this from his hourly rate.

   $9 \cdot 0.15 = \$1.35$

   $9 - \$1.35 = \$7.65$

Student Page 68

3. The price of a car was decreased from $13,000 to $11,830. The price decreased by what percentage?

   The correct answer is A. Calculate the price decrease and then what percentage this represents of the original price.

   $13,000 - 11,830 = \$1,170$

   $\dfrac{1,170}{13,000} = 0.09$, or 9%

4. A TV has an original price of $489.99 before taxes. It goes on sale for 35% below the original price. What is the new price (rounded to the nearest cent) of the TV, before taxes?

   The correct answer is G. Calculate the price after the reduction using the percent decrease formula.

   $489.99 - 489.99(0.35) = \$318.49$

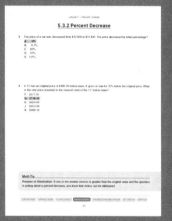

Student Page 69

Process of Elimination: If one of the answer choices is greater than the original value and the question is asking about a percent decrease, you know that choice can be eliminated.

5.3.3 Percent Increase and Decrease

▶ Show students the following problem on the slide. Have students break into pairs based on where they are seated. Give students 1 minute to discuss how they would approach this problem. After, have students come back together as a class and call on a few pairs to offer their suggestions on how to approach the problems. What steps would they need to take? Write the solutions on the board and have students copy them down into the designated portion of their workbooks.

Price of dishwasher: $300

20% discount: $300 · 0.2 = $60

Total: $300 − $60 = $240

Sale price of dishwasher: $240

5% sales tax: $240 · 0.05 = $12

Total: $240 + $12 = $252

MasteryPrep

5.3.3 Percent Increase and Decrease

You are trying to buy a dishwasher, and you see that one is on sale for 20% off. The original price of the dishwasher is $300. What would you pay for the dishwasher if there was a 5% sales tax added to the discounted price?

Price of dishwasher: $300
20% discount: $300 · 0.20 = $60
Total: $300 − $60 = $240

Sale price of dishwasher: $240
5% sales tax: $240 · 0.05 = $12
Total: $240 + $12 = $252

| Entrance Ticket | Learning Targets | Quick Check | Percent Increase | Percent Decrease | Percent Increase and Decrease | ACT Practice | Exit Ticket |

5.3.3 Percent Increase and Decrease

▶ Ask students, still in their pairs, to discuss any rules they can come up with for how to approach these types of problems (which have both percent increases and decreases). Give students one minute to discuss.

▶ Come together as a class and call on one pair to raise their hands and offer their answers. Guide a discussion toward the correct answer, and then have students write down the following principle in the designated portion of their workbooks:

When dealing with problems that have both percent increase and percent decrease, handle the problem **chronologically** (do whichever comes first and then do the next step).

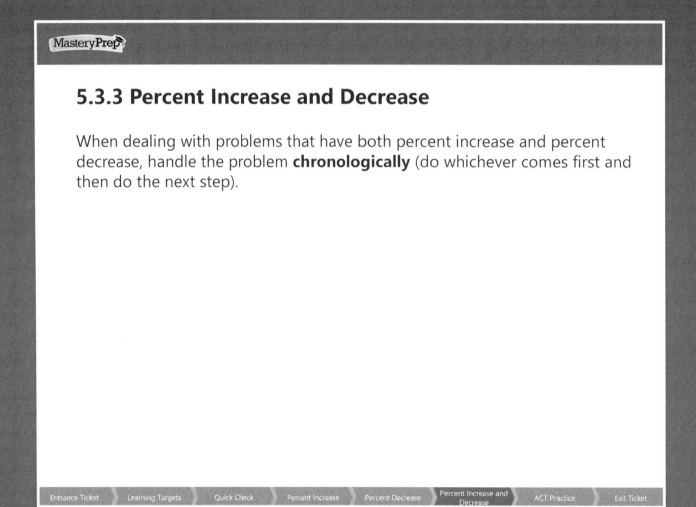

MasteryPrep

5.3.3 Percent Increase and Decrease

When dealing with problems that have both percent increase and percent decrease, handle the problem **chronologically** (do whichever comes first and then do the next step).

Entrance Ticket   Learning Targets   Quick Check   Percent Increase   Percent Decrease   Percent Increase and Decrease   ACT Practice   Exit Ticket

5.3.3 Percent Increase and Decrease

▶ Next, have students independently work on the following three practice problems in their workbooks. Give them 5 minutes.

▶ After, have students come together as a class and call on one student per question to write their solutions on the board. Go over each answer with the class, correcting any that are wrong.

1. Margaret always makes sure to bring coupons to the store. While shopping for cereal, she finds a box that is discounted by 12% from its normal price of $4.30. Margaret has a coupon that takes an additional 4% off the already discounted price. After a sales tax of 6% on the final price, how much does Margaret spend on the box of cereal?

   The correct answer is B. Calculate the 12% discount and subtract from the original price. Repeat with the additional 4% discount, and then calculate the 6% sales tax from this final discounted price and add it to the discounted cost for the final answer.

   $4.30 · 0.12 ≈ $0.52

   $4.30 − $0.52 = $3.78

   $3.78 · 0.04 ≈ $0.15

   $3.78 − $0.15 = $3.63

   $3.63 · 0.06 ≈ $0.22

   $3.63 + $0.22 = $3.85

Student Page 70

2. Alicia went shopping to buy some new clothes. She bought a shirt and a scarf that totaled $41.50, but she had a coupon for 50% off her total purchase before tax. What was the final price Alicia paid for her clothes after the 7% tax was added? Round your answer to the nearest cent.

   The correct answer is G. Calculate the coupon discount and subtract it from the original price. Then calculate the sales tax and add it to the discounted price.

   $41.50 · 0.5 = $20.75

   $41.50 − $20.75 = $20.75

   $20.75 · 0.07 = $1.45

   $20.75 + $1.45 = $22.20

Student Page 71

3. Carl went out to eat with his family for his birthday. The bill was $87.42, but Carl had a 10% off coupon. If Carl gave a 20% tip, what was the final price he paid for the meal?

   The correct answer is C. Calculate the coupon discount and subtract from the original price. Then calculate the tip and add to the discounted price.

   $87.42 · 0.1 = $8.742

   $87.42 − $8.742 = $78.678

   $78.678 · 0.2 = $15.735

   $78.68 + $15.735 = $94.41

5.4 ACT Practice

▶ Have students work on questions from the ACT practice sets here. Pacing should be 3 minutes per practice set or 60 seconds per question.

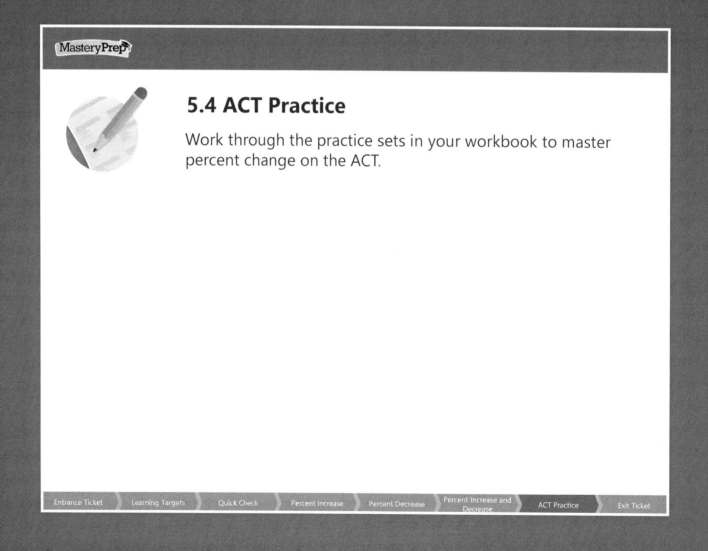

MasteryPrep

5.4 ACT Practice

Work through the practice sets in your workbook to master percent change on the ACT.

Entrance Ticket   Learning Targets   Quick Check   Percent Increase   Percent Decrease   Percent Increase and Decrease   ACT Practice   Exit Ticket

5.4.1 Set One

1. Kirk is getting a raise of 5% due to inflation. His normal salary is $56,000 per year. Which of the following calculations gives Kirk's new salary, in dollars?
   A. 56,000 + 5
   B. 56,000 + 56,000(0.05)
   C. 56,000 + 56,000(0.50)
   D. 56,000 + 56,000(5)
   E. 56,000(.05)

1. **The correct answer is B.** The calculation will be represented by Kirk's original salary plus the amount of his raise.

   56,000 + 56,000(0.05)

2. A bed frame normally weighs 60 pounds. A new, stronger material increases the durability of the frame but makes it weigh 30% more. How many pounds does the new frame weigh?
   F. 63
   G. 66
   H. 78
   J. 90
   K. 102

2. **The correct answer is H.** Calculate the increase in weight and then add it to the original weight.

   60 · 0.3 = 18

   60 + 18 = 78

3. Mifflin Paper Company just upgraded to a heavier cardstock paper for its $42.00 business cards. To compensate for the increase in quality, Mifflin Paper Company is raising its prices by 19%. What is the new price of business cards?
   A. $42.19
   B. $43.90
   C. $47.50
   D. $48.88
   E. $49.98

3. **The correct answer is E.** Calculate the amount of the price increase and add it to the original price.

   $42.00 · 0.19 = $7.98

   $42.00 + $7.98 = $49.98

5.4.2 Set Two

4. The table below shows average milk prices at the local grocery store for the past 5 years.

Year	Price
2011	$2.36
2012	$2.45
2013	$3.15
2014	$2.50
2015	$3.40

From 2010 to 2011, the average price of a gallon of milk increased by 14%. What was the average price of a gallon of milk in 2010?

F. $2.07
G. $2.11
H. $2.22
J. $2.30
K. $2.69

4. **The correct answer is F.** Work backward to calculate the price of a gallon of milk in 2010.

$x + 0.14x = \$2.36$

$1.14x = \$2.36$

$x \approx \$2.07$

5. The table below shows the delivery charge per mile for Polly's Pizzeria over the past 3 months.

Month 1	Month 2	Month 3
$0.50	$0.36	$0.45

By how much did the delivery charge increase from Month 2 to Month 3?

A. 9%
B. 12%
C. 18%
D. 25%
E. 80%

5. **The correct answer is D.** Calculate how much the delivery charge increased between Month 2 and Month 3, and then calculate how much of the original charge (in Month 2) this represents.

$\$0.45 - \$0.36 = \$0.09$

$\dfrac{\$0.09}{\$0.36} = 25\%$

6. Employees at Anderson Manufacturing receive a raise of 4.5% at the end of each year. An employee with an annual salary of $46,000.00 this year will have what annual salary next year?

F. $46,004.50
G. $46,045.00
H. $48,070.00
J. $56,682.00
K. $64,722.00

6. **The correct answer is H.** Calculate the percent raise that the employee will receive, and then add it to the original salary.

$\$46,000 \cdot 0.045 \approx \$2,070$

$\$46,000 + \$2,070 = \$48,070$

5.4.3 Set Three

7. Barry bought a new car for $15,000. The value of the car depreciated by 25% after driving off the lot. After a year of driving the car, the value depreciated by an additional 15%. What percentage of the original value is the car now worth? Round your answer to the nearest percentage.

   A. 4%
   B. 10%
   C. 40%
   D. 46%
   E. 64%

7. **The correct answer is E.** Calculate the 25% depreciation and subtract from the original price. Repeat with this new amount for the additional 15% depreciation, and then calculate the percentage this new price represents of the original price.

   $15,000 \cdot 0.25 = $3,750

   $15,000 − $3,750 = $11,250

   $11,250 \cdot 0.15 = $1,687.50

   $11,250 − $1,687.50 = $9,562.50

   $\dfrac{\$9,562.50}{\$15,000}$ = 63.75%, or approximately 64%

8. The table below gives prices for different services at Quick Wash.

Wash	Vacuum	Wax	Shine
$12.00	$4.00	$15.00	$10.00

   Albert took his car to Quick Wash for a wash, wax, and shine. He paid full price for the wash and shine but got 25% off the wax. How much did Albert spend at Quick Wash?

   F. $11.25
   G. $27.75
   H. $33.25
   J. $34.50
   K. $37.00

8. **The correct answer is H.** Calculate the discount Albert received off the wax and subtract from the original price. Then add to the other prices that Albert paid.

   $15 \cdot 0.25 = $3.75

   $15 − $3.75 = $11.25 for the wax.

   $11.25 + $12.00 + $10.00 = $33.25

9. Shelly wants to tell her friend how large of a sale a local store is having, but she forgets the discount amount. All Shelly knows is that she bought a shirt for $6 that normally costs $10. Shelly can tell her friend that the store has decreased prices by how much?

   A. 4%
   B. 20%
   C. 24%
   D. 35%
   E. 40%

9. **The correct answer is E.** Calculate the number of dollars the shirt was discounted and then calculate the percentage it represents of the original price.

   $10 − $6 = $4

   $\dfrac{4}{10}$ = 40%

5.4.4 Set Four

10. Polka Dot Boutique is having a sale of 15% off previously marked down items. Gwen finds a pair of jeans originally priced at $45.00 and marked down by 25%. She must pay a 6% sales tax on the final price of the jeans. How much does Gwen spend at Polka Dot Boutique?

F. $28.62
G. $30.41
H. $33.00
J. $33.99
K. $51.68

10. The correct answer is G. Calculate the 25% discount off the original price and then subtract it from the original. Repeat with the 15% additional discount and then calculate the sales tax. Add this to the total.

$45.00 · 0.25 = $11.25

$45.00 − $11.25 = $33.75

$33.75 · 0.15 ≈ $5.06

$33.75 − $5.06 = $28.69

$28.69 · 0.06 = $1.72

$28.69 + $1.72 = $30.41

11. At a gas station, all chips are marked down 10%. A customer brings a bag of chips with a regular price of $2.19 to the register. After the 7% sales tax on the final price, how much does the customer pay for the bag of chips? Round your answer to the nearest cent.

A. $2.02
B. $2.09
C. $2.11
D. $2.22
E. $2.24

11. The correct answer is C. Calculate the discount and subtract from the original price. Then calculate the sales tax and add to this total.

$2.19 · 0.1 ≈ $0.22

$2.19 − $0.22 = $1.97

$1.97 · 0.07 ≈ $0.14

$1.97 + $0.14 = $2.11

12. A number is decreased by 50%, and the resulting number is then increased by 300%. The original number is what percentage of the final number?

F. 20%
G. 25%
H. 40%
J. 50%
K. 400%

12. The correct answer is J. Let 100 represent this number for the purposes of the problem. Decreased by 50%, this would then be 50. 50 increased by 300% = 50 + (3.00)(50) = 50 + 150 = 200. The original number, 100, is 50% of 200.

5.4.5 Set Five

13. A bakery is having a *buy 4, get 1 free* sale on cakes. This sale is equivalent to what percentage off the regular price of all 5 cakes?
    A. 1%
    B. 10%
    C. 20%
    D. 25%
    E. 40%

13. **The correct answer is C.** For the purpose of the question, assume that each cake is $2. In this sale, you would get 5 cakes for $8 (which would normally cost $10). This represents $2 off the regular price, or 20% off the regular price.

14. In order for Carlton's Car Dealership to make a profit, it must mark up the dealer price of cars by 14%. After the increase, a new sedan at Carl's Car Dealership is marked to sell for $14,600. What is the dealer price of the sedan?
    F. $12,807
    G. $12,556
    H. $13,114
    J. $13,200
    K. $14,586

14. **The correct answer is F.** Work backward to calculate the dealer price of the sedan.

    $x + 0.14x = \$14{,}600$

    $1.14x = \$14{,}600$

    $x \approx \$12{,}807$

15. The school faculty is having a catered meeting. The catering service charges a $40.00 fee up front. The school buys $33.00 worth of pasta and $45.50 worth of sandwiches. The catering service expects an 18% tip on the food subtotal. How much does the school end up paying for the whole catered meeting?
    A. $ 64.37
    B. $ 92.63
    C. $104.37
    D. $132.63
    E. $139.83

15. **The correct answer is D.** Calculate the total cost of food, and then the tip that will be required (which is only based on the total cost of food). Add these amounts together, along with the $40 fee.

    $\$33 + \$45.50 = \$78.50$

    $\$78.50 \cdot 0.18 = \$14.13$

    $\$78.50 + \$14.13 + \$40.00 = \$132.63$

Lesson 5 – Percent Change

Sum It Up

Percent Change

Percent
Parts per 100

Percent Increase
Initial value + (Initial value)(Percent increase) = Value after increase

---

Percent Decrease
Initial value – (Initial value)(Percent decrease) = Value after decrease

---

Percent Increase and Decrease
Handle the problem chronologically (do the calculation that comes first, and then do the other)

Tips and Techniques

Process of Elimination: If you get stuck, look at the numbers in the problem and make as many eliminations as you can based on the size of the answer choices.

Entrance Ticket | Learning Targets | Percent Increase | Percent Decrease | Percent Increase and Decrease | ACT Practice | Sum It Up

77

Student Page 77

136

5.5 Exit Ticket

▶ Students complete the three questions on their exit ticket.

Students are timed 3 minutes for the three questions (60 seconds per question). There is no break between questions.

Name _____   Date _____

Exit Ticket

1. A deli made $320,000 in revenue last year. Due to increased popularity of the deli, the owner predicts that revenue will increase by 23% next year. How much revenue does the owner think the deli will generate next year?

   A. $320,230
   B. $322,300
   C. $343,000
   D. $393,600
   E. $422,400

DO YOUR FIGURING HERE.

2. Barney made $1,400 from his investments last year but is taxed at a 12% rate for his investment earnings. How much money did Barney earn from his investments last year after taxes?

   F. $1,232
   G. $1,258
   H. $1,352
   J. $1,372
   K. $1,388

3. Miles is shopping for a new computer. He finds a computer with an original price of $325.00 but finds that it is 15% off. After paying a 7% sales tax, how much does Miles spend on his new computer?

   A. $295.59
   B. $303.00
   C. $330.36
   D. $399.91
   E. $469.63

Answered Correctly
___ / 3

MasteryPrep

5.5 Exit Ticket

Solve the questions on your exit ticket.

5.5 Exit Ticket Review

▶ Students work the first question.

1. **The correct answer is D.** Calculate the projected revenue increase and then add to last year's revenue total.

    $320,000 · 0.23 = $73,600

    $320,000 + $73,600 = $393,600

5.5 Exit Ticket Review

1. A deli made $320,000 in revenue last year. Due to increased popularity of the deli, the owner predicts that revenue will increase by 23% next year. How much revenue does the owner think the deli will generate next year?

    A. $320,230

    B. $322,300

    C. $343,000

    D. $393,600

    E. $422,400

Entrance Ticket | Learning Targets | Quick Check | Percent Increase | Percent Decrease | Percent Increase and Decrease | ACT Practice | Exit Ticket

5.5 Exit Ticket Review

▶ Students work the second question.

2. **The correct answer is F.** Calculate the amount Barney pays in taxes and subtract it from the original.

$1,400 · 0.12 = $168

$1,400 − $168 = $1,232

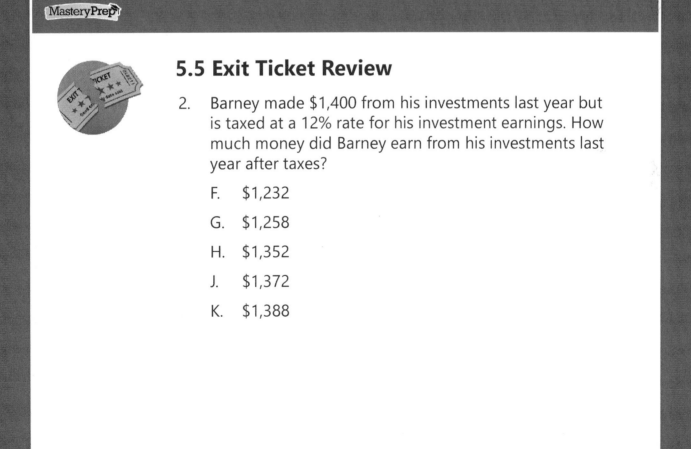

MasteryPrep

5.5 Exit Ticket Review

2. Barney made $1,400 from his investments last year but is taxed at a 12% rate for his investment earnings. How much money did Barney earn from his investments last year after taxes?

F. $1,232

G. $1,258

H. $1,352

J. $1,372

K. $1,388

| Entrance Ticket | Learning Targets | Quick Check | Percent Increase | Percent Decrease | Percent Increase and Decrease | ACT Practice | Exit Ticket |

5.5 Exit Ticket Review

▶ Students work the third question.

> 3. **The correct answer is A.** Calculate the discount that Miles used and subtract from the original price. Then calculate the sales tax and add to this value.
>
> $325.00 · 0.15 = $48.75
>
> $325.00 − $48.75 = $276.25
>
> $276.25 · 0.07 ≈ $19.34
>
> $276.25 + $19.34 = $295.59

▶ After all three questions are completed, students exchange papers. Solve the three exit items step by step on the board. Students grade using their red pens and then return papers to their classmates.

▶ After solving the three exit items, revisit the learning targets slide. Students again assess their knowledge and confidence on the same 1 to 4 scale that they used at the beginning of the lesson. Students write this number in the designated area at the start of the lesson in their workbooks, along with any comments or questions they might have.

▶ Finally, to close the lesson, have students return to the cover page of the lesson and write a caption for the picture there. The caption should be a one-sentence summary of the lesson, a main rule or tip they want to remember, or an explanation of how the picture relates to the topic. If there is additional time, students can share and compare their captions with the class.

5.5 Exit Ticket Review

3. Miles is shopping for a new computer. He finds a computer with an original price of $325.00 but finds that it is 15% off. After paying a 7% sales tax, how much does Miles spend on his new computer?

   A. $295.59

   B. $303.00

   C. $330.36

   D. $399.91

   E. $469.63

Fractions

This lesson will show students how to add, subtract, multiply, and divide fractions and mixed numbers, from simple to complex multi-step problems.

ACT Standards:

N 202. Recognize equivalent fractions and fractions in lowest terms

N 501. Order fractions

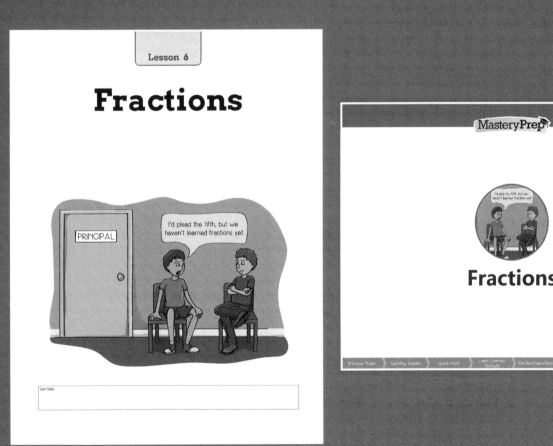

Student Page 79

6.1 Entrance Ticket

▶ Have students try the following three ACT practice questions. Students should work independently. Once the entrance ticket has been completed, review the questions with the students and have them share their answers. Give students the correct answers to the questions, as well as a step-by-step demonstration of how to solve the problems, but do not go into detailed explanation. This will serve as an introduction to the lesson content but is not intended to be the main lesson.

1. **The correct answer is B.** Count the shaded squares and set this number over the total, 64.

$$\frac{24}{64} = \frac{12}{32} = \frac{6}{16} = \frac{3}{8}$$

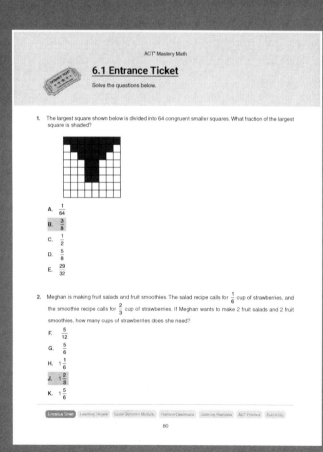

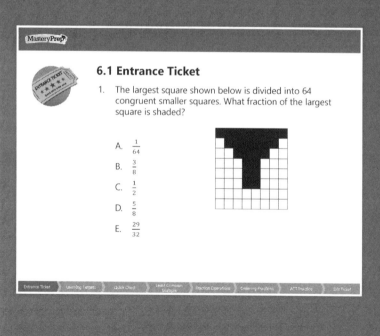

Student Page 80

6.1 Entrance Ticket

2. **The correct answer is J.** Multiply both quantities needed by 2 and then add.

$$\frac{1}{6} \cdot 2 = \frac{2}{6} = \frac{1}{3}$$

$$\frac{2}{3} \cdot 2 = \frac{4}{3}$$

$$\frac{1}{3} + \frac{4}{3} = \frac{5}{3} = 1\frac{2}{3}$$

MasteryPrep

6.1 Entrance Ticket

2. Meghan is making fruit salads and fruit smoothies. The salad recipe calls for $\frac{1}{6}$ cup of strawberries, and the smoothie recipe calls for $\frac{2}{3}$ cup of strawberries. If Meghan wants to make 2 fruit salads and 2 fruit smoothies, how many cups of strawberries does she need?

    F. $\frac{5}{12}$

    G. $\frac{5}{6}$

    H. $1\frac{1}{6}$

    J. $1\frac{2}{3}$

    K. $1\frac{5}{6}$

Entrance Ticket　Learning Targets　Quick Check　Least Common Multiple　Fraction Operations　Ordering Fractions　ACT Practice　Exit Ticket

6.1 Entrance Ticket

3. **The correct answer is B.** First, find the number of students going to college. Then multiply by one-half to determine how many of those are going to an in-state college.

$$482 \cdot \frac{5}{8} = 301.25$$

$$301.25 \cdot \frac{1}{2} = 150.625 \approx 150$$

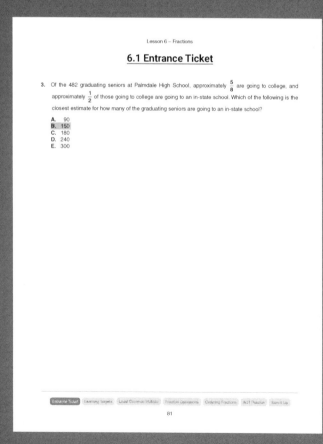

Student Page 81

6.2 Learning Targets

▶ Review learning targets with your students, displayed on the slide and in their workbooks.

▶ After reviewing the learning targets, ask students to assess their knowledge and confidence level on these targets. They should rate themselves on a scale of 1 to 4, with 1 being not confident or uncertain, and 4 being completely confident or certain. They should circle this number in the designated section of their workbooks.

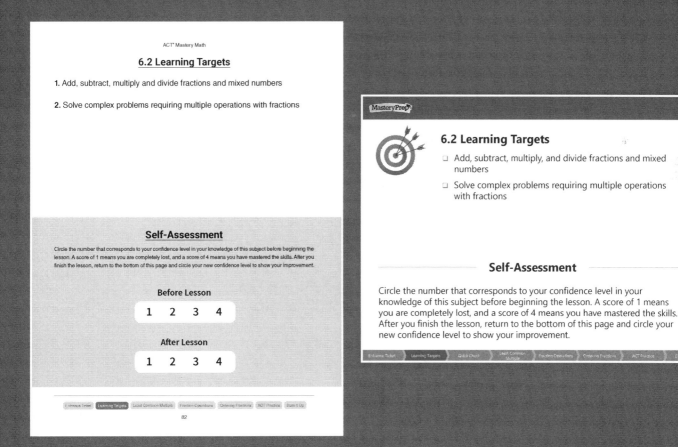

Student Page 82

6.2 Quick Check

▸ Teacher Dialogue: **Define _fraction_.**

Fraction: A number that represents a part of a whole; expressed as the division of one whole number by another

▸ Teacher Dialogue: **Define _numerator_.**

Numerator: The top number of a fraction

▸ Teacher Dialogue: **Define _denominator_.**

Denominator: The bottom number of a fraction

▸ Present students with the following examples of reciprocals:

$$\text{For 3, the reciprocal is } \frac{1}{3}.$$

$$\text{For } \frac{3}{4}, \text{ the reciprocal is } \frac{4}{3}.$$

$$\text{For } -\frac{11}{7}, \text{ the reciprocal is } -\frac{7}{11}.$$

▸ Teacher Dialogue: **Based on these examples, what is the definition of a reciprocal?**

Reciprocal: A number that is related to another number so that their product is equal to 1

6.2 Quick Check

▶ Present students with the following examples of a least common multiple (LCM):

> For 2 and 3, the LCM is 6.
>
> For 4 and 6, the LCM is 12.
>
> For 3 and 15, the LCM is 15.

▶ Teacher Dialogue: **Based on these examples, what is the definition of** *least common multiple (LCM)?*

<u>**Least Common Multiple (LCM):**</u> For any given two numbers, the lowest number that has both as factors

▶ Present students with the following examples of a least common denominator (LCD):

> For $\dfrac{2}{3}$ and $\dfrac{1}{2}$, the LCD is 6 (could rewrite fractions as $\dfrac{4}{6}$ and $\dfrac{3}{6}$).
>
> For $\dfrac{1}{4}$ and $\dfrac{2}{5}$, the LCD is 20 (could rewrite fractions as $\dfrac{5}{20}$ and $\dfrac{8}{20}$).
>
> For $\dfrac{3}{4}$ and $\dfrac{11}{12}$, the LCD is 12 (could rewrite fractions as $\dfrac{9}{12}$ and $\dfrac{11}{12}$).

▶ Teacher Dialogue: **Based on these examples, what is the definition of the** *least common denominator (LCD)?*

<u>**Least Common Denominator (LCD):**</u> The smallest denominator two fractions can share, found by calculating the least common multiple (LCM) of the denominators

▶ Teacher Dialogue: **As we will see later in the lesson, the LCD is essential when adding and subtracting fractions.**

6.2 Quick Check

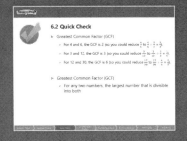

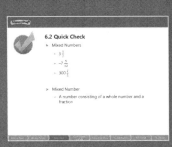

▶ Present students with the following examples of a greatest common factor (GCF):

For 4 and 6, the GCF is 2 (so you could reduce $\dfrac{4}{6}$ to $\dfrac{4}{6} \div \dfrac{2}{2} = \dfrac{2}{3}$).

For 3 and 12, the GCF is 3 (so you could reduce $\dfrac{3}{12}$ to $\dfrac{3}{12} \div \dfrac{3}{3} = \dfrac{1}{4}$).

For 12 and 30, the GCF is 6 (so you could reduce $\dfrac{12}{30}$ to $\dfrac{12}{30} \div \dfrac{6}{6} = \dfrac{2}{5}$).

▶ Teacher Dialogue: **Based on these examples, what is the definition of the greatest common factor (GCF)?**

<u>Greatest Common Factor (GCF):</u> For any two numbers, the largest number that is divisible into both

▶ Teacher Dialogue: **The GCF is used in reducing fractions to lowest terms.**

▶ Present students with the following examples of mixed numbers:

$$3\frac{1}{2}$$

$$-7\frac{5}{12}$$

$$300\frac{2}{5}$$

▶ Teacher Dialogue: **Define *mixed number*.**

<u>Mixed number:</u> A number consisting of a whole number and a fraction

6.2 Quick Check

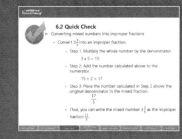

▶ Show students how to convert mixed numbers to improper fractions.

▶ First, review with students the basics of converting mixed numbers to improper fractions. Remind students that an improper fraction is a fraction whose numerator is larger than the denominator.

▶ Work this example for them.

Convert $3\frac{2}{5}$ to an improper fraction.

Step 1: Multiply the whole number by the denominator.
$$3 \cdot 5 = 15$$

Step 2: Add the number calculated above to the numerator.
$$15 + 2 = 17$$

Step 3: Place the number calculated in Step 2 above the original denominator in the mixed fraction.
$$\frac{17}{5}$$

Thus, you can write the mixed number $3\frac{2}{5}$ as the improper fraction $\frac{17}{5}$.

6.3.1 Least Common Multiple

▶ Separate the class into teams. Tell students to raise their hands when they know the least common multiple (LCM) of the two numbers presented. Students earn points for their teams by correctly identifying the LCMs.

▶ Do one test to familiarize students with the concept of the game. Write "2, 3" on the board and have them find the LCM.

Correct answer: 6.

▶ When students are comfortable with the format, present the following problems:

3, 5

LCM: 15

4, 6

LCM: 12

10, 12

LCM: 60

5, 8

LCM: 40

2, 5, 7

LCM: 70

3, 6, 22

LCM: 66

4, 12, 15

LCM: 60

▶ At the end of the game, tally the points that each team received and declare a winner.

Student Page 83

6.3.1 Least Common Multiple

1) 3, 5
   LCM: 15
2) 4, 6
   LCM: 12
3) 10, 12
   LCM: 60
4) 5, 8
   LCM: 40
5) 2, 5, 7
   LCM: 70
6) 3, 6, 22
   LCM: 66
7) 4, 12, 15
   LCM: 60

6.3.2 Fraction Operations

▸ Next, move into some practice to help students solidify their skills in adding fractions.

▸ Write the following problem on the board and work through the problem step by step for the students, showing all work. Work through the problem in silence.

$$\frac{1}{2} + \frac{1}{3}$$

$$\frac{3}{6} + \frac{2}{6}$$

$$\frac{5}{6}$$

▸ When finished, ask a student volunteer to come to the board and explain the steps to the class. Then review the steps as stated on the slide.

Be sure students know that when converting, they must multiply the numerator and denominator by the same number.

MasteryPrep

6.3.2 Fraction Operations

$$\frac{1}{2} + \frac{1}{3}$$

▸ Step 1: Find the lowest common denominator and convert the fractions to get the same denominator.

▸ $\frac{3}{6} + \frac{2}{6}$

▸ Step 2: Add the two fractions together and simplify if necessary. Add the numerators while keeping the denominator constant.

▸ $\frac{5}{6}$

6.3.2 Fraction Operations

▶ Next, write the following problem on the board:

$$\frac{2}{5} - \frac{1}{8}$$

▶ Have a student come up to work the problem in silence on the board. After each step, stop the student and ask volunteers from the class to explain (or question) what the student has done. Refine the student responses as necessary; otherwise, see if students can explain each step. Then, review the steps as stated on the slide.

MasteryPrep

6.3.2 Fraction Operations

$$\frac{2}{5} - \frac{1}{8}$$

▶ Step 1: Find the lowest common denominator and convert the fractions to get the same denominator.

$$\frac{16}{40} - \frac{5}{40}$$

▶ Step 2: Subtract the two fractions and simplify if necessary.

$$\frac{11}{40}$$

Entrance Ticket Learning Targets Quick Check Least Common Multiple Fraction Operations Ordering Fractions ACT Practice Exit Ticket

6.3.2 Fraction Operations

► Finally, write the following problem on the board.

$$\frac{7}{9} + \frac{1}{4} - \frac{2}{5}$$

► Have a student come up to work the problem in silence on the board. After each step, stop the student and ask volunteers from the class to explain (or question) what the student has done. Refine the student responses as necessary; otherwise, see if students can explain each step. Then, review the steps as stated on the slide.

MasteryPrep

6.3.2 Fraction Operations

$$\frac{7}{9} + \frac{1}{4} - \frac{2}{5}$$

▶ Step 1: Find the lowest common denominator and convert the fractions to get the same denominator.

  $\dfrac{140}{180} + \dfrac{45}{180} - \dfrac{72}{180}$

▶ Step 2: Add the first two fractions together, subtract the third fraction, and simplify if necessary.

▶ $\dfrac{113}{180}$

6.3.2 Fraction Operations

▶ Next, give students six addition/subtraction problems with different denominators. Have them work on each problem independently.

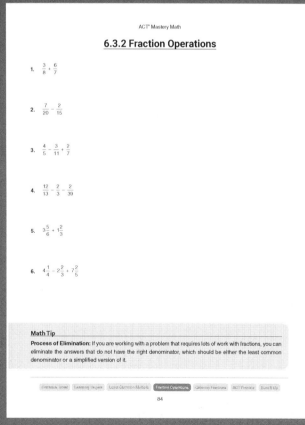

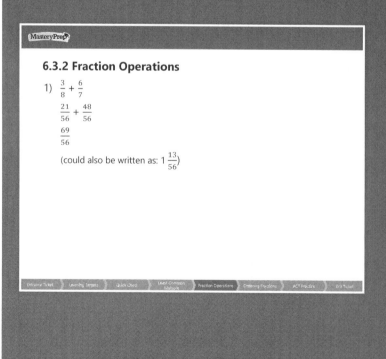

Student Page 84

6.3.2 Fraction Operations

▶ Once students have finished the problems, ask a student volunteer for the correct answer to each problem. If students have questions on any particular problem, work the problem on the board or have a student volunteer work the problem.

1. $\dfrac{3}{8} + \dfrac{6}{7}$

   $\dfrac{21}{56} + \dfrac{48}{56}$

   $\dfrac{69}{56}$

   (can also be written as: $1\dfrac{13}{56}$)

2. $\dfrac{7}{20} - \dfrac{2}{15}$

   $\dfrac{21}{60} - \dfrac{8}{60}$

   $\dfrac{13}{60}$

3. $\dfrac{4}{5} - \dfrac{3}{11} + \dfrac{2}{7}$

   $\dfrac{308}{385} - \dfrac{105}{385} + \dfrac{110}{385}$

   $\dfrac{313}{385}$

6.3.2 Fraction Operations

4. $\dfrac{12}{13} - \dfrac{2}{3} - \dfrac{2}{39}$

$\dfrac{36}{39} - \dfrac{26}{39} - \dfrac{2}{39}$

$\dfrac{8}{39}$

5. $3\dfrac{5}{6} + 1\dfrac{2}{3}$

$\dfrac{23}{6} + \dfrac{5}{3}$

$\dfrac{23}{6} + \dfrac{10}{6}$

$\dfrac{33}{6}$, which can be reduced to $\dfrac{11}{2}$.

(can also be written as $5\dfrac{1}{2}$)

6. $4\dfrac{1}{4} - 2\dfrac{2}{3} + 7\dfrac{2}{5}$

$\dfrac{17}{4} - \dfrac{8}{3} + \dfrac{37}{5}$

$\dfrac{255}{60} - \dfrac{160}{60} + \dfrac{444}{60}$

$\dfrac{539}{60}$, which can also be written as $8\dfrac{59}{60}$.

If you are not sure how to solve a problem, it is always helpful to narrow down your answer choices using the process of elimination. When it comes to fractions, you can eliminate the answer options that don't have the right denominator, which should be either the least common denominator or a simplified version of it.

6.3.2 Fraction Operations

▶ Write $\frac{1}{2} \div \frac{1}{4}$ on the board.

▶ Teacher Dialogue: **Restate the problem $\frac{1}{2} \div \frac{1}{4}$ in a different way.**

Students may come up with answers such as the following:

$$\frac{\left(\frac{1}{2}\right)}{\left(\frac{1}{4}\right)} \text{ or } \frac{1}{2} \cdot \frac{4}{1}$$

The latter is the target response. If students do not come up with this, write it on the board for the next discussion.

▶ Teacher Dialogue: **What happened when we converted the problem into multiplication? What stayed the same, and what changed? How did it change?**

Allow students to volunteer some points. Then reveal the steps as given on the slide.

1. Keep the first fraction.
2. Change the operation from division to multiplication.
3. Flip the second fraction to its reciprocal.

Have students write down the above steps in their workbooks.

▶ Teacher Dialogue: **Any fraction can be rewritten as a division problem: numerator ÷ denominator. An easy way to remember is to say, "Keep, change, flip!"**

▶ Next, silently model solving a "fraction of a fraction" problem on the board.

$$\frac{3}{4} \div \frac{2}{5} \qquad \frac{3}{4} \cdot \frac{5}{2} \qquad \frac{15}{8}$$

▶ Ask for feedback from the whole class on the correct steps used. They should follow the steps enumerated above.

Keep the first fraction as is: $\frac{3}{4}$

Change the operation from division to multiplication: ·

Flip the second fraction: $\frac{5}{2}$

Multiply the numerators and denominators: $\frac{3}{4} \cdot \frac{5}{2} = \frac{15}{8}$

Student Page 85

6.3.2 Fraction Operations

▶ Have students solve the five "fraction of a fraction" problems in their workbooks. Students should work independently.

▶ Once students have finished, go through each question, asking a student volunteer to give the answer and write the work on the board. Correct answers and steps for solving are given in the slide.

1. $\dfrac{1}{2} \div \dfrac{3}{4}$

    $\dfrac{1}{2} \cdot \dfrac{4}{3}$

    $\dfrac{4}{6}$

    $\dfrac{2}{3}$

2. $\dfrac{4}{5} \div \dfrac{2}{3}$

    $\dfrac{4}{5} \cdot \dfrac{3}{2}$

    $\dfrac{12}{10}$

    $\dfrac{6}{5}$

3. $\dfrac{7}{11} \div \dfrac{1}{22}$

    $\dfrac{7}{11} \cdot \dfrac{22}{1}$

    $\dfrac{154}{11}$

    $\dfrac{14}{1}$

    14

4. $\dfrac{5}{7} \div \dfrac{6}{13}$

    $\dfrac{5}{7} \cdot \dfrac{13}{6}$

    $\dfrac{65}{42}$

5. $\dfrac{3}{5} \div \dfrac{5}{12}$

    $\dfrac{3}{5} \cdot \dfrac{12}{5}$

    $\dfrac{36}{25}$

6.3.3 Ordering Fractions

▶ Teacher Dialogue: **Write down a fraction of your choosing, using no numerals over 9 in the numerator and no numerals over 25 in the denominator.**

Call on two individual students and write their fractions on the board, reducing to lowest terms if necessary.

▶ Teacher Dialogue: **Which fraction is larger?**

Make students justify their answers. Even if students give an incorrect response, have them attempt to explain their answer so they learn through trial and error.

▶ Add a third student's fraction to the board and ask students where it should go on the list, if ordering from smallest to largest. Have students write the fractions in numerical order in the three blanks in their workbooks. Do the same with a fourth and a fifth student, again having students write the fractions in order in the blanks in their workbooks.

ACT® Mastery Math

6.3.3 Ordering Fractions

1. $\frac{1}{3}, \frac{5}{12}, \frac{1}{5}, \frac{3}{7}, \frac{4}{13}$

2. $\frac{3}{4}, \frac{1}{6}, \frac{4}{11}, \frac{5}{8}, \frac{1}{9}$

3. $\frac{1}{2}, \frac{7}{8}, \frac{2}{7}, \frac{1}{5}, \frac{2}{3}$

4. $\frac{4}{9}, -\frac{2}{3}, \frac{1}{12}, -\frac{4}{5}, \frac{3}{10}$

5. $\frac{7}{10}, -0.5, -\frac{1}{3}, \frac{5}{12}, 0.45$

Math Tip

Process of Elimination: If an ACT math question asks you to order fractions, begin with the first choice and compare two fractions at a time. As soon as you find one fraction in the wrong sequence, eliminate that answer choice. Don't waste time checking other fractions within that choice. If all of the comparisons work in a choice, you have found the correct answer.

Student Page 86

6.3.3 Ordering Fractions
Complete the class activity with your teacher's instruction.

6.3.3 Ordering Fractions

► Go over and emphasize strategies listed on the slide that students can use when ordering fractions.

1. Convert the fractions so that they have common denominators.

2. Convert fractions to decimals using a calculator.

3. Use values of simpler fractions in order to compare them.

► Inform students that they will take part in a small competition. They should pair up.

► Display the lists of randomly ordered fractions one at a time. The numbers are also listed in their workbooks. Students will have to write the fractions displayed on the slide in numerical order, from smallest to largest, on their whiteboards. The first pair to hold the paper up with the correct order earns a point. After earning this point, team members must justify their answers to the rest of the class. This will repeat for all five sets. The team with the most points wins.

6.3.3 Ordering Fractions

▸ Have students put the fractions in numerical order and justify their process after each question. Review the correct answers as you go. Students should write the correct answers in their workbooks.

1. $\dfrac{1}{3}, \dfrac{5}{12}, \dfrac{1}{5}, \dfrac{3}{7}, \dfrac{4}{13}$ becomes $\dfrac{1}{5}, \dfrac{4}{13}, \dfrac{1}{3}, \dfrac{5}{12}, \dfrac{3}{7}$

2. $\dfrac{3}{4}, \dfrac{1}{6}, \dfrac{4}{11}, \dfrac{5}{8}, \dfrac{1}{9}$ becomes $\dfrac{1}{9}, \dfrac{1}{6}, \dfrac{4}{11}, \dfrac{5}{8}, \dfrac{3}{4}$

3. $\dfrac{1}{2}, \dfrac{7}{8}, \dfrac{2}{7}, \dfrac{1}{5}, \dfrac{2}{3}$ becomes $\dfrac{1}{5}, \dfrac{2}{7}, \dfrac{1}{2}, \dfrac{2}{3}, \dfrac{7}{8}$

4. $\dfrac{4}{9}, -\dfrac{2}{3}, \dfrac{1}{12}, -\dfrac{4}{5}, \dfrac{3}{10}$ becomes $-\dfrac{4}{5}, -\dfrac{2}{3}, \dfrac{1}{12}, \dfrac{3}{10}, \dfrac{4}{9}$

5. $\dfrac{7}{10}, -0.5, -\dfrac{1}{3}, \dfrac{5}{12}, 0.45$ becomes $-0.5, -\dfrac{1}{3}, \dfrac{5}{12}, 0.45, \dfrac{7}{10}$

▸ After the last set, announce the winning team(s) and ask students if they have any questions.

> **Process of Elimination:** If an ACT question asks you to order fractions, start with the first choice and compare two fractions at a time. As soon as you find the wrong order, eliminate that choice and move on without checking the other fractions. If each comparison works, that is the correct answer.

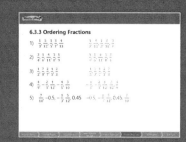

6.4 ACT Practice

▶ Have students work on questions from the ACT practice sets here. Pacing should be 3 minutes per practice set or 60 seconds per question.

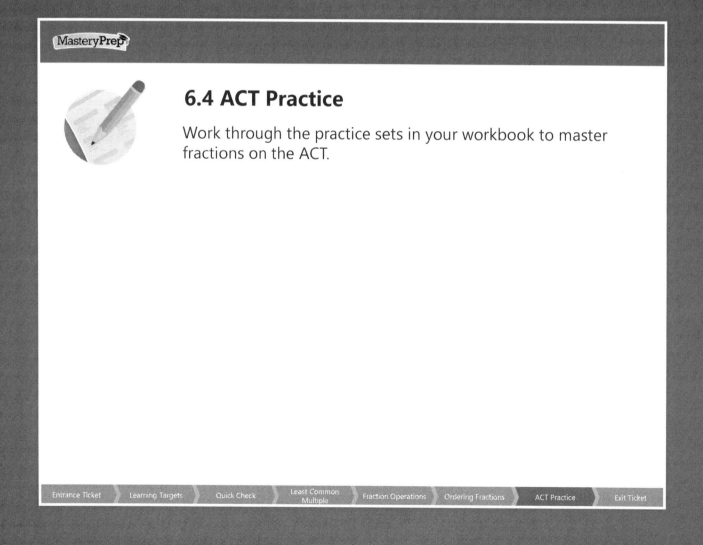

MasteryPrep

6.4 ACT Practice

Work through the practice sets in your workbook to master fractions on the ACT.

Entrance Ticket 〉 Learning Targets 〉 Quick Check 〉 Least Common Multiple 〉 Fraction Operations 〉 Ordering Fractions 〉 ACT Practice 〉 Exit Ticket

6.4.1 Set One

1. Lebron played $2\frac{1}{2}$ games of basketball on Friday and $3\frac{1}{3}$ games of basketball on Saturday. What is the total number of games Lebron played during those 2 days?

   A. $5\frac{1}{6}$

   B. $5\frac{1}{5}$

   C. $5\frac{1}{3}$

   D. $5\frac{2}{3}$

   E. $5\frac{5}{6}$

1. **The correct answer is E.** Convert the two mixed numbers into improper fractions and add.

$$2\frac{1}{2} + 3\frac{1}{3}$$

$$\frac{5}{2} + \frac{10}{3}$$

$$\frac{15}{6} + \frac{20}{6} = \frac{35}{6}$$

$$5\frac{5}{6}$$

2. Scotty and Tyler are training for a pizza-eating contest. They are trying to eat 6 pizzas in total. So far, Scotty has eaten $2\frac{3}{4}$ pizzas and Tyler has eaten $1\frac{7}{8}$ pizzas. How much more pizza do they have left to eat?

   F. $\frac{3}{4}$

   G. $1\frac{3}{8}$

   H. $1\frac{3}{4}$

   J. $2\frac{3}{8}$

   K. $4\frac{5}{8}$

2. **The correct answer is G.** Convert the mixed numbers into improper fractions and subtract from 6.

$$6 - 2\frac{3}{4} - 1\frac{7}{8}$$

$$6 - \frac{11}{4} - \frac{15}{8}$$

$$\frac{48}{8} - \frac{22}{8} - \frac{15}{8}$$

$$\frac{11}{8} = 1\frac{3}{8}$$

3. Which of the following fractions is equal to $\dfrac{1}{12^{30}} - \dfrac{1}{12^{31}}$?

A. $\dfrac{1}{12^{31}}$

B. $\dfrac{1}{12^{32}}$

C. $\dfrac{1}{12^{60}}$

D. $\dfrac{11}{12^{31}}$

E. $\dfrac{11}{12^{61}}$

3. **The correct answer is D.** Convert the first fraction so that each shares a common denominator and subtract.

$$\dfrac{1}{12^{30}} - \dfrac{1}{12^{31}}$$

$$\dfrac{12}{12^{31}} - \dfrac{1}{12^{31}}$$

$$\dfrac{11}{12^{31}}$$

6.4.2 Set Two

4. $\dfrac{1}{3 + \dfrac{1}{1 + \dfrac{1}{4}}} = ?$

    F. $\dfrac{4}{17}$

    G. $\dfrac{5}{19}$

    H. $\dfrac{5}{12}$

    J. $\dfrac{19}{5}$

    K. $\dfrac{17}{4}$

4. The correct answer is G. Add the fractions in the denominator and simplify.

$$\dfrac{1}{3 + \dfrac{1}{1 + \dfrac{1}{4}}} = \dfrac{1}{3 + \dfrac{1}{\dfrac{5}{4}}}$$

$$\dfrac{1}{3 + \dfrac{4}{5}} = \dfrac{1}{\dfrac{19}{5}} = \dfrac{5}{19}$$

---

5. What fraction of $3\dfrac{1}{2}$ is $1\dfrac{1}{6}$?

    A. $\dfrac{1}{2}$

    B. $\dfrac{1}{3}$

    C. $\dfrac{1}{4}$

    D. $\dfrac{1}{8}$

    E. $\dfrac{1}{12}$

5. The correct answer is B. Convert the numbers into improper fractions, then determine what number $3\dfrac{1}{2}$ would have to be multiplied by to equal $1\dfrac{1}{6}$.

$$3\dfrac{1}{2} = \dfrac{7}{2} \text{ and } 1\dfrac{1}{6} = \dfrac{7}{6}$$

$$\dfrac{7}{2}x = \dfrac{7}{6}$$

$$x = \dfrac{7}{6} \cdot \dfrac{2}{7} = \dfrac{14}{42} = \dfrac{1}{3}$$

---

6. The expression $\dfrac{4 + \dfrac{1}{8}}{1 + \dfrac{1}{16}}$ is equal to:

    F. 3

    G. $3\dfrac{15}{17}$

    H. $4\dfrac{49}{128}$

    J. $5\dfrac{3}{16}$

    K. 8

6. The correct answer is G. Add the numbers in the numerator and the numbers in the denominator, then simplify.

$$\dfrac{4 + \dfrac{1}{8}}{1 + \dfrac{1}{16}} = \dfrac{\dfrac{32}{8} + \dfrac{1}{8}}{\dfrac{16}{16} + \dfrac{1}{16}} = \dfrac{\dfrac{33}{8}}{\dfrac{17}{16}}$$

$$\dfrac{33}{8} \cdot \dfrac{16}{17} = \dfrac{66}{17} = 3\dfrac{15}{17}$$

6.4.3 Set Three

7. Which of the following lists orders $\frac{7}{9}$, 0.79, $\frac{2}{3}$, $\frac{7}{10}$, 0.71, and $\frac{3}{4}$ from least to greatest?

A. $\frac{7}{9}$, 0.79, $\frac{2}{3}$, $\frac{7}{10}$, 0.71, $\frac{3}{4}$

B. $\frac{7}{10}$, $\frac{2}{3}$, 0.71, $\frac{7}{9}$, $\frac{3}{4}$, 0.79

C. $\frac{7}{10}$, $\frac{2}{3}$, 0.71, $\frac{3}{4}$, $\frac{7}{9}$, 0.79

D. $\frac{2}{3}$, $\frac{7}{10}$, 0.71, $\frac{3}{4}$, $\frac{7}{9}$, 0.79

E. $\frac{2}{3}$, $\frac{3}{4}$, $\frac{7}{9}$, 0.71, $\frac{7}{10}$, 0.79

7. **The correct answer is D.** Order the fractions from smallest to largest, converting to a common denominator (or to a decimal) where necessary.

$\frac{7}{9}$, 0.79, $\frac{2}{3}$, $\frac{7}{10}$, 0.71, $\frac{3}{4}$

$\frac{2}{3}$, $\frac{7}{10}$, 0.71, $\frac{3}{4}$, $\frac{7}{9}$, 0.79

8. Madeline is trying to measure the edge of a table with a tape measure. The table is somewhere between $32\frac{1}{4}$ inches and $32\frac{3}{8}$ inches. Which of the following could be the exact measurement of the table?

F. $32\frac{1}{16}$

G. $32\frac{3}{16}$

H. $32\frac{1}{4}$

J. $32\frac{5}{16}$

K. $32\frac{7}{16}$

8. **The correct answer is J.** Choose the number with a fraction between $\frac{1}{4}$ and $\frac{3}{8}$. $\frac{1}{4} = \frac{4}{16}$ and $\frac{3}{8} = \frac{6}{16}$, so $\frac{5}{16}$ is between these two fractions.

9. Which of the following inequalities is true for the fractions $\frac{2}{5}$, $\frac{5}{13}$, and $\frac{3}{7}$?

A. $\frac{5}{13} < \frac{2}{5} < \frac{3}{7}$

B. $\frac{5}{13} < \frac{3}{7} < \frac{2}{5}$

C. $\frac{2}{5} < \frac{3}{7} < \frac{5}{13}$

D. $\frac{2}{5} < \frac{5}{13} < \frac{3}{7}$

E. $\frac{3}{7} < \frac{2}{5} < \frac{5}{13}$

9. **The correct answer is A.** Place the fractions in order from least to greatest, converting to common denominators (or decimals) if necessary.

$$\frac{2}{5}, \frac{5}{13}, \frac{3}{7}$$

$$\frac{5}{13} < \frac{2}{5} < \frac{3}{7}$$

10. Of the 627 coins in Jacob's coin jar, approximately $\frac{4}{5}$ are silver, and approximately $\frac{1}{10}$ of those coins that are silver are dimes. Which of the following is the closest estimate for the number of dimes in Jacob's coin jar?

F. 50
G. 100
H. 125
J. 250
K. 500

10. The correct answer is F. First, calculate how many silver coins are in the jar. Then calculate how many of them are dimes.

$$\frac{4}{5} \cdot 627 = 501.6$$

$$\frac{1}{10} \cdot 501.6 = 50.16 \approx 50$$

11. When Elton was cleaning his garage, he found 2 bottles of motor oil. According to the labels, the capacity of the larger bottle was three times the capacity of the smaller bottle. He estimated that both the smaller bottle and the larger bottle were about $\frac{3}{4}$ full of motor oil. He poured all the motor oil from the smaller bottle into the larger bottle. Then, about how full was the larger bottle?

A. $\frac{1}{4}$ full

B. $\frac{9}{16}$ full

C. $\frac{7}{8}$ full

D. Completely full

E. Overflowing

11. The correct answer is D. The larger bottle can hold $3x$ amount of motor oil, and the smaller bottle can hold x. Both bottles are $\frac{3}{4}$ full, so the larger bottle contains $\frac{3}{4} \cdot 3x = \frac{9x}{4}$, and the smaller bottle contains $\frac{3}{4} \cdot x = \frac{3x}{4}$. If the smaller amount is added to the larger, you get $\frac{9x}{4} + \frac{3x}{4} = \frac{12x}{4} = 3x$, which is the total capacity of the larger bottle. Thus, the larger bottle is completely full.

12. Pablo works in a factory and has to cut a rectangular metal rod into small cubes. The rod that he needs to cut is $1\frac{1}{4}$ inches by $1\frac{1}{4}$ inches by 8 feet (shown below), and he will cut it so that he will have cubes $1\frac{1}{4}$ inches on a side. He must allow an extra $\frac{1}{2}$ inch for each cut because his saw blade is $\frac{1}{2}$ inch wide. Assuming that the metal rod has no flaws, what is the maximum number of cubes he can make from his 8-foot piece of metal?

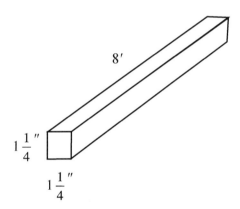

F. 46
G. 55
H. 58
J. 102
K. 118

12. **The correct answer is G.** For every cut, an additional half inch is needed in the calculations, except for the last cube. This is because the last cut of the rod will cut both the second to last cube and the last cube. In other words, the last cube does not need a cut of its own.

Ex: _____cut_____cut_____ (two cuts for three pieces)

First determine the length of the rod in inches: 8 feet · 12 inches/foot = 96 inches.

Subtract the length of one cube without the cut dimension of 0.5 inches factored in. 96 - 1.25 inches = 94.75 inches.

For each additional piece, add 0.5 inches to its length to account for the blade. 1.25 + 0.5 = 1.75 inches. Divide the remaining length of the rod by the length of the cube and blade. 94.75 ÷ 1.75 = 54.1428. This means 54 total cubes can be made. Do not forget to add the cube already accounted for, for a total of 55 cubes.

6.4.5 Set Five

13. Zack is taking inventory of loaves of bread at the grocery store where he works. There are 20 loaves in a full case, and Zack has 3 partially filled cases: 1 case is $\frac{1}{2}$ full, 1 case is $\frac{1}{4}$ full, and 1 case is $\frac{2}{5}$ full. How many total loaves of bread are in the 3 partially filled cases?

A. 11
B. 16
C. 19
D. 23
E. 30

13. The correct answer is D. Multiply each fraction by 20 and then add.

$$\frac{1}{2} \cdot 20 = 10$$

$$\frac{1}{4} \cdot 20 = 5$$

$$\frac{2}{5} \cdot 20 = 8$$

$$10 + 5 + 8 = 23$$

14. Which of the following gives the fractions $-\frac{5}{7}$, $-\frac{9}{11}$, and $-\frac{3}{4}$ in order from least to greatest?

F. $-\frac{5}{7}, \ -\frac{9}{11}, \ -\frac{3}{4}$

G. $-\frac{3}{4}, \ -\frac{9}{11}, \ -\frac{5}{7}$

H. $-\frac{3}{4}, \ -\frac{5}{7}, \ -\frac{9}{11}$

J. $-\frac{9}{11}, \ -\frac{5}{7}, \ -\frac{3}{4}$

K. $-\frac{9}{11}, \ -\frac{3}{4}, \ -\frac{5}{7}$

14. The correct answer is K. Order the fractions from smallest to largest, keeping in mind that the larger the negative number, the farther to the left that number is on a number line. Convert to a common denominator (or decimal) if necessary.

$$-\frac{5}{7}, \ -\frac{9}{11}, \ -\frac{3}{4}$$

$$-\frac{9}{11} < -\frac{3}{4} < -\frac{5}{7}$$

15. Savion is eating a pizza for lunch. He eats $\frac{5}{8}$ of it and gives the remaining pizza to his 2 coworkers. What fraction of the whole pizza will each of Savion's coworkers get if they share the remaining pizza equally?

A. $\frac{1}{16}$

B. $\frac{1}{8}$

C. $\frac{3}{16}$

D. $\frac{3}{8}$

E. $\frac{3}{2}$

15. **The correct answer is C.** If Savion eats $\frac{5}{8}$ of the pizza, then $\frac{3}{8}$ is left. Multiply $\frac{3}{8}$ by $\frac{1}{2}$ to figure out how much each of his coworkers will get to eat.

$$\frac{3}{8} \cdot \frac{1}{2} = \frac{3}{16}$$

ACT® Mastery Math

Sum It Up

Fractions

Fraction
A number that represents a part of a whole

Numerator
The top number of a fraction

Denominator
The bottom number of a fraction

Reciprocal
A number that is related to another number so that their product is equal to 1

Least Common Multiple (LCM)
For any two numbers, the lowest number that has both as factors

Least Common Denominator (LCD)
The smallest denominator two fractions can share

Greatest Common Factor (GCF)
For any two numbers, the largest number that is divisible into both

Mixed Number
A number consisting of a whole number and a fraction

Tips and Techniques

Process of Elimination: Eliminate any answers that either have the wrong denominators or break the order asked for in the question.

Entrance Ticket   Learning Targets   Least Common Multiple   Fraction Operations   Ordering Fractions   ACT Practice   Sum It Up

6.5 Exit Ticket

▶ Students complete the three questions on their exit ticket.

Students are timed 3 minutes for the three questions (60 seconds per question). There is no break between questions.

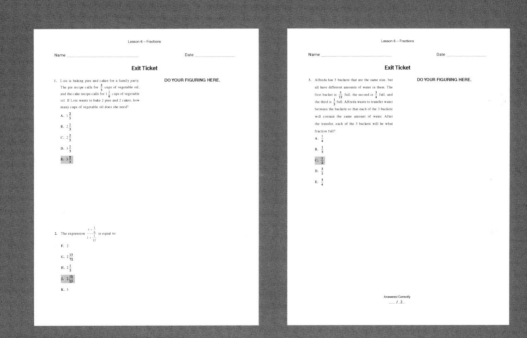

6.5 Exit Ticket Review

▶ Students work the first question.

1. **The correct answer is E.** Multiply the amounts required in each recipe by 2 and add.

$$\frac{2}{3} \cdot 2 = \frac{4}{3} = \frac{8}{6}$$

$$\frac{7}{6} \cdot 2 = \frac{14}{6}$$

$$\frac{8}{6} + \frac{14}{6} = \frac{22}{6} = 3\frac{4}{6} = 3\frac{2}{3}$$

MasteryPrep

6.5 Exit Ticket Review

1. Lois is baking pies and cakes for a family party. The pie recipe calls for $\frac{2}{3}$ cups of vegetable oil, and the cake recipe calls for $1\frac{1}{6}$ cups of vegetable oil. If Lois wanted to make 2 pies and 2 cakes, how many cups of vegetable oil does she need?

   A. $1\frac{2}{3}$

   B. $2\frac{1}{3}$

   C. $2\frac{2}{3}$

   D. $3\frac{1}{3}$

   E. $3\frac{2}{3}$

Entrance Ticket ⟩ Learning Targets ⟩ Quick Check ⟩ Least Common Multiple ⟩ Fraction Operations ⟩ Ordering Fractions ⟩ ACT Practice ⟩ Exit Ticket

6.5 Exit Ticket Review

► Students work the second question.

2. **The correct answer is J.** Add the numerator and denominator and simplify.

$$\frac{3 + \dfrac{1}{6}}{1 + \dfrac{1}{12}} = \frac{\dfrac{18}{6} + \dfrac{1}{6}}{\dfrac{12}{12} + \dfrac{1}{12}} = \frac{\dfrac{19}{6}}{\dfrac{13}{12}}$$

$$\frac{19}{6} \cdot \frac{12}{13} = \frac{38}{13} = 2\frac{12}{13}$$

MasteryPrep

6.5 Exit Ticket Review

2. The expression $\dfrac{3 + \frac{1}{6}}{1 + \frac{1}{12}}$ is equal to:

F. 2

G. $2\dfrac{13}{72}$

H. $2\dfrac{1}{2}$

J. $2\dfrac{12}{13}$

K. 3

Entrance Ticket   Learning Targets   Quick Check   Least Common Multiple   Fraction Operations   Ordering Fractions   ACT Practice   Exit Ticket

6.5 Exit Ticket Review

▶ Students work the third question.

> 3. **The correct answer is C.** Add the amounts together and divide by 3.
>
> $$\frac{5}{12} + \frac{3}{4} + \frac{1}{3}$$
>
> $$\frac{5}{12} + \frac{9}{12} + \frac{4}{12} = \frac{18}{12}$$
>
> $$\frac{18}{12} \div 3 = \frac{6}{12} = \frac{1}{2}$$

▶ After all three questions are completed, students exchange papers. Solve the three exit items step by step on the board. Students grade using their red pens and then return papers to their classmates.

▶ After solving the three exit items, revisit the learning targets slide. Students again assess their knowledge and confidence on the same 1 to 4 scale that they used at the beginning of the lesson. Students write this number in the designated area at the start of the lesson in their workbooks, along with any comments or questions they might have.

▶ Finally, to close the lesson, have students return to the cover page of the lesson and write a caption for the picture there. The caption should be a one-sentence summary of the lesson, a main rule or tip they want to remember, or an explanation of how the picture relates to the topic. If there is additional time, students can share and compare their captions with the class.

Operations

This lesson will cover how to solve word problems involving a variety of operations including addition, subtraction, multiplication, and division.

ACT Standards:

AF 302. Solve some routine two-step arithmetic problems

AF 401. Solve routine two-step or three-step arithmetic problems involving concepts such as rate and proportion, tax added, percentage off, and estimating by using a given average value in place of actual values

AF 501. Solve multistep arithmetic problems that involve planning or converting commonly derived units of measure (e.g., feet per second to miles per hour)

AF 601. Solve word problems containing several rates, proportions, or percentages

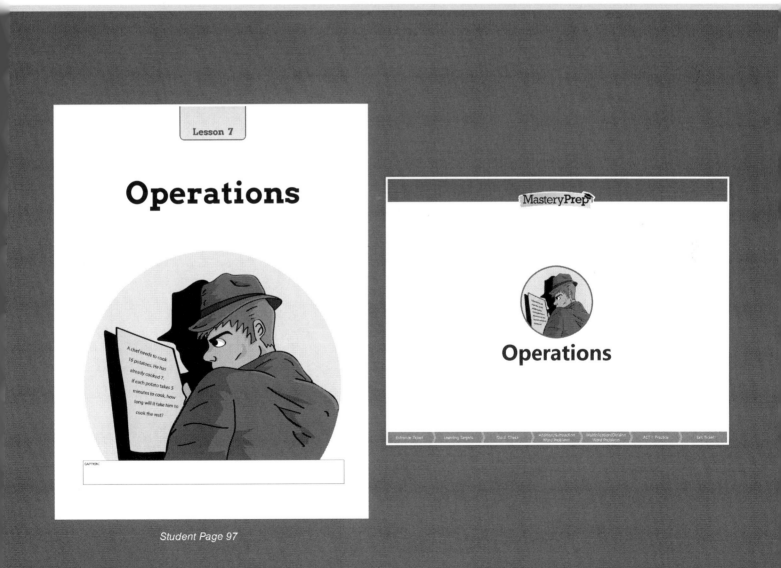

Student Page 97

7.1 Entrance Ticket

▶ Have students try the following three ACT practice questions. Students should work independently. Once the entrance ticket has been completed, review the questions with the students and have them share their answers. Give students the correct answers to the questions, as well as a step-by-step demonstration of how to solve the problems, but do not go into detailed explanation. This will serve as an introduction to the lesson content but is not intended to be the main lesson.

1. **The correct answer is A.** Translate the word problem into an expression and solve.

   Speed = miles/hour

   $$\frac{1{,}000 \text{ miles}}{2.5 \text{ hours}} = 400 \text{ miles/hour}$$

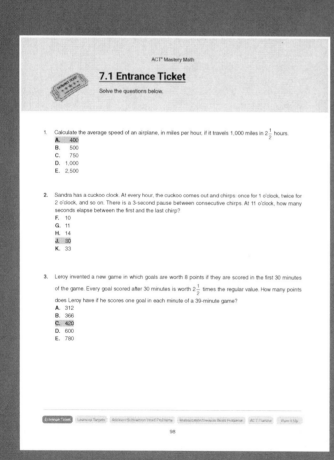

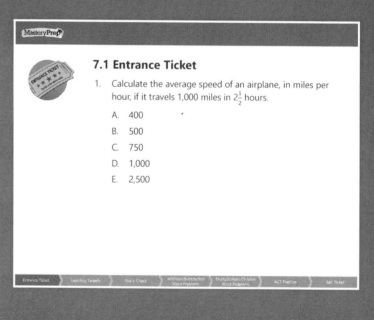

Student Page 98

7.1 Entrance Ticket

2. **The correct answer is J.** At 11:00, the cuckoo clock will chirp 11 times. This means, in between the 11 chirps, there will be 10 3-second pauses. $3 \cdot 10 = 30$, so there will be 30 seconds between the first and last chirp.

7.1 Entrance Ticket

2. Sandra has a cuckoo clock. At every hour, the cuckoo comes out and chirps: once for 1 o'clock, twice for 2 o'clock, and so on. There is a 3-second pause between consecutive chirps. At 11 o'clock, how many seconds elapse between the first and the last chirp?

   F. 10

   G. 11

   H. 14

   J. 30

   K. 33

7.1 Entrance Ticket

3. **The correct answer is C.** Translate the word problem into an equation and solve. If goals scored in the first 30 minutes are worth 8 points, goals scored after that are worth $2.5 \cdot 8 = 20$ points.

$30 \cdot 8 = 240$

$9 \cdot 20 = 180$

$240 + 180 = 420$

7.1 Entrance Ticket

3. Leroy invented a new game in which goals are worth 8 points if they are scored in the first 30 minutes of the game. Every goal scored after 30 minutes is worth $2\frac{1}{2}$ times the regular value. How many points does Leroy have if he scores one goal in each minute of a 39-minute game?

   A. 312

   B. 366

   C. 420

   D. 600

   E. 780

Entrance Ticket · Learning Targets · Quick Check · Addition/Subtraction Word Problems · Multiplication/Division Word Problems · ACT Practice · Exit Ticket

7.2 Learning Targets

► Review learning targets with your students, displayed on the slide and in their workbooks.

► After reviewing the learning targets, ask students to assess their knowledge and confidence level on these targets. They should rate themselves on a scale of 1 to 4, with 1 being not confident or uncertain, and 4 being completely confident or certain. They should circle this number in the designated section of their workbooks.

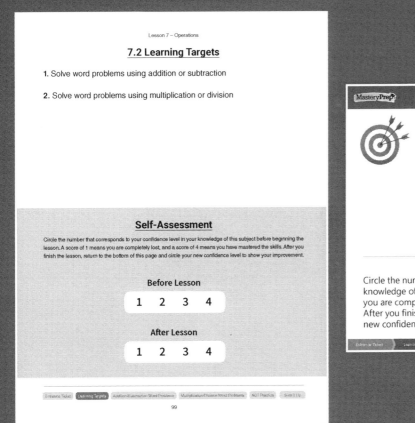

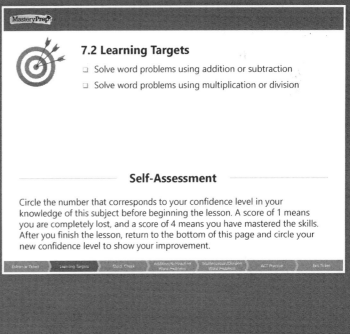

Student Page 99

7.2 Quick Check

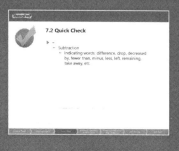

► Show students the following operation signs on the slide. Have them identify each sign and then brainstorm as many words as possible that might be used in word problems to indicate these signs. Write all correct guesses on the board.

Addition

Potential indicating words:

sum, combined, plus, added to, total of, more, both, in all, raise, etc.

Subtraction

Potential indicating words:

difference, drop, decreased by, fewer than, minus, less, left, remaining, take away, etc.

Multiplication

Potential indicating words:

product, of, multiplied by, times, triple, twice, etc.

Division

Potential indicating words:

per, divided by, out of, half, etc.

7.3.1 Addition/Subtraction Word Problems

▶ Break students into pairs. Have each pair designate one person the "translator" and the other the "problem solver."

▶ The translator's job is to translate the word problems in the workbook into a language that the problem solver can understand in order to solve. The solver only "speaks" equations, so the translator must give the solver equations instead of the words in the problems.

▶ Students will switch roles throughout the lesson.

▶ Teacher Dialogue: **What is the first thing the translator must do when presented with a new word problem?**

First identify the operations in the problem.

▶ Have students copy the steps of the process listed on the slide into the relevant portion of their workbooks.

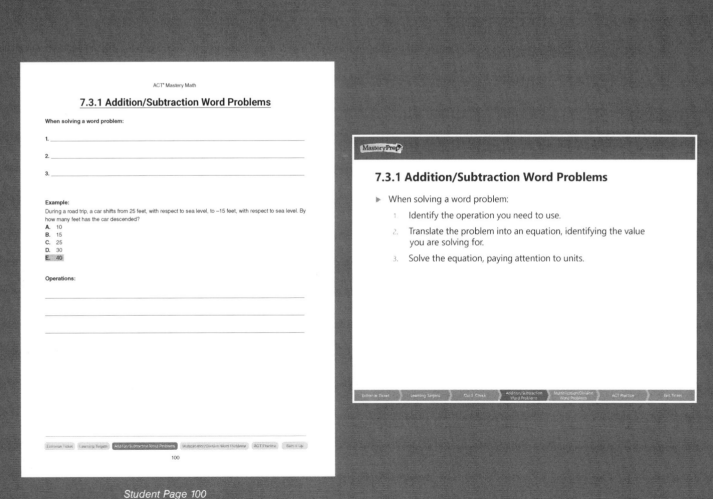

Student Page 100

7.3.1 Addition/Subtraction Word Problems

▶ Now tell students that they will work with their partners to translate and solve a series of new problems, competing against one another. First, show them the example on a slide.

▶ Teacher Dialogue: **Does this problem require addition or subtraction?**

Students should recognize that in this problem, the sea level changes from 25 feet to −15 feet, so in order to find the difference, they must subtract −15 from 25:

25 − (−15) = 25 + 15 = 40 feet

So, the correct answer is E.

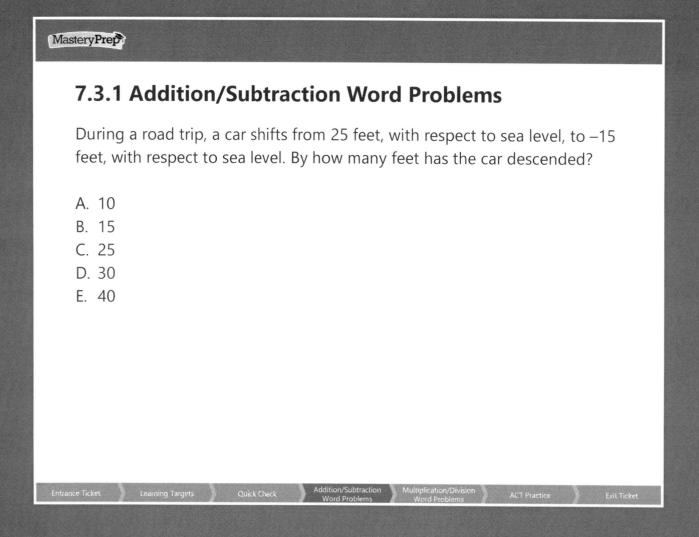

MasteryPrep

7.3.1 Addition/Subtraction Word Problems

During a road trip, a car shifts from 25 feet, with respect to sea level, to −15 feet, with respect to sea level. By how many feet has the car descended?

A. 10
B. 15
C. 25
D. 30
E. 40

Entrance Ticket | Learning Targets | Quick Check | Addition/Subtraction Word Problems | Multiplication/Division Word Problems | ACT Practice | Exit Ticket

Lesson 7 – Operations

7.3.1 Addition/Subtraction Word Problems

1. When the Jackson family boarded a plane for vacation, the temperature at the airport was 27° Celsius. When they landed at the next airport, the temperature was –12° Celsius. If – denotes a drop in temperature and + denotes a rise in temperature, which of the following best describes the change in temperature from the time the Jackson family left for vacation until they arrived?
   A. +39°C
   B. +15°C
   C. +5°C
   D. –15°C
   E. –39°C

2. Before the Johnson family lit a fire on their camping trip, the temperature at the campsite was 27° Celsius. When the fire was at full blaze, the temperature was –11° Celsius. If – denotes a drop in temperature and + denotes a rise in temperature, which of the following best describes the change in temperature from the time before the Johnson family lit the fire until it was at full blaze?
   F. +38°C
   G. +36°C
   H. +16°C
   J. –16°C
   K. –38°C

3. What is the value of 873 + 155 + 107, rounded to the nearest hundred?
   A. 1,200
   B. 1,100
   C. 1,000
   D. 900
   E. 800

4. What is the value of 322 + 724 + 808, rounded to the nearest hundred?
   F. 1,600
   G. 1,700
   H. 1,800
   J. 1,900
   K. 2,000

Entrance Ticket · Learning Targets · Addition/Subtraction Word Problems · Multiplication/Division Word Problems · ACT Practice · Sum It Up

7.3.1 Addition/Subtraction Word Problems

▶ Students will now begin the competition. If possible, instruct the problem solvers to turn their chairs around so they are facing their translators. The translators should all be facing forward, toward the slides while the problem solvers should have their backs toward the slides.

▶ Show the translators the following problems on the slides; they will then have to translate this problem into an equation for the problem solvers to solve, writing it down on their whiteboards or paper. The problem solvers will solve the problem and hold up their hands once they are finished. The teacher will check the answer and award a point to every team that correctly solved the problem. After three questions, have the problem solvers and translators switch roles.

▶ After each question, have one of the teams that calculated the correct answer come up and write their work on the board. Students who calculated an incorrect answer should pay attention to where in the process they went wrong—the translation or the calculation. Repeat this process for each of the problems.

If you do not have access to a projector, the problems are repeated in the book. Make sure the translators are looking at the problems in the book and the problem solvers are using the blank page or a personal whiteboard to write down their answers.

1. **The correct answer is E.** Translate the word problem into an expression and solve.

$-12°C - 27°C = -39°C$

7.3.1 Addition/Subtraction Word Problems

2. **The correct answer is K.** Translate the word problem into an expression and solve.

$-11°C - 27°C = -38°C$

7.3.1 Addition/Subtraction Word Problems

2. Before the Johnson family lit a fire on their camping trip, the temperature at the campsite was 27° Celsius. When the fire was at full blaze, the temperature was −11° Celsius. If − denotes a drop in temperature and + denotes a rise in temperature, which of the following best describes the change in temperature from the time before the Johnson family lit the fire until it was at full blaze?

F. +38°
G. +36°
H. +16°
J. −16°
K. −38°

Entrance Ticket Learning Targets Quick Check Addition/Subtraction Word Problems Multiplication/Division Word Problems ACT Practice Exit Ticket

7.3.1 Addition/Subtraction Word Problems

3. **The correct answer is B.** First, add the three numbers, and then round to the nearest hundred.

    873 + 155 + 107 = 1,135

    Rounded to the nearest hundred, 1,135 is approximately 1,100.

7.3.1 Addition/Subtraction Word Problems

3. What is the value of 873 + 155 + 107, rounded to the nearest hundred?

    A. 1,200
    B. 1,100
    C. 1,000
    D. 900
    E. 800

Entrance Ticket   Learning Targets   Quick Check   Addition/Subtraction Word Problems   Multiplication/Division Word Problems   ACT Practice   Exit Ticket

188

7.3.1 Addition/Subtraction Word Problems

4. **The correct answer is J.** First, add the three numbers, and then round to the nearest hundred.

322 + 724 + 808 = 1,854

Rounded to the nearest hundred, 1,854 is approximately 1,900.

7.3.1 Addition/Subtraction Word Problems

4. What is the value of 322 + 724 + 808, rounded to the nearest hundred?

   F. 1,600
   G. 1,700
   H. 1,800
   J. 1,900
   K. 2,000

| Entrance Ticket | Learning Targets | Quick Check | Addition/Subtraction Word Problems | Multiplication/Division Word Problems | ACT Practice | Exit Ticket |

ACT® Mastery Math

7.3.1 Addition/Subtraction Word Problems

5. At 11 a.m., the temperature is −10°C. Meteorologists predict that the temperature will decrease 3°C per hour for the next 4 hours. What should be the temperature at 3 p.m. ?
   A. −22°C
   B. −13°C
   C. −7°C
   D. −6°C
   E. 2°C

6. At 3 p.m., the temperature in the park is 76°F. For the next 2 hours, the temperature decreases 6°F per hour. What is the temperature at 5 p.m. ?
   F. 64°F
   G. 70°F
   H. 74°F
   J. 82°F
   K. 88°F

Math Tip

Show Your Work: Most of the word problems that focus on operations have the easiest math you will find on the test. However, it is easy to make mistakes on these problems if you are not careful. Make sure you show your work, even if you think the question is simple. That way you will avoid needless mistakes.

Entrance Ticket | Learning Targets | Addition/Subtraction Word Problems | Multiplication/Division Word Problems | ACT Practice | Sum It Up

102

Student Page 102

190

7.3.1 Addition/Subtraction Word Problems

5. **The correct answer is A.** Translate the word problem into an equation and solve.

$(-3°C)(4) = -12°C$

$-10°C - 12°C = -22°C$

7.3.1 Addition/Subtraction Word Problems

5. At 11 a.m., the temperature is –10°C. Meteorologists predict that the temperature will decrease 3°C per hour for the next 4 hours. What should be the temperature at 3 p.m.?

    A. –22°C
    B. –13°C
    C. –7°C
    D. –6°C
    E. 2°C

7.3.1 Addition/Subtraction Word Problems

6. **The correct answer is F.** Translate the word problem into an equation and solve.

$(-6°C)(2) = -12°C$

$76°C - 12°C = 64°C$

> **Show Your Work:** Most of the word problems that focus on operations have the easiest math you will find on the test. However, the ACT writers know that you will try to answer these questions mentally, and they expect you to make errors. Make sure you show your work, even if you think the question is easy. That way you won't make any simple mistakes.

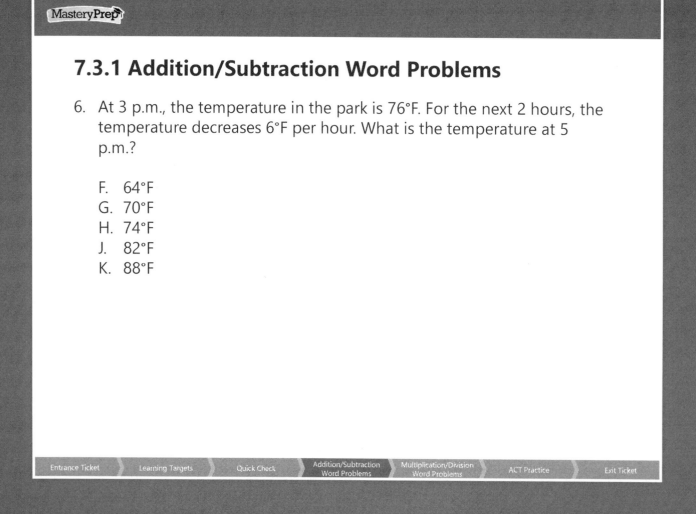

MasteryPrep

7.3.1 Addition/Subtraction Word Problems

6. At 3 p.m., the temperature in the park is 76°F. For the next 2 hours, the temperature decreases 6°F per hour. What is the temperature at 5 p.m.?

F. 64°F
G. 70°F
H. 74°F
J. 82°F
K. 88°F

Entrance Ticket | Learning Targets | Quick Check | Addition/Subtraction Word Problems | Multiplication/Division Word Problems | ACT Practice | Exit Ticket

7.3.2 Multiplication/Division Word Problems

▶ Teacher Dialogue: **What are the most important things to keep in mind when solving multiplication word problems?**

Call on a few students to offer their answers. Write their suggestions on the board, then show the tips on the slide. Have students copy them down in the designated portion of their workbooks. Students should recognize that the following points are essential:

When solving multiplication word problems:

1. Identify the two things that you are multiplying together.

2. Don't forget to make sure the units are the same.

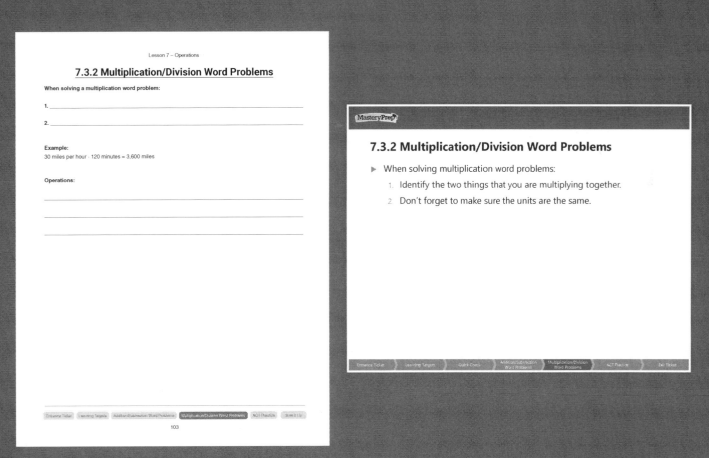

Student Page 103

7.3.2 Multiplication/Division Word Problems

▸ Show students the example on the slide.

▸ Teacher Dialogue: **What is wrong with this example?**

  Give students 1 minute to discuss the question in pairs. Come back together as a class and call on a few students to offer their answers. Students should recognize that they cannot multiply miles per hour by minutes, as the units don't cancel.

▸ Show this on the slide:

$$\frac{miles}{hour} \cdot minutes$$

▸ Teacher Dialogue: **Just like in the fraction $\frac{3x}{3}$, where 3 cancels because it appears on both the top and the bottom of the fraction, we can cancel units as well when they appear both on the top and bottom. But in the above example, no units are the same, so they cannot cancel.**

7.3.2 Multiplication/Division Word Problems

▶ Teacher Dialogue: **What unit could we change minutes to in the problem in order to solve it?**

Minutes can be changed to hours.

120 minutes = 2 hours

30 miles per hour · 2 hours = 60 miles

(Units: $\frac{\text{miles}}{\text{hour}}$ · hours = miles)

7.3.2 Multiplication/Division Word Problems

▶ Minutes can be changed to hours.

▶ 120 minutes = 2 hours

▶ 30 miles per hour · 2 hours = 60 miles

▶ (Units: $\frac{miles}{hour}$ · hours = miles)

7.3.2 Multiplication/Division Word Problems

▸ As extra practice, show students the following problem on the slide. Give students 1 minute to discuss and work on the problem in their pairs.

▸ Come back together as a class and call on one pair to explain their work. Solicit feedback from the class, revising their answer until correct. Then reveal the correct answer process on the slide.

Students should recognize that in this problem, they are given the rate (what they are multiplying by) and the time (what they are multiplying). Now all they need to do is make sure their units match and then multiply them together to find the total length:

15 weeks · 7 days/week = 15 · 7 = 105 days

15.5 pounds/day · 105 days = 15.5 · 105 = 1,837.5 pounds

ACT® Mastery Math

7.3.2 Multiplication/Division Word Problems

1. A snail traveled for exactly 25 seconds at an average speed of 0.80 meters per minute. Which of the following is closest to the total distance, in meters, traveled by the snail?
   A. 1.0
   B. 0.7
   C. 0.4
   D. 0.3
   E. 0.2

2. A taxi driver traveled at an average speed of 35 miles per hour and arrived at her destination in exactly 15 minutes. Which of the following is closest to the total number of miles she traveled?
   F. 5
   G. 7
   H. 9
   J. 15
   K. 18

3. Riding a bike at a constant pace of 30 seconds per third mile, how many minutes would it take to ride 4 miles?
   A. 6.0
   B. 3.6
   C. 2.0
   D. 1.5
   E. 1.2

4. Jogging at a constant pace of 150 seconds per quarter mile, how long would it take to run 3 miles, in minutes?
   F. 30.0
   G. 13.5
   H. 12.0
   J. 7.5
   K. 5.0

Entrance Ticket   Learning Targets   Addition/Subtraction Word Problems   Multiplication/Division Word Problems   ACT Practice   Sum It Up

7.3.2 Multiplication/Division Word Problems

▶ Students will now begin the second round of the competition. Repeat the process used for the first round.

1. **The correct answer is D.** Translate the word problem into an equation and solve.

25 seconds · 1 minute/60 seconds = $\dfrac{5}{12}$ minutes

$\dfrac{5}{12}$ minutes · 0.80 meters/minute ≈ 0.3 meters

7.3.2 Multiplication/Division Word Problems

1. A snail traveled for exactly 25 seconds at an average speed of 0.80 meters per minute. Which of the following is closest to the total distance, in meters, traveled by the snail?

   A. 1.0
   B. 0.7
   C. 0.4
   D. 0.3
   E. 0.2

7.3.2 Multiplication/Division Word Problems

2. **The correct answer is H.** Translate the word problem into an equation and solve.

    15 minutes · 1 hour/60 minutes = 0.25 hours

    0.25 hours · 35 miles/hour = 8.75 miles, or approximately 9 miles.

7.3.2 Multiplication/Division Word Problems

2. A taxi driver traveled at an average speed of 35 miles per hour and arrived at her destination in exactly 15 minutes. Which of the following is closest to the total number of miles she traveled?

    F. 5
    G. 7
    H. 9
    J. 15
    K. 18

Entrance Ticket · Learning Targets · Quick Check · Addition/Subtraction Word Problems · Multiplication/Division Word Problems · ACT Practice · Exit Ticket

7.3.2 Multiplication/Division Word Problems

3. **The correct answer is A.** Translate the word problem into an equation and solve.

    30 seconds · 1 minute/60 seconds = 0.5 minutes

    4 miles · 3 "third miles"/1 mile = 12 "third miles"

    12 "third miles" · 0.5 minutes/"third mile" = 6.0 minutes

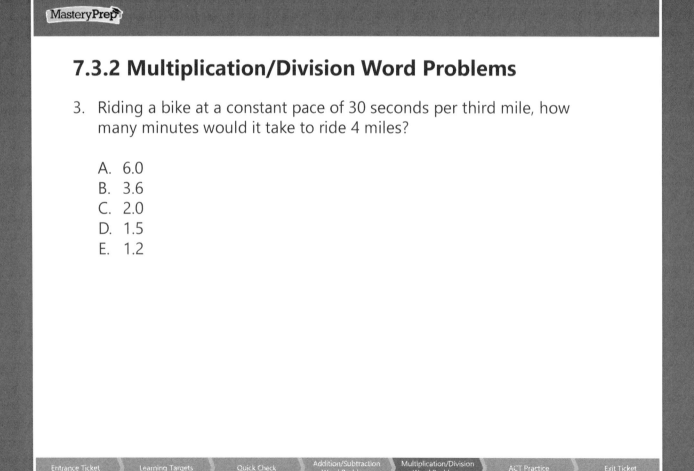

7.3.2 Multiplication/Division Word Problems

4. **The correct answer is F.** Translate the word problem into an equation and solve.

150 seconds · 1 minute/60 seconds = 2.5 minutes

3 miles · 4 "quarter miles"/1 mile = 12 "quarter miles"

12 "quarter miles" · 2.5 minutes/"quarter mile" = 30.0 minutes

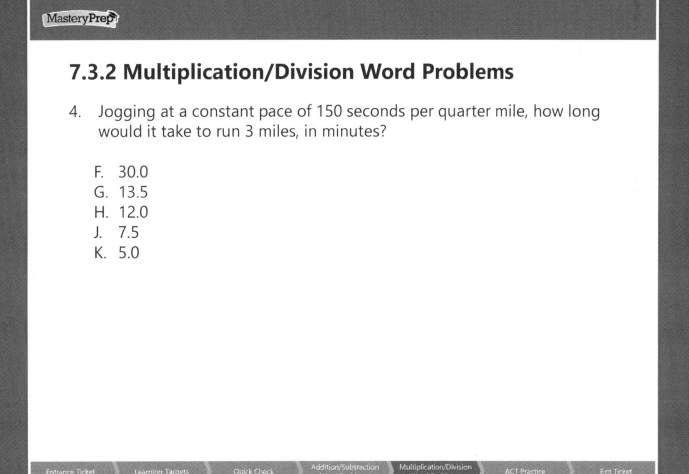

MasteryPrep

7.3.2 Multiplication/Division Word Problems

4. Jogging at a constant pace of 150 seconds per quarter mile, how long would it take to run 3 miles, in minutes?

F. 30.0
G. 13.5
H. 12.0
J. 7.5
K. 5.0

Entrance Ticket   Learning Targets   Quick Check   Addition/Subtraction Word Problems   Multiplication/Division Word Problems   ACT Practice   Exit Ticket

7.3.2 Multiplication/Division Word Problems

5. Chet rents a car for a month. It costs a $260 fixed charge to rent the car for one month and $8 for every 100 miles driven in it. Chet drove 3,000 miles in the rental car. What was his total bill for the car?
    A. $ 270
    B. $ 287
    C. $ 500
    D. $2,700
    E. $2,960

6. A small hardware store pays for the electricity it uses. The monthly cost is a fixed charge of $200 plus $12 for every 100 units of electricity used. Last month, the store used 1,200 units of electricity. What was the total cost of electricity for the store last month?
    F. $ 144
    G. $ 214.40
    H. $ 344
    J. $1,440
    K. $1,640

Math Tip

Show Your Work: Many multiplication word problems will try to confuse you with different kinds of units. Be sure to set the problem up by labeling all of the units before you start your calculations.

Entrance Ticket   Learning Targets   Addition/Subtraction Word Problems   Multiplication/Division Word Problems   ACT Practice   Sum It Up

7.3.2 Multiplication/Division Word Problems

5. **The correct answer is C.** Translate the word problem into an equation and solve.

   3,000 miles · 8 dollars/100 miles = 240 dollars

   $240 + $260 = $500

7.3.2 Multiplication/Division Word Problems

5. Chet rents a car for a month. It costs a $260 fixed charge to rent the car for one month and $8 for every 100 miles driven in it. Chet drove 3,000 miles in the rental car. What was his total bill for the car?

   A. $270
   B. $287
   C. $500
   D. $2,700
   E. $2,960

Entrance Ticket   Learning Targets   Quick Check   Addition/Subtraction Word Problems   Multiplication/Division Word Problems   ACT Practice   Exit Ticket

7.3.2 Multiplication/Division Word Problems

6. **The correct answer is H.** Translate the word problem into an equation and solve.

    1,200 units electricity · 12 dollars/100 units electricity = 144 dollars

    $144 + $200 = $344

Show Your Work: Many multiplication word problems will try to confuse you with different kinds of units. Be sure to set up the problem with all of the units labeled before you start your calculations.

7.3.2 Multiplication/Division Word Problems

6. A small hardware store pays for the electricity it uses. The monthly cost is a fixed charge of $200 plus $12 for every 100 units of electricity used. Last month, the store used 1,200 units of electricity. What was the total cost of electricity for the store last month?

    F. $144
    G. $214.40
    H. $344
    J. $1,440
    K. $1,640

7.3.2 Multiplication/Division Word Problems

▶ Show students the following problem on the slide.

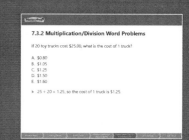

▶ Teacher Dialogue: **Whenever you know the total value of a group of things, you can use division to figure out the value of one thing.**

▶ Call on a few students to offer their suggestions on how to approach the problem. Choose one student to come up and solve the problem on the board, soliciting feedback from the class until the correct answer is found. Students should come up with:

25 ÷ 20 = 1.25, so the cost of 1 truck is $1.25.

This can also be taught through setting up proportions. Your students may have a good grasp of proportions, and it may be an easier way to help them remember that they are supposed to divide:

$$\frac{\$25.00}{20 \text{ toy trucks}} = \frac{x}{1 \text{ toy truck}} \rightarrow 20x = 25 \rightarrow x = 1.25, \text{ or } \$1.25.$$

ACT® Mastery Math

7.3.2 Multiplication/Division Word Problems

1. Bud needs to grow 700 roses for the local farmers market. If Bud knows that the seeds he is planting will yield, on average, 1.25 roses per square foot, Bud needs to plant how many square feet of seeds?
   A. 125
   B. 280
   C. 560
   D. 700
   E. 875

2. A cyclist traveled at an average speed of 18 miles per hour and finished her bike ride in exactly 4 minutes. Which of the following is closest to the number of miles she traveled?
   F. 1
   G. 2
   H. 4
   J. 5
   K. 9

3. A vintage baseball card was purchased 6 years ago for $1,860. The card is currently valued at $2,400. What was the card's average increase in value per year?
   A. $ 90
   B. $270
   C. $310
   D. $350
   E. $400

4. Anna bought her motorcycle 8 years ago for $5,320. It is now worth $2,840. What is the average decrease in value of the motorcycle per year?
   F. $ 310
   G. $ 355
   H. $ 620
   J. $ 665
   K. $1,240

Entrance Ticket · Learning Targets · Addition/Subtraction Word Problems · **Multiplication/Division Word Problems** · ACT Practice · Sum It Up

106

Student Page 106

206

7.3.2 Multiplication/Division Word Problems

▶ Students will now begin the division round of their competition. After each question, have one of the teams that calculated the correct answer come up and write their work on the board. Students who calculated an incorrect answer should pay attention to where in the process they went wrong—the translation or the calculation. Repeat this process for each of the problems.

1. **The correct answer is C.** Translate the word problem into an equation and solve.

   700 roses ÷ 1.25 roses/square foot = 560 square feet

7.3.2 Multiplication/Division Word Problems

1. Bud needs to grow 700 roses for the local farmers market. If Bud knows that the seeds he is planting will yield, on average, 1.25 roses per square foot, Bud needs to plant how many square feet of seeds?

   A. 125
   B. 280
   C. 560
   D. 700
   E. 875

Entrance Ticket   Learning Targets   Quick Check   Addition/Subtraction Word Problems   Multiplication/Division Word Problems   ACT Practice   Exit Ticket

7.3.2 Multiplication/Division Word Problems

2. **The correct answer is F.** Translate the word problem into an equation and solve.

$$4 \text{ minutes} \cdot 1 \text{ hour}/60 \text{ minutes} = \frac{1}{15} \text{ hours}$$

$$\frac{1}{15} \text{ hours} \cdot 18 \text{ miles/hour} = 1.2 \text{ miles, or approximately 1 mile.}$$

MasteryPrep

7.3.2 Multiplication/Division Word Problems

2. A cyclist traveled at an average speed of 18 miles per hour and finished her bike ride in exactly 4 minutes. Which of the following is closest to the number of miles she traveled?

   F. 1
   G. 2
   H. 4
   J. 5
   K. 9

Entrance Ticket | Learning Targets | Quick Check | Addition/Subtraction Word Problems | Multiplication/Division Word Problems | ACT Practice | Exit Ticket

7.3.2 Multiplication/Division Word Problems

3. **The correct answer is A.** Translate the word problem into an equation and solve.

$2,400 - $1,860 = $540

$$\frac{\$540}{6 \text{ years}} = \$90 \text{ increase/year}$$

MasteryPrep

7.3.2 Multiplication/Division Word Problems

3. A vintage baseball card was purchased 6 years ago for $1,860. The card is currently valued at $2,400. What was the card's average increase in value per year?

A. $90
B. $270
C. $310
D. $350
E. $400

Entrance Ticket | Learning Targets | Quick Check | Addition/Subtraction Word Problems | Multiplication/Division Word Problems | ACT Practice | Exit Ticket

7.3.2 Multiplication/Division Word Problems

4. **The correct answer is F.** Translate the word problem into an equation and solve.

$5,320 − $2,840 = $2,480

$$\frac{\$2,480}{8 \text{ years}} = \$310 \text{ decrease/year}$$

7.3.2 Multiplication/Division Word Problems

4. Anna bought her motorcycle 8 years ago for $5,320. It is now worth $2,840. What is the average decrease in value of the motorcycle per year?

   F. $310
   G. $355
   H. $620
   J. $665
   K. $1,240

Entrance Ticket   Learning Targets   Quick Check   Addition/Subtraction Word Problems   Multiplication/Division Word Problems   ACT Practice   Exit Ticket

Lesson 7 – Operations

7.3.2 Multiplication/Division Word Problems

5. Cole wants to work enough hours to buy a necklace that costs $370 dollars. He earns $11.25 per hour, and he has already worked 24 hours. What is the minimum number of whole hours that Cole must work in order to afford the necklace?

    A. 7
    B. 8
    C. 9
    D. 16
    E. 33

6. José wants to work enough hours to make at least $93 dollars this week (before taxes are deducted). He has a job that pays $7.25 per hour and has already worked 7 hours. If José can only work in full-hour increments, how many more full hours must he work to meet his weekly goal?

    F. 4
    G. 5
    H. 6
    J. 7
    K. 13

Entrance Ticket   Learning Targets   Addition/Subtraction Word Problems   Multiplication/Division Word Problems   ACT Practice   Sum It Up

107

Student Page 107

211

7.3.2 Multiplication/Division Word Problems

5. **The correct answer is C.** Translate the word problem into an equation and solve.

24 hours · 11.25 dollars/1 hour = 270 dollars

$370 − $270 = $100 left to earn

$$\frac{\$100}{\$11.25 \, / \, hour} \approx 9 \text{ more hours of work}$$

7.3.2 Multiplication/Division Word Problems

5. Cole wants to work enough hours to buy a necklace that costs $370 dollars. He earns $11.25 per hour, and he has already worked 24 hours. What is the minimum number of whole hours that Cole must work in order to afford the necklace?

   A. 7
   B. 8
   C. 9
   D. 16
   E. 33

Entrance Ticket   Learning Targets   Quick Check   Addition/Subtraction Word Problems   Multiplication/Division Word Problems   ACT Practice   Exit Ticket

212

7.3.2 Multiplication/Division Word Problems

6. **The correct answer is H.** Translate the word problem into an equation and solve.

   7 hours · 7.25 dollars/1 hour = 50.75 dollars

   $93 − $50.75 = $42.25 left to earn

   $$\frac{\$42.25}{\$7.25 \text{ / hour}} \approx 6 \text{ more hours of work}$$

▶ After, have students write down their pair's score and add it to their running total. Declare a winner.

7.3.2 Multiplication/Division Word Problems

6. José wants to work enough hours to make at least $93 dollars this week (before taxes are deducted). He has a job that pays $7.25 per hour and has already worked 7 hours. If José can only work in full-hour increments, how many more full hours must he work to meet his weekly goal?

   F. 4
   G. 5
   H. 6
   J. 7
   K. 13

Entrance Ticket | Learning Targets | Quick Check | Addition/Subtraction Word Problems | Multiplication/Division Word Problems | ACT Practice | Exit Ticket

7.4 ACT Practice

► Have students work on questions from the ACT practice sets here. Pacing should be 3 minutes per practice set or 60 seconds per question.

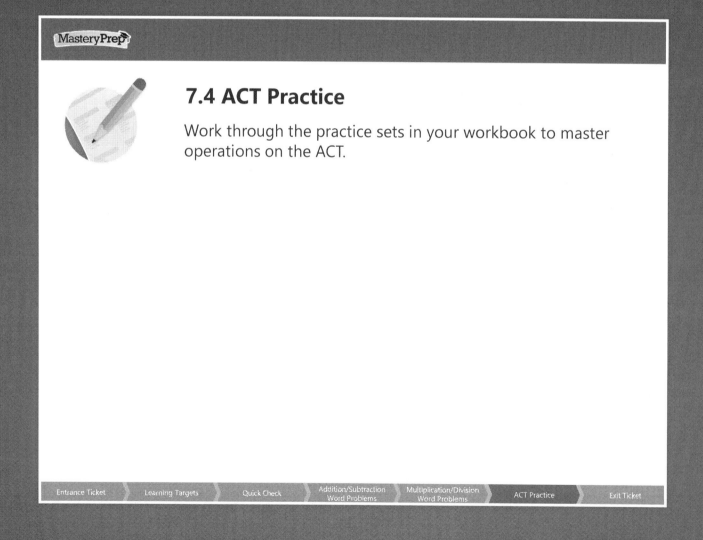

7.4.1 Set One

1. What is the value of 668 + 575 + 453, rounded to the nearest hundred?

    A. 1,100
    B. 1,200
    C. 1,500
    D. 1,600
    E. 1,700

1. **The correct answer is E.** Add the numbers together and then round to the nearest hundred. 668 + 575 + 453 = 1,696, or approximately 1,700

2. An object placed in a super-cooling freezer cools from 33°F to –18°F. By how many degrees Fahrenheit has it cooled?

    F. 18°F
    G. 15°F
    H. 33°F
    J. 51°F
    K. 52°F

2. **The correct answer is J.** Translate the word problem into an equation and solve.

    33°F – (–18°F) = 51°F

3. At 4:00 a.m., the temperature is –17°F. The temperature decreases 3°F per hour. What is the temperature at 6:00 a.m. ?

    A. –23°F
    B. –20°F
    C. –17°F
    D. –14°F
    E. –11°F

3. **The correct answer is A.** Translate the word problem into an equation and solve.

    4:00 am to 6:00 am = 2 hours

    2 · 3°F = 6°F

    –17°F – 6°F = –23°F

7.4.2 Set Two

4. When Kaitlyn went to bed, the temperature was 36°F. When she woke up the next morning, the temperature was −9°F. If + represents a rise in temperature and − represents a drop in temperature, which of the following best illustrates the temperature change from the time Kaitlyn went to bed to the time she woke up?

   F. −45°F
   G. −27°F
   H. −12°F
   J.   27°F
   K.   45°F

4. **The correct answer is F.** Translate the word problem into an equation and solve.

   −9°F − 36°F = −45°F

---

5. If boxes of pasta sell at $0.88 per box or 4 boxes for $3.00, how much is saved, to the nearest cent, on each box by buying the boxes 4 at a time?

   A. 12¢
   B. 13¢
   C. 39¢
   D. 52¢
   E. 53¢

5. **The correct answer is B.** Translate the word problem into an equation and solve.

   $0.88 · 4 boxes = $3.52

   $3.52 − $3.00 = $0.52

   $0.52 ÷ 4 = $0.13/box

---

6. Hair grows at an average rate of 0.5 inches per month. Courtney refused to cut her hair from the time she was 8 years old until she was 20 years old. If Courtney's hair grew at the average rate, approximately how many inches did her hair grow during the time she refused to cut her hair?

   F.   4
   G.   6
   H. 14
   J. 72
   K. 78

6. **The correct answer is J.** Translate the word problem into an equation and solve.

   20 − 8 = 12

   0.5 inches/month · 12 months/year = 6 inches/year

   12 years · 6 inches/year = 72 inches

7.4.3 Set Three

7. Matt purchased a car for $31,400. Four years later, the car is worth $24,700. What was the car's average decrease in value per year?

A. $1.675
B. $2,233
C. $3,350
D. $3,375
E. $5,000

7. **The correct answer is A.** Translate the word problem into an equation and solve.

$31,400 – $24,700 = $6,700

$6,700 ÷ 4 = $1,675 value decrease per year

8. Owen purchased 2 boxes of 16-ounce bottles of soap. Each box contained 10 bottles of soap. Owen could have purchased the same amount of soap by purchasing how many 20-ounce bottles?

F. 8
G. 10
H. 16
J. 20
K. 24

8. **The correct answer is H.** Translate the word problem into an equation and solve.

2 · 16 · 10 = 320 ounces

320 ÷ 20 = 16 bottles

9. A dog adoption agency is holding a function on the weekend at which families can adopt puppies. On Friday, 3 puppies were adopted; 7 puppies were adopted on Saturday; and 6 were adopted on Sunday. By the end of the weekend, the agency was left with 2 more than a quarter of the puppies they originally had. How many puppies did the adoption agency originally have?

A. 20
B. 21
C. 22
D. 23
E. 24

9. **The correct answer is E.** Translate the word problem into an equation and solve.

$x - 3 - 7 - 6 = 0.25x + 2$

$x - 16 = 0.25x + 2$

$0.75x = 18$

$x = 24$

7.4.4 Set Four

10. Charles ran 30 feet in 4 seconds. At this rate, how many *yards* can Charles run in 3 *minutes* ?

    F. 120
    G. 270
    H. 360
    J. 450
    K. 600

10. The correct answer is J. Translate the word problem into an equation and solve.

1 yard = 3 feet

4 seconds · 1 minute/60 seconds = $\frac{1}{15}$ minutes

So, Charlie can run 10 yards per $\frac{1}{15}$ minutes

3 minutes ÷ $\frac{1}{15}$ minutes = 45

45 · 10 = 450 yards

11. Joe Watson is a car mechanic who has earned $14,875 doing one car inspection per day since he started working 175 days ago. Joe decides to take off for vacation, and his temporary replacement charges $135 per inspection at one inspection per day. While Joe Watson is on vacation, how many more dollars do the customers spend per day on car inspections?

    A. 40
    B. 50
    C. 60
    D. 75
    E. 85

11. The correct answer is B. Translate the word problem into an equation and solve.

$14,875 ÷ 175 = 85

$135 − $85 = $50

12. Carlos was accepted to a university that has a tuition cost of $33,000 per year. He took out a loan from the bank for the entire $33,000 and made loan payments of $415 per month for 8 years. After the 8-year period, how much more than the tuition cost did Carlos pay?

    F. $6,840
    G. $4,980
    H. $4,860
    J. $3,320
    K. $3,120

12. The correct answer is F. Translate the word problem into an equation and solve.

8 years · 12 months/year = 96 months

$415 · 96 = $39,840

$39,840 − $33,000 = $6,840

7.4.5 Set Five

---

13. Jay has 12 classic cars in his garage. He paid $3,500 for each car 5 years ago. The cars are currently worth $4,200 each. How much more must the average value of the cars rise for the combined value of these 12 cars to be exactly $10,800 more than Jay paid for them?

  A. $200.00
  B. $700.00
  C. $800.50
  D. $841.67
  E. $958.33

13. The correct answer is A. Translate the word problem into an equation and solve.

$3,500 · 12 = $42,000

$42,000 + $10,800 = $52,800

$52,800 ÷ 12 = $4,400

Current average = $4,200

$4,400 − $4,200 = $200.00

---

14. Trevor and his siblings want to get professional pictures taken for their parents' anniversary. They spend the day finding the location with the best price. They have exactly $150 to spend on the photographs. Snap! Photo Center charges a general fee of $75 and $1.25 per photo proof. Say Gouda Photo Center charges a general fee of $60 and $1.50 per photo proof. Which photo center, if either, allows Trevor and his siblings to get more photo proofs, and how many more proofs?

  F. Snap!, 25
  G. Snap!, 90
  H. Say Gouda, 10
  J. Say Gouda, 15
  K. Trevor and his siblings would get the same maximum number of proofs from each photo center.

14. The correct answer is K. Calculate the number of proofs you would be able to get in each photo center with $150 to spend.

Snap! Photo Center:

$150 = 75 + 1.25x$

$75 = 1.25x$

$60 = x$

Say Gouda Photo Center:

$150 = 60 + 1.50x$

$90 = 1.50x$

$60 = x$

So, Trevor and his siblings would get the same number of proofs from the two photo centers.

---

15. A train leaves the station traveling at 40 miles per hour. A second train leaves the station traveling at 60 miles per hour. The second train leaves the station 2 hours after the first train leaves. Both trains stop traveling 4 hours after the first train left. Together, the two trains traveled how many miles?

  A. 160
  B. 200
  C. 240
  D. 280
  E. 400

15. The correct answer is D. The first train travels 4 hours at 40 miles per hour, or 4 hours · 40 miles/hour = 160 miles. The second train travels for 4 − 2 = 2 hours at 60 miles per hour, or 2 hours · 60 miles/hour = 120 miles. 160 + 120 = 280 miles total.

Lesson 7 – Operations

Sum It Up

Operations

Indicating Words:

Addition
Sum, combined, plus, added to, total of, more, both, in all, raise, etc.

Subtraction
Difference, drop, decreased by, fewer than, minus, less, left, remaining, take away, etc.

Multiplication
Product, of, multiplied by, times, triple, twice, etc.

Division
Per, divided by, out of, half, etc.

Solving Word Problems:

When solving a word problem:
1. Identify the operation you need to use.
2. Translate the problem into an equation, identifying the value you are solving for.
3. Solve the equation, paying attention to units.

When solving multiplication word problems:
1. Identify the two things that you are multiplying together.
2. Make sure the units are the same.

When solving division word problems:
Set up a proportion if it helps you keep track of units and how different parts relate to one another.

Tips and Techniques

Show Your Work: Be sure to set up all the units and solve the questions carefully. Remember that the easier the question is, the more likely you are to make a simple mistake. Be sure to show your work.

Entrance Ticket Learning Targets Addition/Subtraction Word Problems Multiplication/Division Word Problems ACT Practice Sum It Up

113

Student Page 113

220

7.5 Exit Ticket

► Students complete the three questions on their exit ticket.

Students are timed 3 minutes for the three questions (60 seconds per question). There is no break between questions.

Lesson 7 – Operations

Name _____   Date _____

Exit Ticket

1. On his trek across the globe, Gary experienced temperatures as cold as –12° and temperatures as hot as 115°. The lowest temperature that Gary experienced was how many degrees Fahrenheit less than the highest temperature?

DO YOUR FIGURING HERE.

   A. 127°F
   B. 117°F
   C. 107°F
   D. 103°F
   E. 83°F

2. Ms. Clipner had 15 days to prepare her seventh-grade class for their next math exam. On the first day, she gave the class 7 math problems to complete. Each day following, Ms. Clipner gave the class 5 more math problems to solve in preparation. How many problems did Ms. Clipner give the class for review?

   F. 26
   G. 72
   H. 77
   J. 82
   K. 156

3. The Terra family sold its heavily wooded land to a lumber company for $350,000 at a rate of $700 dollars per acre. If the property averages 8 trees per acre, which of the following is closest to the number of trees on the land?

   A. 63
   B. 500
   C. 3,500
   D. 4,000
   E. 5,608

Answered Correctly
_____ / 3

MasteryPrep

7.5 Exit Ticket

Solve the questions on your exit ticket.

Entrance Ticket | Learning Targets | Quick Check | Addition/Subtraction Word Problems | Multiplication/Division Word Problems | ACT Practice | Exit Ticket

7.5 Exit Ticket Review

▶ Students work the first question.

1. **The correct answer is A.** Translate the word problem into an equation and solve.

   115°F − (−12°F) = 127°F

7.5 Exit Ticket Review

1. On his trek across the globe, Gary experienced temperatures as cold as −12° and temperatures as hot as 115°. The lowest temperature that Gary experienced was how many degrees Fahrenheit less than the highest temperature?

   A. 127°F

   B. 117°F

   C. 107°F

   D. 103°F

   E. 83°F

Entrance Ticket   Learning Targets   Quick Check   Addition/Subtraction Word Problems   Multiplication/Division Word Problems   ACT Practice   Exit Ticket

7.5 Exit Ticket Review

▶ Students work the second question.

2. The correct answer is H. Translate the word problem into an equation and solve.

$7 + 5(15 - 1)$

$7 + 5(14)$

$7 + 70 = 77$

7.5 Exit Ticket Review

2. Ms. Clipner had 15 days to prepare her seventh grade class for their next math exam. On the first day, she gave the class 7 math problems to complete. Each day following, Ms. Clipner gave the class 5 more math problems to solve in preparation. How many problems did Ms. Clipner give the class for review?

F.   26

G.   72

H.   77

J.   82

K.   156

| Entrance Ticket | Learning Targets | Quick Check | Addition/Subtraction Word Problems | Multiplication/Division Word Problems | ACT Practice | Exit Ticket |

7.5 Exit Ticket Review

▶ Students work the third question.

  3. The correct answer is D. Translate the word problem into an equation and solve.

  $350,000 ÷ $700/acre = 500 acres

  500 · 8 = 4,000 trees

▶ After all three questions are completed, students exchange papers. Solve the three exit items step by step on the board. Students grade using their red pens and then return papers to their classmates.

▶ After solving the three exit items, revisit the learning targets slide. Students again assess their knowledge and confidence on the same 1 to 4 scale that they used at the beginning of the lesson. Students write this number in the designated area at the start of the lesson in their workbooks, along with any comments or questions they might have.

▶ Finally, to close the lesson, have students return to the cover page of the lesson and write a caption for the picture there. The caption should be a one-sentence summary of the lesson, a main rule or tip they want to remember, or an explanation of how the picture relates to the topic. If there is additional time, students can share and compare their captions with the class.

7.5 Exit Ticket Review

3. The Terra family sold its heavily wooded land to a lumber company for $350,000 at a rate of $700 dollars per acre. If the property averages 8 trees per acre, which of the following is closest to the number of trees on the land?

  A. 63

  B. 500

  C. 3,500

  D. 4,000

  E. 5,608

Entrance Ticket   Learning Targets   Quick Check   Addition/Subtraction Word Problems   Multiplication/Division Word Problems   ACT Practice   Exit Ticket

Substitution

This lesson will cover concepts such as the order of operations and how to substitute numbers of unknown quantities (variables) in equations.

ACT Standards:

A 301. Substitute whole numbers for unknown quantities to evaluate expressions

A 401. Evaluate algebraic expressions by substituting integers for unknown quantities

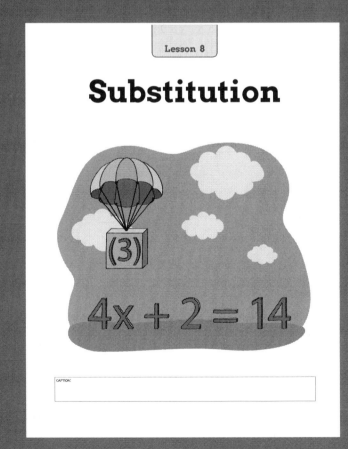

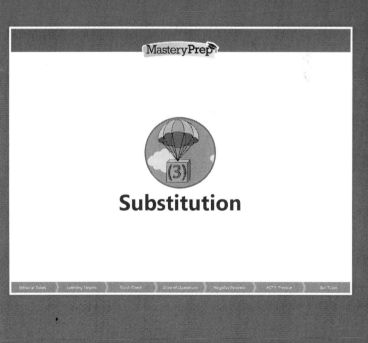

Student Page 115

8.1 Entrance Ticket

▶ Have students try the following three ACT practice questions. Students should work independently. Once the entrance ticket has been completed, review the questions with the students and have them share their answers. Give students the correct answers to the questions, as well as a step-by-step demonstration of how to solve the problems, but do not go into detailed explanation. This will serve as an introduction to the lesson content but is not intended to be the main lesson.

1. **The correct answer is D.** Substitute -2 for x in the equation.

   $-2 + 4 = 2$

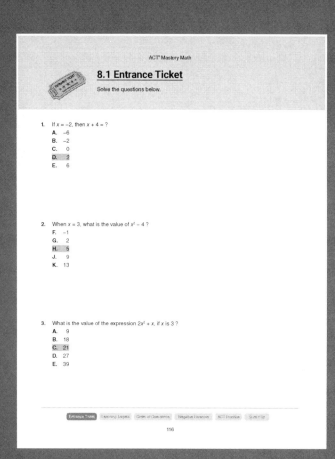

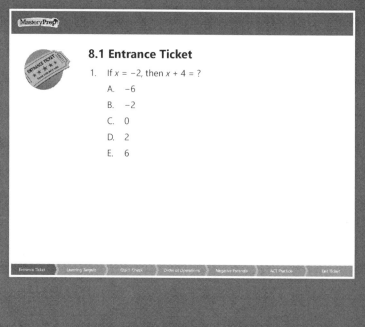

Student Page 116

8.1 Entrance Ticket

2. **The correct answer is H.** Substitute 3 for *x* in the equation.

$3^2 - 4$

$9 - 4 = 5$

8.1 Entrance Ticket

2. When $x = 3$, what is the value of $x^2 - 4$?

F.   −1

G.   2

H.   5

J.   9

K.   13

8.1 Entrance Ticket

3. **The correct answer is C.** Substitute 3 for *x* in the equation.

$2(3)^2 + 3$

$2(9) + 3$

$18 + 3 = 21$

8.1 Entrance Ticket

3. What is the value of the expression $2x^2 + x$, if *x* is 3 ?

   A. 9

   B. 18

   C. 21

   D. 27

   E. 39

Entrance Ticket | Learning Targets | Quick Check | Order of Operations | Negative Paranoia | ACT Practice | Exit Ticket

8.2 Learning Targets

▶ Review learning targets with your students, displayed on the slide and in their workbooks.

▶ After reviewing the learning targets, ask students to assess their knowledge and confidence level on these targets. They should rate themselves on a scale of 1 to 4, with 1 being not confident or uncertain, and 4 being completely confident or certain. They should circle this number in the designated section of their workbooks.

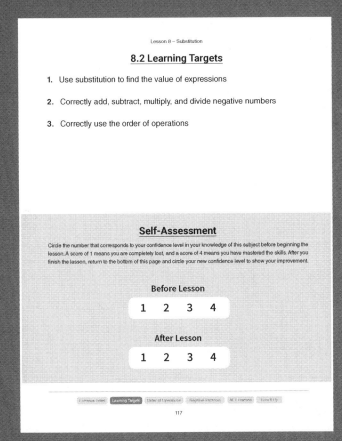

Student Page 117

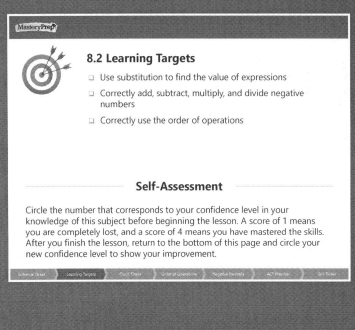

8.2 Quick Check

▶ Teacher Dialogue: **Define *value*.**

   <u>Value:</u> A number or measurement

▶ Teacher Dialogue: **Define *expression*.**

   <u>Expression:</u> A group of numbers, symbols, and operations that indicate a value

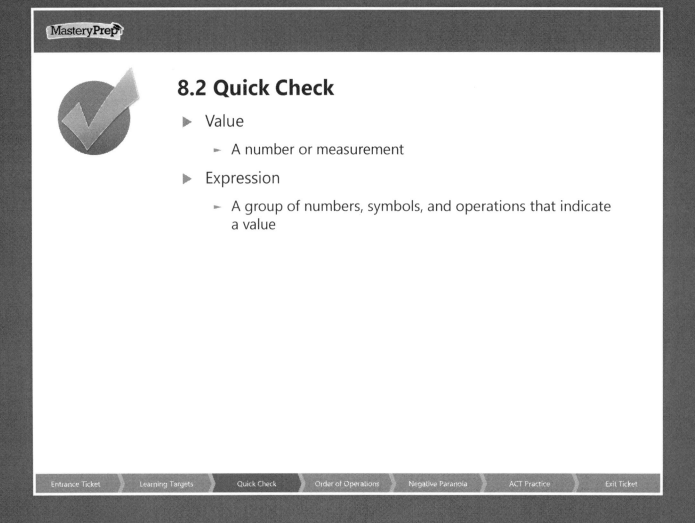

8.3.1 Order of Operations

▶ Teacher Dialogue: **Math has an important set of rules for order. If it didn't, there would be no way to agree on how to solve an expression. There is a shortcut for remembering the order of operations for the ACT. The shortcut is called PEMDAS.**

Student Page 118

▶ Present the order of operations acronym PEMDAS to the students. Explain what each piece means, and then teach them the mnemonic device "Please Excuse My Dear Aunt Sally." Have students copy the order of operations details into their workbooks.

> **P** = Parentheses
>
> **E** = Exponentiation
>
> **M** = Multiplication
>
> **D** = Division
>
> **A** = Addition
>
> **S** = Subtraction

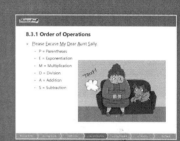

▶ Teacher Dialogue: **Which operation comes first: exponentiation or multiplication?**

Exponentiation

▶ Teacher Dialogue: **Which operation comes first: multiplication or division?**

It depends; those operations are worked left to right, regardless of the operation. For example, $3 \cdot 2 \div 3 = 2$, but $3 \div 2 \cdot 3 = 4.5$.

▶ Teacher Dialogue: **Are there any other operations like this?**

Addition and subtraction

8.3.1 Order of Operations

▶ Have students try the three practice problems in their workbooks, then review the correct answers. Ask individual students to call out the steps for each example to check understanding. If students are unsure, model the steps by working out the problem on the board.

1. **The answer is C.** Plug 6 in for *x* and solve.

   $2(6)^2 - 11(6)$

   $2(36) - 66$

   $72 - 66 = 6$

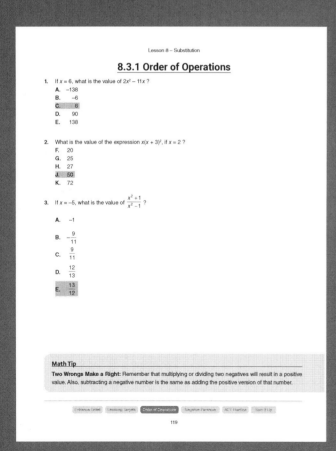

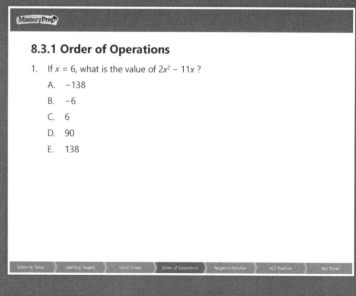

Student Page 119

8.3.1 Order of Operations

2. **The answer is J.** Plug 2 in for x and solve.

$2 \cdot (2 + 3)^2$

$2 \cdot (5)^2$

$2 \cdot 25 = 50$

3. **The answer is E.** Plug -5 in for x and solve.

$$\frac{(-5)^2 + 1}{(-5)^2 - 1}$$

$$\frac{25 + 1}{25 - 1}$$

$$\frac{26}{24} = \frac{13}{12}$$

The best way to keep track of the operations you've already completed is to show your work. Otherwise, you might make a careless error. The expressions and equations are engineered to trick you. That is why you must show your work as much as possible.

8.3.2 Negative Paranoia

▶ Teacher Dialogue: **If you've ever seen a horror movie, you'd recognize this popular scene: one of the side characters is looking for something or someone, so they walk into a broken down house in the middle of the night, all alone. Meanwhile, we all know that the monster is waiting in the shadows, and then we all know what happens next.**

▶ Teacher Dialogue: **How many times have you seen this scene and thought to yourself 'Get out of there!' or even 'this is why you don't go into creepy houses in the middle of the night'? This is how I feel on the ACT. Specifically, when using negative numbers.**

▶ Display the sample problem from the slide deck or write it on the board.

If $x = -2$, what is $-3(x)^2 + 4$?

▶ Teacher Dialogue: **Most of you right off the bat see the negative, probably the $x = -2$. The problem is once you get into the question, it is easy to forget about two things: what happens when you square a negative and the -3. If you overlook just one of them, you will miss this question.**

▶ Teacher Dialogue: **Almost every substitution question on the ACT is also testing your understanding of negative numbers. In order to be successful, you need to keep two things in mind: know your rules for negatives and be paranoid about them.**

Student Page 120

8.3.2 Negative Paranoia

$6 + (-2) = 4$

Adding a Negative: If you add a negative, subtract the value instead.

$6 - (-2) = 8$

Subtracting a Negative: If you subtract a negative, make it positive and add it instead.

$6 \times (-2) = -12$

$$\frac{6}{-2} = -3$$

Multiplying or Dividing a Negative by a Positive: If you multiply or divide a negative by a positive, the resulting value is negative.

$(-6) \times (-2) = 12$

$$\frac{-6}{-2} = 3$$

Multiplying or Dividing a Negative by a Negative: If you multiply or divide a negative by a negative, the resulting value is positive.

$(-2)^2 = 4$

Raising a Negative to an Even Power: If you square a negative, or raise it to any even power, the resulting value is positive.

$(-2)^3 = -8$

Raising a Negative to an Odd Power: If you cube a negative, or raise it to any odd power, the resulting value is negative.

▶ Teacher Dialogue: **Now that you've reviewed the rules for negatives, it is time to put them into action.**

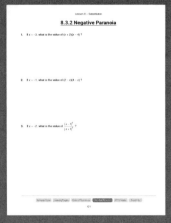

Student Page 121

8.3.2 Negative Paranoia

▶ Have the students complete three questions that use a mixture of the negative rules. Before they calculate their answers, they should circle each time a negative appears in the question. When they solve, they should show their work and be prepared to discuss how the negative rules functioned in each question.

1. If $x = -3$, what is the value of $(x + 2)(x - 4)$?

   Plug -3 in for x and solve.

   $((-3) + 2)((-3) - 4)$

   $(-1)(-7) = 7$

   This question tests multiplying a negative by a negative as well as adding to and subtracting from a negative.

2. If $x = -1$, what is the value of $(2 - x)(4 - x)$?

   Plug -1 in for x and solve:

   $(2 - (-1))(4 - (-1))$

   $(3)(5) = 15$

   This question tests subtracting a negative value.

3. If $x = -2$, what is the value of $\dfrac{(x - 1)^2}{(x + 1)^3}$?

   Plug -2 in for x and solve:

   $$\frac{((-2) - 1)^2}{((-2) + 1)^3}$$

   $$\frac{(-3)^2}{(-1)^3}$$

   $$\frac{9}{-1} = -9$$

   This question tests raising a negative to an even and an odd power as well as dividing a positive by a negative.

8.4 ACT Practice

▶ Have students work on questions from the ACT practice sets here. Pacing should be 3 minutes per practice set or 60 seconds per question.

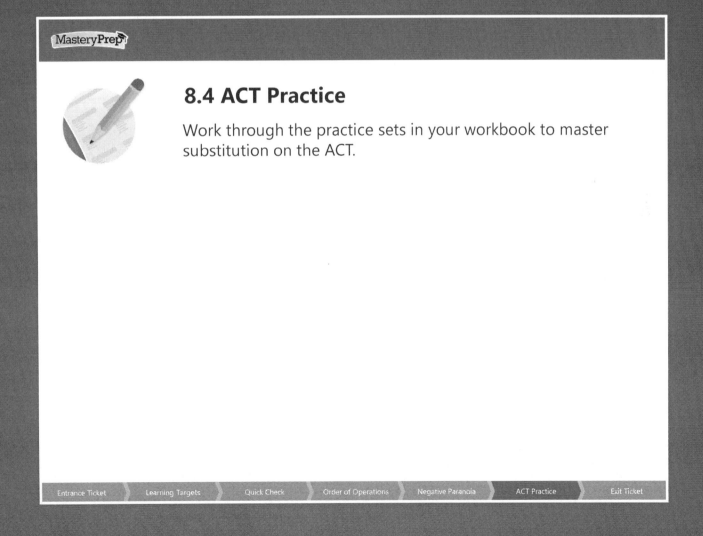

8.4.1 Set One

1. If $a = 0.3$ and $b = 0.9$, then $a^2b^2 = ?$
   A. 0.0729
   B. 0.09
   C. 0.243
   D. 0.27
   E. 0.81

1. **The correct answer is A.** Plug 0.3 in for a and 0.9 for b.

$(0.3)^2(0.9)^2$

$(0.09)(0.81) = 0.0729$

2. What is the value of the expression $2c(c + 3)^2$ if $c = 2$?
   F.   5
   G.   20
   H.   25
   J.   40
   K.   100

2. **The correct answer is K.** Plug 2 in for c.

$2(2)(2+3)^2$

$4(5)^2$

$4(25) = 100$

3. Given that $x = \dfrac{1}{3}$ and $y = \dfrac{1}{4}$, what is the value of

$2\left(\dfrac{1}{x} - \dfrac{1}{y}\right)$?

   A. –2

   B. $\dfrac{1}{6}$

   C. 2

   D. 7

   E. 14

3. **The correct answer is A.** Plug $\dfrac{1}{3}$ in for x and $\dfrac{1}{4}$ for y.

$2\left(\dfrac{1}{\left(\dfrac{1}{3}\right)} - \dfrac{1}{\left(\dfrac{1}{4}\right)}\right)$

$2(3 - 4)$

$2(-1) = -2$

8.4.2 Set Two

4. What is the value of the expression $(a - b)^3$ when $a = 3$ and $b = 4$?

   F. -3
   G. -1
   H. 1
   J. 3
   K. 27

4. **The correct answer is G.** Plug 3 in for a and 4 for b.

$$(3 - 4)^3$$
$$(-1)^3 = -1$$

5. If $x = 6$ and $y = 3$, what is the value of the following expression?

$$\frac{y^2 (x+y)^2 (y-x)}{y(x-y)}$$

   A. -243
   B. -81
   C. 27
   D. 81
   E. 243

5. **The correct answer is A.** Plug 6 in for x and 3 for y.

$$\frac{3^2 (6 + 3)^2 (3 - 6)}{3(6 - 3)}$$

$$\frac{9(9^2)(-3)}{3(3)}$$

$$\frac{9(81)(-3)}{9}$$

$$\frac{-2,187}{9} = -243$$

6. If $a = 2$, $b = 5$, and $c = -1$, what is the value of $\frac{ab - ac}{c^3}$?

   F. -20
   G. -12
   H. -8
   J. 8
   K. 12

6. **The correct answer is G.** Plug 2 in for a, 5 for b, and -1 for c.

$$\frac{(2)(5) - (2)(-1)}{(-1)^3}$$

$$\frac{10 - (-2)}{-1}$$

$$\frac{12}{-1} = -12$$

8.4.3 Set Three

7. What is the value of the expression $(2x + y)(2x - y)$ when $x = 4$ and $y = -5$?
   A. -9
   B. 9
   C. 13
   D. 16
   E. 39

7. **The correct answer is E.** Plug 4 in for x and -5 for y.

   $(2(4) + -5)(2(4) - (-5))$

   $(8 + -5)(8 + 5)$

   $(3)(13) = 39$

8. If $x = -3$, what is the value of $\dfrac{x^2 + x}{x^2 - x}$?

   F. -2

   G. -1

   H. $\dfrac{1}{2}$

   J. $\dfrac{3}{4}$

   K. 2

8. **The correct answer is H.** Plug -3 in for x.

   $$\dfrac{(-3)^2 + -3}{(-3)^2 - (-3)}$$

   $$\dfrac{9 + -3}{9 + 3}$$

   $$\dfrac{6}{12} = \dfrac{1}{2}$$

9. What is the value of $50 - 3(x^2 - y^2) + x$ when $x = 6$ and $y = -4$?
   A. -145
   B. -6
   C. -4
   D. 26
   E. 44

9. **The correct answer is C.** Plug 6 in for x and -4 for y.

   $50 - 3(6^2 - (-4)^2) + 6$

   $50 - 3(36 - 16) + 6$

   $50 - 3(20) + 6$

   $50 - 60 + 6$

   $-10 + 6 = -4$

8.4.4 Set Four

10. If $y = -4$, what is the value of $\dfrac{y^2 + 2}{y^2 - 2}$?

   F. $-\dfrac{5}{3}$

   G. -1

   H. $\dfrac{7}{9}$

   J. $\dfrac{9}{7}$

   K. $\dfrac{5}{3}$

10. The correct answer is J. Plug -4 in for y.

$$\frac{(-4)^2 + 2}{(-4)^2 - 2}$$

$$\frac{16 + 2}{16 - 2}$$

$$\frac{18}{14} = \frac{9}{7}$$

---

11. If $x = 15$, $y = -3$, and $z = -2$, what is the value of $\dfrac{x - y}{yz} + x$?

   A. 2
   B. 3
   C. 17
   D. 18
   E. 45

11. The correct answer is D. Plug 15 in for x, -3 for y, and -2 for z.

$$\frac{15 - (-3)}{(-3)(-2)} + 15$$

$$\frac{15 + 3}{(6)} + 15$$

$$\frac{18}{6} + 15$$

$$3 + 15 = 18$$

---

12. If $a = -2$, $b = 3$, and $c = 6$, then $3a^2b^2 - 4ac + c^2 = ?$

   F. 36
   G. 48
   H. 96
   J. 192
   K. 228

12. The correct answer is J. Plug -2 in for a, 3 for b, and 6 for c.

$$3(-2)^2(3)^2 - 4(-2)(6) + 6^2$$

$$3(4)(9) - (-48) + 36$$

$$108 + 48 + 36$$

$$156 + 36 = 192$$

8.4.5 Set Five

13. If $a = 11$, $b = 3$, and $c = -3$, what does $(a + b - c)(b + c)$ equal?

   A. -17
   B. -11
   C. 0
   D. 17
   E. 102

13. The correct answer is C. Plug 11 in for a, 3 for b, and -3 for c.

$$(11 + 3 - (-3))(3 + -3)$$
$$(17)(0) = 0$$

---

14. If $q = -1$, $r = 4$, and $s = 7$, what does $(q + r - s)(r - q)$ equal?

   F. -60
   G. -20
   H. -12
   J. -10
   K. -6

14. The correct answer is G. Plug -1 in for q, 4 for r, and 7 for s.

$$(-1 + 4 - 7)(4 - (-1))$$
$$(-4)(5) = -20$$

---

15. If $f = -3$, $g = -5$, and $h = 7$, what does $(f + g + h)(2f + h)$ equal?

   A. -13
   B. -11
   C. -1
   D. 1
   E. 11

15. The correct answer is C. Plug -3 in for f, -5 for g, and 7 for h.

$$(-3 + -5 + 7)(2(-3) + 7)$$
$$(-1)(1) = -1$$

Lesson 8 – Substitution

Sum It Up

Substitution

Value
A number or measurement

Expression
A group of numbers, symbols, and operations that indicate a value

Tips and Techniques

Show Your Work: Many answer choices are designed to catch your mistakes and cause you to lose out on points. That is why you must show your work whenever you solve.

Two Wrongs Make a Right: Remember that multiplying or dividing two negatives will result in a positive value. Also, subtracting a negative number is the same as adding the positive version of that number.

8.5 Exit Ticket

▶ Students complete the three questions on their exit ticket.

Students are timed 3 minutes for the three questions (60 seconds per question). There is no break between questions.

Lesson 8 – Substitution

Name _____   Date _____

Exit Ticket

1. The only solution to the equation $(x-4)(x-10) = k$ is $x = 7$. What is the value of k?
   A. −14
   B. −9
   C. 0
   D. 9
   E. 28

   DO YOUR FIGURING HERE.

2. If $x = -2$, what is the value of $6x^2 - x + 16$?
   F. −34
   G. −30
   H. −18
   J. 62
   K. 66

3. If $x = -4$, what is the value of $\dfrac{x^2-1}{x-1}$?

   A. $-\dfrac{17}{5}$

   B. −3

   C. $\dfrac{9}{5}$

   D. $\dfrac{17}{5}$

   E. 5

   Answered Correctly
   ____ / 3

8.5 Exit Ticket Review

▶ Students work the first question.

1. **The correct answer is B**. Plug 7 in for x.

   $(7 - 4)(7 - 10)$

   $(3)(-3) = -9$

MasteryPrep

8.5 Exit Ticket

1. The only solution to the equation is $(x - 4)(x - 10) = k$ is $x = 7$. What is the value of k?

   A. −14

   B. −9

   C. 0

   D. 9

   E. 28

| Entrance Ticket | Learning Targets | Quick Check | Order of Operations | Negative Paranoia | ACT Practice | Exit Ticket |

8.5 Exit Ticket Review

▶ Students work the second question.

2. **The correct answer is G.** Plug −2 in for x.

$6(-2)^3 - (-2) + 16$

$6(-8) + 2 + 16$

$-48 + 18 = -30$

MasteryPrep

8.5 Exit Ticket

2. If $x = -2$, what is the value of $6x^3 - x + 16$?

    F.   −34

    G.   −30

    H.   −18

    J.   62

    K.   66

Entrance Ticket   Learning Targets   Quick Check   Order of Operations   Negative Paranoia   ACT Practice   Exit Ticket

8.5 Exit Ticket Review

▸ Students work the third question.

   3. **The correct answer is B.** Plug −4 in for *x*.

$$\frac{(-4)^2 - 1}{(-4) - 1}$$

$$\frac{16 - 1}{-4 - 1}$$

$$\frac{15}{-5}$$

$$-3$$

▸ After all three questions are completed, students exchange papers. Solve the three exit items step by step on the board. Students grade using their red pens and then return papers to their classmates.

▸ After solving the three exit items, revisit the learning targets slide. Students again assess their knowledge and confidence on the same 1 to 4 scale that they used at the beginning of the lesson. Students write this number in the designated area at the start of the lesson in their workbooks, along with any comments or questions they might have.

▸ Finally, to close the lesson, have students return to the cover page of the lesson and write a caption for the picture there. The caption should be a one-sentence summary of the lesson, a main rule or tip they want to remember, or an explanation of how the picture relates to the topic. If there is additional time, students can share and compare their captions with the class.

Averages, Median, Mode, and Range

This lesson will cover concepts and skills involved in calculating the average of a set of values. It will also teach students how to distinguish between mean, median, mode, and range.

ACT Standards:

S 201. Calculate the average of a list of positive whole numbers

S 301. Calculate the average of a list of numbers

S 302. Calculate an average based on the number of data values and the sum of the data values

S 401. Calculate the missing data value given the average and all other data values

S 501. Calculate an average based on the frequency counts of all the data values

S 601. Calculate or use a weighted average

S 701. Distinguish between mean, median, and mode for a list of numbers

Additional materials needed: deck of cards

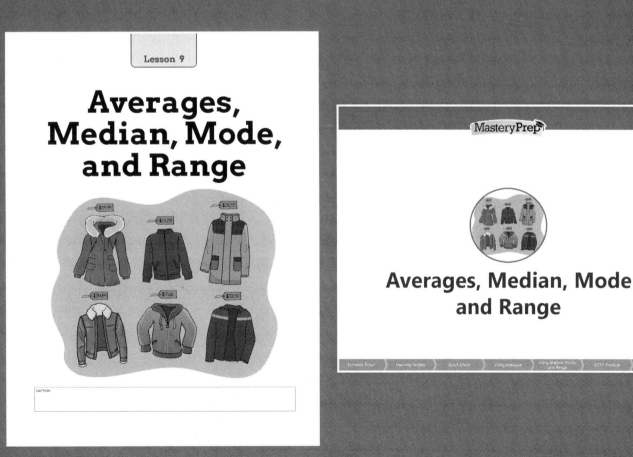

Student Page 129

9.1 Entrance Ticket

► Have students try their hand at the following three ACT practice questions. Students should work independently. Once the entrance ticket has been completed, review the questions with the students and have them share their answers. Give students the correct answers to the questions, as well as a step-by-step demonstration of how to solve the problems, but do not go into detailed explanation. This will serve as an introduction to the lesson content but is not intended to be the main lesson.

1. **The correct answer is C.** The average can be found by adding all of the prices and then dividing by 7.

($3.58 + $3.24 + $3.30 + $3.58 + $3.53 + $3.55 + $3.76 = $24.54; $24.54 ÷ 7 ≈ $3.51).

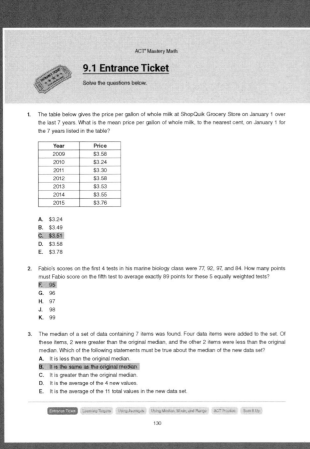

Student Page 130

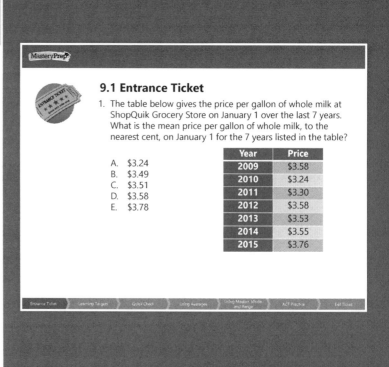

9.1 Entrance Ticket

2. **The correct answer is F.** The average can be found by solving for the sum of the five tests: $\frac{x}{5} = 89$, so $x = 445$. Then subtract the four test scores Fabio already scored: $445 - (77 + 92 + 97 + 84) = 95$.

9.1 Entrance Ticket

2. Fabio's scores on the first 4 tests in his marine biology class were 77, 92, 97, and 84. How many points must Fabio score on the fifth test to average exactly 89 points for these 5 equally weighted tests?

F. 95
G. 96
H. 97
J. 98
K. 99

9.1 Entrance Ticket

3. **The correct answer is B.** Because the median is the middle value of a set of data, the median will remain the same if 2 greater numbers and 2 smaller numbers (as compared to the original median) are added to the set.

9.1 Entrance Ticket

3. The median of a set of data containing 7 items was found. Four data items were added to the set. Of these items, 2 were greater than the original median, and the other 2 items were less than the original median. Which of the following statements must be true about the median of the new data set?

A. It is less than the original median.
B. It is the same as the original median.
C. It is greater than the original median.
D. It is the average of the 4 new values.
E. It is the average of the 11 total values in the new data set.

9.2 Learning Targets

▶ Review learning targets with your students, displayed on the slide and in their workbooks.

▶ After reviewing the learning targets, ask students to assess their knowledge and confidence level on these targets. They should rate themselves on a scale of 1 to 4, with 1 being not confident or uncertain, and 4 being completely confident or certain. They should circle this number in the designated section of their workbooks.

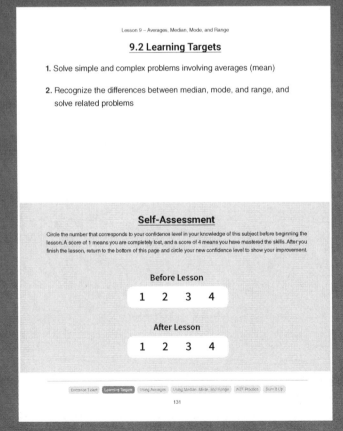

Student Page 131

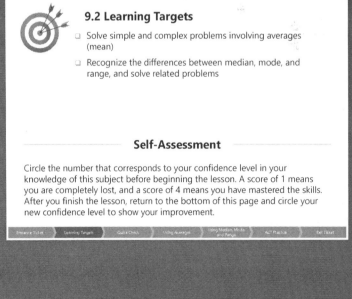

9.2 Quick Check

▶ Teacher Dialogue: **Define *data*.**

<u>Data:</u> Pieces of information that can be used for research or analysis

▶ Teacher Dialogue: **What are some examples of data?**

Potential answers include a set of test scores, scientific results from a study, a list of stock prices, etc.

MasteryPrep

9.2 Quick Check

▶ Data

  ▸ Pieces of information that can be used for research or analysis

  ▸ Examples: test scores, scientific results from a study, list of stock prices, etc.

Entrance Ticket | Learning Targets | Quick Check | Using Averages | Using Median, Mode, and Range | ACT Practice | Exit Ticket

9.3.1 Using Averages

▶ Next, make averages relatable to something that students know. Choose five students to each provide a hypothetical number of points scored by a basketball player, anywhere between 0 and 50. Explain to the class that each point total represents the player's scoring in one of five basketball games played.

▶ Write each number on the board, and then tell students to take out their white boards. Have students race to find the average of the five numbers, instructing them to raise one hand when they are finished.

Call on the first student to raise his or her hand, but don't allow the winner to speak until the majority of students have raised their hands as well.

You may also want to remember the second and third students who raise their hands, just in case the first student's answer is incorrect.

Have the winning student explain how he/she reached his/her answer. Reinforce to the class that to calculate the average, one must add all the values in a set and then divide that sum by the number of values—in this example, 5.

▶ Next, write the average number under each of the five different values on the board in order to illustrate that *an average is merely equalizing each data value without changing the sum of the data values*, just like students did getting the number of apples in each basket down to 7. Tell students that the averages of both sets (the raw data and the five identical numbers written below) are the same to reinforce this.

▶ Teacher Dialogue: **What does this average represent?**

The player's points-per-game average

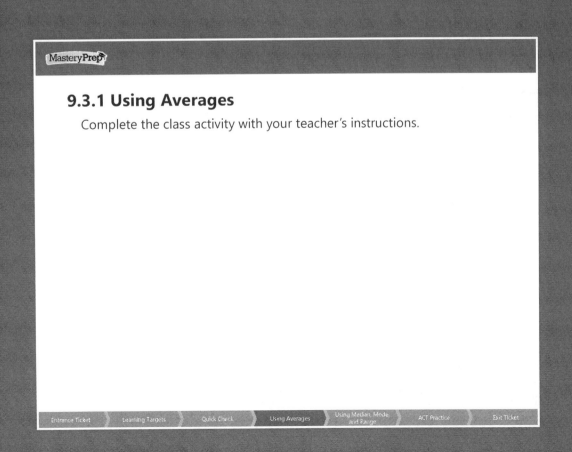

9.3.1 Using Averages

▶ Now have students complete the same activity with a few other scenarios.

▶ **Scenario 1—Science Test Scores**

▶ Teacher Dialogue: **A student wants to calculate his average, or mean, test score based on the eight exams his teacher gave that semester.**

▶ Have students use the space in their workbooks to do their calculations. (Calculators are allowed.) Remind students to raise their hands when they have an answer. When everyone is ready, show them the following numbers: 72, 93, 85, 87, 91, 88, 90, 82

Call on the first student to raise his or her hand, but don't allow the winner to speak until a majority of students have raised their hands as well.

You may also want to remember the second and third students who raise their hands, just in case the first student's answer is incorrect.

▶ Have the winning student explain how he/she reached his/her answer.

$$\frac{72 + 93 + 85 + 87 + 91 + 88 + 90 + 82}{8}$$

$$\frac{688}{8}$$

$$86$$

▶ Teacher Dialogue: **How do you calculate average here?**

Add all the values in a set and then divide that sum by the number of values—in this example, 8.

▶ Teacher Dialogue: **An average is merely equalizing each data value without changing the sum of the data values. So, if the student in this scenario had gotten an 86 on each of his eight exams, what would the average be?**

The average would be the same (86).

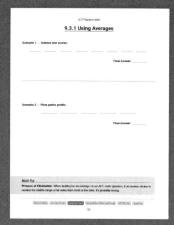

Student Page 132

9.3.1 Using Averages

▶ **Scenario 2—Pizza Parlor Profits**

▶ Teacher Dialogue: **A local pizza parlor owner is trying to calculate his average weekly profits over the past five weeks.**

▶ Show them the following numbers: −$200, $145, $298, $0, $427

  Call on the first student to raise his or her hand, but don't allow the winner to speak until a majority of students have raised their hands as well.

▶ Have the winning student explain how he/she reached his/her answer.

$$\frac{-\$200 + \$145 + \$298 + \$0 + \$427}{5}$$

$$\frac{\$670}{5}$$

$$\$134$$

▶ Teacher Dialogue: **How do you calculate average here?**

  Add all the values in a set, and then divide that sum by the number of values—in this example, 5.

▶ Teacher Dialogue: **An average is merely equalizing each data value without changing the sum of the data values. So, if the pizza parlor had made $134 in profit each of the 5 weeks, what would the average be?**

  The average would be the same ($134).

▶ Teacher Dialogue: **Why was the first value negative?**

  The pizza parlor owner lost money that week. (His costs for pizza ingredients, for example, might have been greater than the money he made in selling pizza slices.)

▶ Teacher Dialogue: **Why was the fourth value zero?**

  This week, the pizza parlor owner neither lost money nor made a profit. (His costs for pizza ingredients, for example, might have been equal to the money he made in selling pizza slices.)

  It is not essential to review these concepts in depth, but make sure that students recognize that both negative values and the number zero can be included when calculating averages, and that each still counts as one distinct term.

> **Process of Elimination:** If an answer is out of the middle range, or far away from **most** of the data, it's probably wrong. Eliminate it if you are stuck, and then make your best guess. Mark and move.

9.3.1 Using Averages

▶ Working Backward with the Formula

▶ Ask five individual students to volunteer a score between 70 and 100 on an imaginary test. Write the scores on the board, and then ask students to pair up. Write the variable x as the score of the sixth test, next to the other numbers.

▶ Teacher Dialogue: **What is the minimum value of the sixth score if the student wants to achieve an average of 86?**

Have students attempt to calculate the minimum value of the sixth score, raising their hands once they have an answer. See if students can figure it out on their own. Call on a few different pairs to offer their answers. Ask one of the pairs to justify their answer, and you can put their work on the board. If it is incorrect, point out what the pair did correctly in their calculations, and then ask another pair to come up and try to justify their answer. Repeat this process until the correct answer and work is demonstrated on the board.

Teacher's Explanation: Below is one possible scenario of a set of numbers and how students may work through the problem. If the students chose the following five test scores:

$$75 \quad 80 \quad 89 \quad 95 \quad 85$$

Then students may calculate the necessary sixth score as follows:

$$75 \quad 80 \quad 89 \quad 95 \quad 85 \quad x$$

$$\frac{75 + 80 + 89 + 95 + 85 + x}{6} = 86$$

$$86\,(6) = 75 + 80 + 89 + 95 + 85 + x$$

$$516 = 75 + 80 + 89 + 95 + 85 + x$$

$$516 = 424 + x$$

$$92 = x$$

The student needs a score of at least 92 on the sixth test in order to receive an average of 86 on the six tests.

Make sure students understand the problem this way: If a student received a score of 86 on all six tests, their average would be 86. Since we are trying to calculate an average of 86 when five of six values are 75, 80, 89, 95, and 85, we need to figure out what value would make the sum of those six numbers the same as the sum of $86 + 86 + 86 + 86 + 86 + 86$, or 6 values of 86 added together. In other words, they could solve the problem as:

$$86 + 86 + 86 + 86 + 86 + 86 = 75 + 80 + 89 + 95 + 85 + x$$

$$516 = 424 + x$$

$$92 = x$$

9.3.1 Using Averages

▶ Have students practice this concept with a few additional practice problems. Instruct students to remain in their pairs.

▶ Teacher Dialogue: **You will need to help out a student, Andy Jackson, as he goes through his senior year. Andy is trying to meet some important goals, and he needs to know exactly what to aim for to help him achieve them.**

▶ Have students do their calculations in the space provided in the workbooks. Once partners have reached an answer, they can write it on their whiteboard and hold it up for the teacher to see. Instruct students that they will race against other teams to determine the missing value in a set, as in the problem they just practiced.

▶ **Scenario 1—Wrestling**

▶ Teacher Dialogue: **Andy is trying to gain weight for a wrestling match he has coming up. In order to gain more muscle, his coach advised him to eat an average of four eggs per day over the course of the next week. It's now Saturday night, and Andy needs to figure out how many eggs he must eat tomorrow to make sure he hits an average of four. How many eggs should Andy eat on Sunday?**

▶ Show students the following data on the slide:

Mon	Tues	Wed	Thurs	Fri	Sat	Sun
5	2	3	4	5	6	x

▶ Call on the first pair to hold up the correct answer. Have that pair come to the board and show their work.

$$\frac{5 + 2 + 3 + 4 + 5 + 6 + x}{7} = 4$$

$$4\,(7) = 5 + 2 + 3 + 4 + 5 + 6 + x$$

$$28 = 5 + 2 + 3 + 4 + 5 + 6 + x$$

$$28 = 25 + x$$

$$3 = x$$

Thus, Andy will need to eat 3 eggs on Sunday.

Student Page 133

259

9.3.1 Using Averages

▶ **Scenario 2—Volunteer Hours**

▶ Teacher Dialogue: **Andy is hoping to win a Community Service Award at his school. In order to qualify, he needs to average 10 hours of volunteering per week for six weeks. How many hours should he volunteer his sixth week in order to make this average and qualify?**

▶ Show students the following data on the slide:

$$7, 11, 8, 15, 10, x$$

▶ Call on the first pair to hold up the correct answer. Have that pair come to the board and show their work.

$$\frac{7 + 11 + 8 + 15 + 10 + x}{6} = 10$$

$$10\,(6) = 7 + 11 + 8 + 15 + 10 + x$$

$$60 = 7 + 11 + 8 + 15 + 10 + x$$

$$60 = 51 + x$$

$$9 = x$$

Thus, Andy needs to volunteer 9 hours the sixth week in order to qualify for the Community Service Award.

> **Plug In:** If you don't know how to set up an average problem, try to plug in the answers. Start with the middle choice and check to see whether it is correct. If it is too big, eliminate it and the other bigger numbers. If it is too small, eliminate it and the other smaller numbers. If it is just right, mark it and move.

9.3.2 Using Median, Mode, and Range

▸ Using a shuffled deck of cards, have nine students each pick a card at random. Let Jacks = 11, Queens = 12, Kings = 13, and Aces = 14. (All other cards will be valued at the number they represent.) Write the value of each card on the board in the order they were picked. Have students write these values in the first row of blanks in their workbook.

   If you don't have a deck of cards, number a few note cards or slips of paper.

▸ Teacher Dialogue: **What is the median value of the data?**

   Ask the students to pair up and discuss the answer. Have each pair write the median on one of their white boards and hold it up. Ask one of the pairs that wrote down the correct answer to explain how they arrived at it.

▸ Have a tenth student pick a card from those remaining in the deck. Ask him or her to write the card numbers on the board in numerical order, adding in the number of the card they just picked. Have students write these 10 values, in order, in the second row of blanks in their workbook.

▸ Teacher Dialogue: **What is the new median of the data?**

   Have students discuss the answer in pairs. Instruct them to write down the median on one of their whiteboards and hold it up. Pick one of the pairs that wrote down the correct answer and ask them to explain how they arrived at it.

   Make sure that students understand that when calculating the median with an even number of data values, students must take the two numbers in the middle and average—in other words, add the two middle values and divide by 2.

▸ Go back to the 10-item data set on the board, making sure there are at least two values that are the same (if necessary, replace one number with a repeat number).

▸ Teacher Dialogue: **What is the mode of the data?**

   Ask the students to pair up and discuss the answer. Have each pair write the mode on one of their whiteboards and hold it up. Ask one of the pairs that wrote down the correct answer to explain how they arrived at it.

Student Page 134

261

9.3.2 Using Median, Mode, and Range

▶ Now add one or more numbers to the set until there are two items that appear equally often but more than any other (for example, three 7s and three 9s).

▶ Teacher Dialogue: **What is the new mode of the data?**

Call on a few pairs randomly to offer their answers. Allow a few different pairs of students to give their thoughts, leading the discussion to the correct conclusion that there may be more than one mode in a set of data.

▶ Teacher Dialogue: **What is the range of the data?**

Instruct students to put the value of the range they determined on their whiteboards and hold them up. Choose one pair who calculated the range correctly to discuss how they arrived at their answer.

▶ Teacher Dialogue: **How do you calculate the range of a set of data?**

Range = Value of largest number − Value of smallest number

9.4 ACT Practice

▶ Have students work on questions from the ACT practice sets here. Pacing should be 3 minutes per practice set or 60 seconds per question.

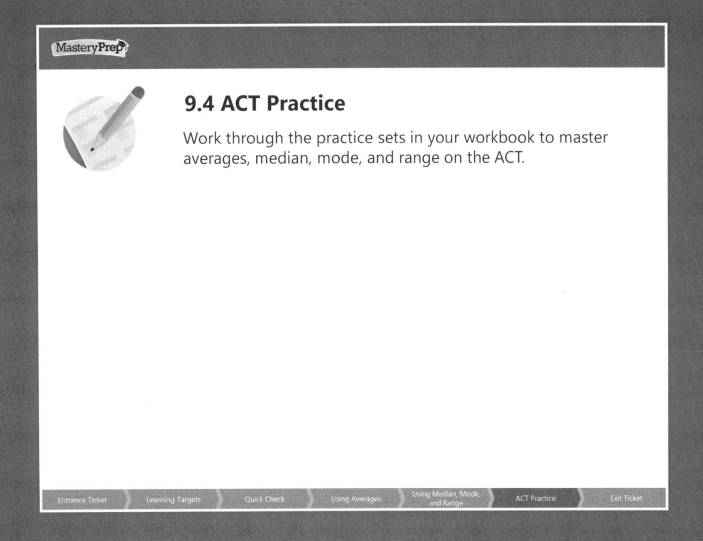

MasteryPrep

9.4 ACT Practice

Work through the practice sets in your workbook to master averages, median, mode, and range on the ACT.

Entrance Ticket | Learning Targets | Quick Check | Using Averages | Using Median, Mode, and Range | ACT Practice | Exit Ticket

9.4.1 Set One

1. For the first 7 days of January, the daily low temperatures for Burlington were 20°, 14°, 9°, 8°, −8°, −11°, and −4° Fahrenheit. What was the average daily low temperature, in degrees Fahrenheit, for those 7 days?

A. −1°
B. 0°
C. 1°
D. 4°
E. 6°

1. **The correct answer is D.** Add all temperatures and divide by 7.

$$\frac{20 + 14 + 9 + 8 + -8 + -11 + -4}{7}$$

$$\frac{28}{7}$$

$$4°$$

2. To determine a student's overall homework score for the semester, Mr. Daley drops the 2 lowest homework scores and takes the average of the remaining homework scores. Payton earned the following homework scores in Mr. Daley's class this semester: 85, 56, 67, 90, 95, 86, 0, 83, 100, and 88. What is the overall homework score that Payton earned in Mr. Daley's class this semester? Round your answer to the nearest tenth of a point.

F. 69.4
G. 77.1
H. 86.8
J. 88.0
K. 99.1

2. **The correct answer is H.** Eliminate the two lowest values, 0 and 56, and find the average of the remaining scores.

$$\frac{85+67+90+95+86+83+100+88}{8}$$

$$\frac{694}{8}$$

$$\approx 86.8$$

3. Sydney earned 91, 93, 93, 94, and 96 points on the 5 essays—each out of a total of 100 points—given so far this semester. How many points must she earn on her sixth essay, which is also out of 100 points, to average 90 points for the six essays assigned this semester?

A. 73
B. 80
C. 86
D. 90
E. 93

3. **The correct answer is A.** Solve for the sum of the 6 essays to earn an average of 90. Then, plug in the other scores and solve for the missing sixth essay score.

$$\frac{x}{6} = 90$$

$$540 = x$$

$$540 = 91 + 93 + 93 + 94 + 96 + x$$

$$x = 73$$

9.4.2 Set Two

4. What is the mean of the following scores? 5, 93, 64, 45, 58, 13, 58

    F. 46
    G. 48
    H. 52
    J. 54
    K. 58

4. **The correct answer is G.** Add the values and divide by 7.

$$\frac{5 + 93 + 64 + 45 + 58 + 13 + 58}{7} = \frac{336}{7} = 48$$

5. What is the average of 4, 4, and 5 ?

    A. 4

    B. $4\frac{1}{3}$

    C. $4\frac{1}{2}$

    D. 5

    E. $5\frac{2}{3}$

5. **The correct answer is B.** Add the values and divide by 3.

$$\frac{4 + 4 + 5}{3} = \frac{13}{3} = 4\frac{1}{3}$$

6. The stem-and-leaf plot below shows the number of points a basketball player with the New Orleans Krewe scored in each of his 15 games.

Stem	Leaf
0	8
1	0 4 7 7 7 8 9
2	3 5 5 6 8
3	1 2

(Note: For example, 20 points would have a stem value of 2 and a leaf value of 0.)

Which of the following is closest to the mean number of points the player scored per game?

    F. 4.7
    G. 15.0
    H. 15.8
    J. 20.0
    K. 20.7

6. **The correct answer is K.** Add all the values and divide by 15.

$$\frac{8 + 10 + 14 + 17 + 17 + 17 + 18 + 19 + 23 + 25 + 25 + 26 + 28 + 31 + 32}{15}$$

$$= \frac{310}{15} \approx 20.7$$

9.4.3 Set Three

7. George was absent for the last accounting test. For those who took the test, the mean was 75.8, the median was 74, and the mode was 81. When George took the test later, his score was different from all the other students' scores, and the class mean went up to exactly 76.6. What effect, if any, did George's score have on the class mode?

A. None, the mode stayed the same.
B. It decreased the mode exactly 0.8 points.
C. It increased the mode exactly 0.8 points.
D. It increased the mode more than 0.8 points.
E. The effect of George's score on the mode cannot be determined from the given information.

7. **The correct answer is A.** The mode is not affected, since the mode is the number that appears most often in a set. Since George's score was not the same as any other student's, his score did not affect the mode of 81.

8. What is the median of the following 9 numbers?
66, 29, 31, 49, 65, 13, 80, 13, 24

F. 13
G. 31
H. 41.1
J. 65
K. 80

8. **The correct answer is G.** The median is the middle value of the set. The numbers in order are 13, 13, 24, 29, 31, 49, 65, 66, 80, meaning the middle number is 31.

9. Julia started exercising August 1 because she wanted to prepare for volleyball season. For 7 days, she recorded the number of pushups she did each day in the table below. What was the range of pushups Julia did during the first 7 days of August?

August	1	2	3	4	5	6	7
Number of pushups	50	75	75	100	130	140	165

A. 75
B. 100
C. 105
D. 115
E. 135

9. **The correct answer is D.** Calculate the range by subtracting the smallest value from the largest one.

165 − 50 = 115

9.4.4 Set Four

10. The table below shows the scoring patterns of 4 different basketball players over the last 5 games. The table gives the number of points each player scored in each game. Which player has the greatest range in points given in the table, and what is that range, in points?

Player A	Player B	Player C	Player D
9	13	15	12
3	22	35	27
7	33	14	22
19	34	24	8
16	23	12	24

   F. Player A; 16
   G. Player B; 21
   H. Player B; 25
   J. Player C; 23
   K. Player D; 19

10. **The correct answer is J.** Calculate the range of each player's score and determine the greatest value.

Player A: 19 − 3 = 16

Player B: 34 − 13 = 21

Player C: 35 − 12 = 23 (Greatest range)

Player D: 27 − 8 = 19

11. The following chart shows the current enrollment for all the youth football teams offered in Arlington.

Division	Team	Enrollment
Cadet	A	35
Junior Peewee	A	32
	B	33
Peewee	A	41
	B	34
	C	36

What is the average number of players enrolled per team in the Peewee division?

   A. 34
   B. 35
   C. 36
   D. 37
   E. 41

11. **The correct answer is D.** Add all the values in the "peewee" teams, A through C, and divide by 3.

$$\frac{41 + 34 + 36}{3} = \frac{111}{3} = 37$$

12. The table below shows information about a car dealership over a 4-year period. The table shows the number of employees on staff, the number of cars sold, and the amount of sales the company made.

Year	Employees	Cars Sold	Sales
2000	39	10	$70,500
2001	40	16	$111,000
2002	44	19	$128,250
2003	51	25	$166,000

To the nearest dollar, what was the average price of a car sold in 2001 ?

F. $2,775
G. $6,640
H. $6,750
J. $6,938
K. $7,050

12. **The correct answer is J.** Divide the total sales in the row labeled "2001" and divide by the number of cars sold, 16.

$$\frac{\$111,000}{16} \approx \$6,938$$

9.4.5 Set Five

13. Caitlin has earned the following scores on four 100-point tests this year: 94, 81, 87, and 90. What score must Caitlin earn on the fifth and final 100-point test to earn an average score of 90 for the 5 tests?
A. 90
B. 92
C. 96
D. 98
E. Caitlin cannot earn an average of 90.

13. The correct answer is D. Solve for the total sum required for Caitlin to earn a 90 average. Then plug in and solve for the missing value.

$$\frac{x}{5} = 90$$
$$450 = x$$
$$450 = 94 + 81 + 87 + 90 + y$$
$$y = 98$$

14. A data set contains 6 numbers and has a mean of 6. Five of the numbers are 8, 7, 5, 9, and 4. What is the sixth number in this data set?
F. 3
G. 4
H. 5
J. 6
K. 7

14. The correct answer is F. Plug in and solve for the missing value.

$$\frac{8 + 7 + 5 + 9 + 4 + x}{6} = 6$$
$$36 = 33 + x$$
$$x = 3$$

15. The table below shows the quarterly sales totals (in thousands of dollars) for a company over a 4-year period. The company's CEO set a sales goal of $140,000 for the quarterly average in 2008. To meet this goal, what must be the minimum fourth-quarter sales in 2008, in thousands of dollars?

Year	Q1	Q2	Q3	Q4
2005	85	89	80	93
2006	100	107	95	115
2007	122	129	125	134
2008	140	143	136	

A. 138
B. 139
C. 140
D. 141
E. 142

15. The correct answer is D. The average of the last row must be 140. Solve for the missing value that would lead to this average.

$$\frac{140 + 143 + 136 + x}{4} = 140$$
$$560 = 419 + x$$
$$141 = x$$

Lesson 9 – Averages, Median, Mode, and Range

Sum It Up

Averages, Median, Mode, and Range

Data
Pieces of information that can be used for research or analysis

Average (or *mean*)
A calculation of the center of a set of data

$$\frac{sum\ of\ all\ data\ items\ in\ a\ set}{total\ number\ of\ data\ items}$$

Median
The middle data item in a set

Mode
The number that appears most often in a data set

Range
The difference between the largest number and the smallest number in a data set

Tips and Techniques

Process of Elimination: If an answer choice is outside the middle range or far away from most of the data, it is probably wrong.

Plug In: If you don't know how to set up an average problem, try to plug in the answers. Start with the middle choice and determine whether it is correct. If it is too big, eliminate it and the bigger numbers. If it is too small, eliminate it and the smaller numbers. If it is just right, mark it and move on.

9.5 Exit Ticket

► Students complete the three questions on their exit ticket.

Students are timed 3 minutes for the three questions (60 seconds per question). There is no break between questions.

Name _____   Date _____

Exit Ticket

1. The stem-and-leaf plot below shows the number of fish caught in Long Island Sound during a 31-day period. What is the median number of fish caught?

DO YOUR FIGURING HERE.

Stem	Leaf
3	1 2 6 6 7 8
4	0 0 2 3 9 9
5	1 1 4 5 7 7 7 9
6	2 2 3 3 6 7 8 8 9
8	0 1 1

(Note: For example, 51 fish would have a stem value of 5 and a leaf value of 1.)

A. 54
B. 55
C. 56
D. 57
E. 58

2. The table below shows the number of points each basketball team scored in 5 of 6 games. After each team plays their 6th game, the average points per game will be calculated for the team. If team A scores 60 points in their 6th game, what is the minimum number of points team B will need to score to have a higher points-per-game average than team A?

Team A	Team B	Team C
44	51	49
48	46	60
45	46	54
56	55	53
50	52	51

F. 51
G. 52
H. 53
J. 54
K. 55

MasteryPrep

9.5 Exit Ticket

Solve the questions on your exit ticket.

Entrance Ticket | Learning Target | Quick Check | Using Averages | Using Median, Mode, and Range | ACT Practice | Exit Ticket

9.5 Exit Ticket Review

▶ Students work the first question.

1. **The correct answer is C.** The median number is the middle value. Eliminate the first and last value, continuing until the middle value is reached. The two middle values are 55 and 57, so they should be averaged to find the median.

$$\frac{55 + 57}{2} = 56$$

MasteryPrep

9.5 Exit Ticket Review

1. The stem-and-leaf plot below shows the number of fish caught in Long Island Sound during a 31-day period. What is the median number of fish caught?

   (Note: For example, 51 fish would have a stem value of 5 and a leaf value of 1.)

   A. 54
   B. 55
   C. 56
   D. 57
   E. 58

Stem	Leaf
3	1 2 6 6 7 8
4	0 0 2 3 9 9
5	1 1 4 5 7 7 7 9
6	2 2 3 3 6 7 8 8 9
8	0 1 1

Entrance Ticket   Learning Targets   Quick Check   Using Averages   Using Median, Mode, and Range   ACT Practice   Exit Ticket

9.5 Exit Ticket Review

▸ Students work the second question.

2. **The correct answer is J.** Calculate the sum of the scores of Team A after the sixth game. Add 1, and then solve for the sixth value Team B would need to beat this total.

$$44 + 48 + 45 + 56 + 50 + 60 = 303$$
$$303 + 1 = 304$$
$$304 = 51 + 46 + 46 + 55 + 52 + x$$
$$54 = x$$

MasteryPrep

9.5 Exit Ticket Review

2. The table below shows the number of points each basketball team scored in 5 of 6 games. After each team plays their 6th game, the average points per game will be calculated for the team. If team A scores 60 points in their 6th game, what is the minimum number of points team B will need to score to have a higher points-per-game average than team A?

F. 51
G. 52
H. 53
J. 54
K. 55

Team A	Team B	Team C
44	51	49
48	46	60
45	46	54
56	55	53
50	52	51

9.5 Exit Ticket Review

► Students work the third question.

3. **The correct answer is B.** Add the number of hours each student watches television and divide by the total students, 26.

$$\frac{5(0) + 8(1) + 7(2) + 4(3) + 2(4)}{26}$$

$$\frac{42}{26}$$

$$\approx 1.6$$

► After all three questions are completed, students exchange papers. Solve the three exit items step by step on the board. Students grade using their red pens and then return papers to their classmates.

► After solving the three exit items, revisit the learning targets slide. Students again assess their knowledge and confidence on the same 1 to 4 scale that they used at the beginning of the lesson. Students write this number in the designated area at the start of the lesson in their workbooks, along with any comments or questions they might have.

► Finally, to close the lesson, have students return to the cover page of the lesson and write a caption for the picture there. The caption should be a one-sentence summary of the lesson, a main rule or tip they want to remember, or an explanation of how the picture relates to the topic. If there is additional time, students can share and compare their captions with the class.

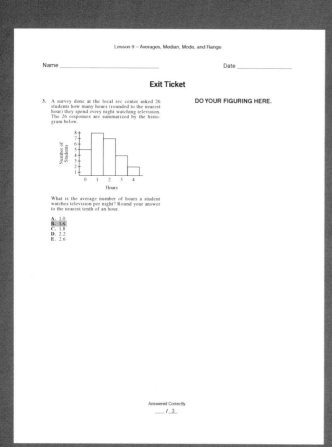

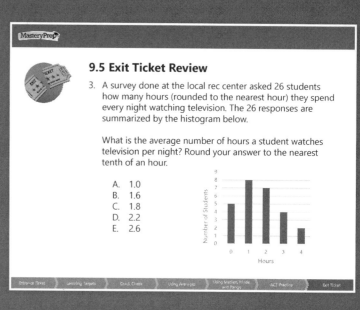

Perimeter and Line Segments

This lesson will cover how to determine the lengths of line segments and the perimeters of shapes.

ACT Standards:

G 202. Calculate the length of a line segment based on the lengths of other line segments that go in the same direction (e.g., overlapping line segments and parallel sides of polygons with only right angles)

G 302. Compute the perimeter of polygons when all side lengths are given

G 403. Compute the area and perimeter of triangles and rectangles in simple problems

G 505. Compute the perimeter of simple composite geometric figures with unknown side lengths

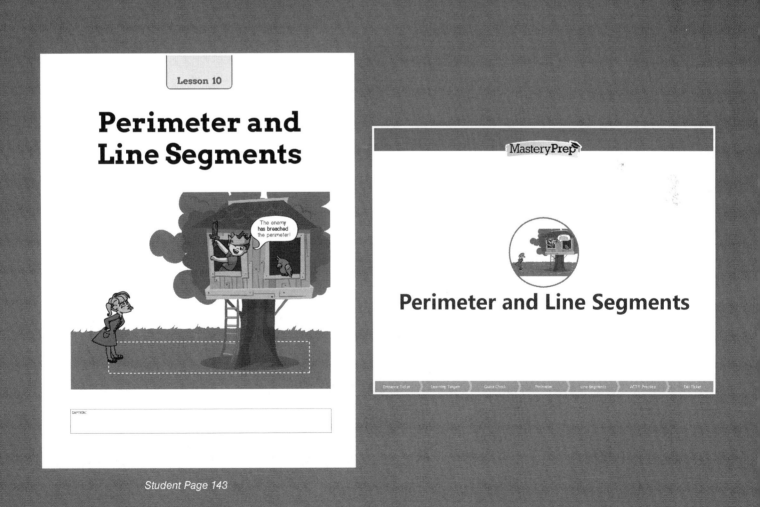

Student Page 143

10.1 Entrance Ticket

▶ Have students complete the following writing prompt presented on the slide. Students should work independently. Once the entrance ticket has been completed, the teacher calls on several students to share their answers and discuss as a class.

What is the perimeter of this room? How did you make your estimate?

Students should estimate the length of each wall of the classroom and find the sum of these estimated lengths.

Note: Students should make estimates <u>without</u> normal measurement tools. Do not tell them how to do it; they should figure out that they can make estimates by counting the tiles on the floor or ceiling, estimating the length of a desk and how many desks might fit along a wall, counting panels on the wall, etc. Teachers need to measure their actual classroom perimeter ahead of time. Recall that the perimeter of a two-dimensional shape is given by the sum of the lengths of its sides.

▶ Do not reveal the actual perimeter to the students. Reveal which student is closest to the actual perimeter.

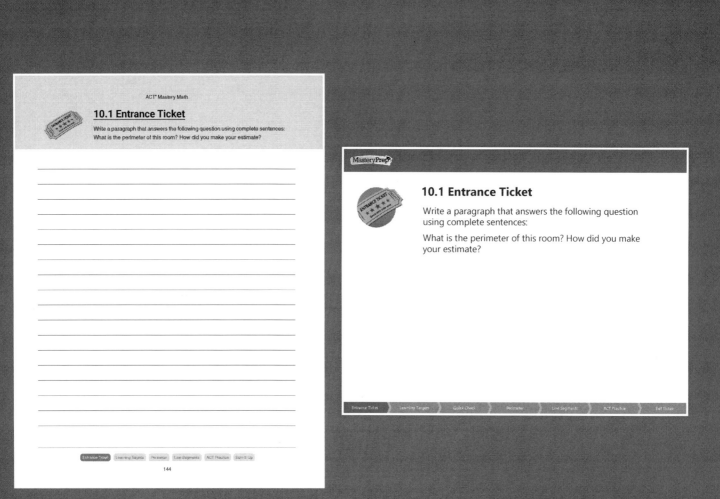

Student Page 144

10.2 Learning Targets

▶ Review learning targets with your students, displayed on the slide and in their workbooks.

▶ After reviewing the learning targets, ask students to assess their knowledge and confidence level on these targets. They should rate themselves on a scale of 1 to 4, with 1 being not confident or uncertain, and 4 being completely confident or certain. They should circle this number in the designated section of their workbooks.

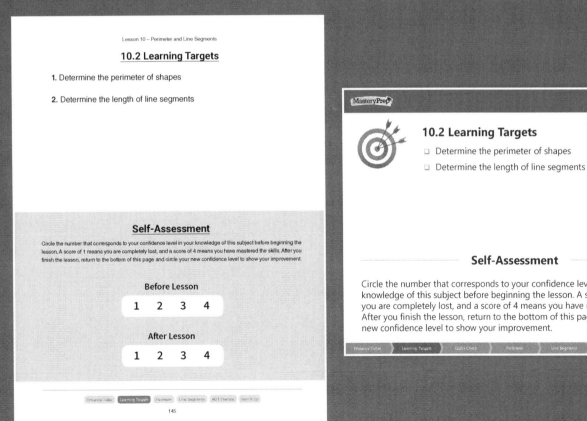

Student Page 145

10.2 Quick Check

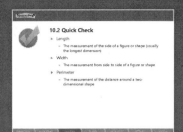

► Make sure the students can define the following terms.

► Teacher Dialogue: **Define *length*.**

   Length: The measurement of the side of a figure or shape

► Teacher Dialogue: **Define *width*.**

   Width: The measurement from side to side of a figure or shape

► Teacher Dialogue: **Define *perimeter*.**

   Perimeter: The measurement of the distance around a two-dimensional shape

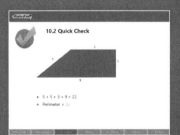

► Teacher Dialogue: **For most two-dimensional shapes, the perimeter can be found by adding the lengths of each side. How would you find the perimeter of the irregular quadrilateral shown?**

   Add the lengths of the sides to find the perimeter.

10.3.1 Perimeter

Tell the students to imagine they are going to turn the classroom into an epic walk-in closet fit for the stars. First, they will be installing shelving all along the walls for shoes and accessories. Tell the students they will need to figure out how much it will cost to redo the shelving for the classroom closet.

▶ Tell them you will answer three (and only three) questions to help them solve the problem.

Acceptable questions include "What is the length of the room?" "What is the width of the room?" "How much does the flooring cost?" etc.

You will not answer the question "What is the perimeter of the classroom?" though. They'll have to figure that out on their own. Remember, you will need to find out the dimensions of the classroom beforehand.

▶ Teacher Dialogue: **Assume that it would cost $14.00 per foot to install shelving along the walls of the classroom.**

▶ Answer the students' questions and give them some time to attempt to figure out the answer. If the students are unable to solve the problem, answer another question for them. (For example, if students did not ask for both dimensions of the room and find themselves unable to get the correct answer, give them an opportunity to ask for the information they need this second time around.) Then review the process for finding the correct answer.

Sum of measurements of the sides of the classroom · $14 per foot = price

▶ Explain to the students that there are many different polygons, but the methods for finding their perimeters are similar.

▶ Teacher Dialogue: **Though there are some shortcuts for all polygons, perimeter can be found by adding the lengths of all the sides. For any polygon, add a number of lengths equal to the number of sides of the polygon. For a triangle, add three numbers; for a pentagon, add five numbers and so on.**

Student Page 146

10.3.1 Perimeter

▶ Teacher Dialogue: **Find the perimeter of the triangle.**

Add the lengths of the sides. The perimeter of the triangle is given by $P = 8 + 15 + 19 = 42$ inches.

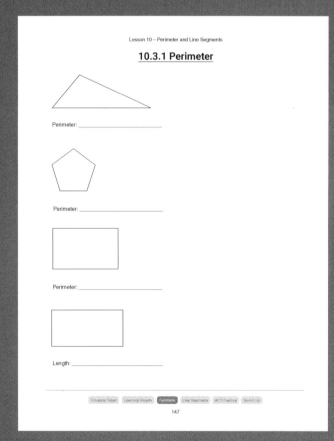

Student Page 147

10.3.1 Perimeter

▶ Teacher Dialogue: **Find the perimeter of the regular pentagon.**

Add the lengths of the sides. The perimeter of the pentagon is $P = 9 + 9 + 9 + 9 + 9 = 45$ cm. Ask the students if they can guess the shortcut. The perimeter of the pentagon can be found more easily with the equation $P = 5(9) = 45$ cm. The perimeter of any regular polygon can be found by multiplying one side length by the number of sides.

▶ Teacher Dialogue: **Find the perimeter of the rectangle.**

As with any polygon, the perimeter can be found by adding the sides. However, rectangles and parallelograms (since they have two equal sides) have a shortcut, a perimeter formula: $P = 2w + 2l$ where w is the width and l is the length. The perimeter of the rectangle is $P = 2(5) + 2(11) = 10 + 22 = 32$ mm.

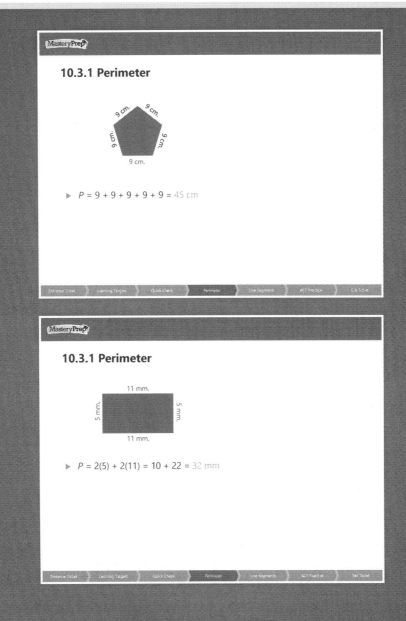

10.3.1 Perimeter

▶ The students may find the above practice to be too easy. Remind them that the ACT test writers take what students know and find easy and try to make it seem complicated and confusing. Examine the next examples.

▶ Teacher Dialogue: **How do you think the length of an unknown side can be found if the perimeter is known?**

Work backward.

▶ Teacher Dialogue: **Find the length of a rectangle if its length is twice its width and the perimeter is 48 inches.**

Plug the information into the perimeter formula to get $48 = 2w + 2(2w) = 6w$. The measure of w is $\frac{48}{6}$ = 8 inches. Since the length of the rectangle is twice its width, then $l = 2w$.

$l = 2(8) = 16$ inches

10.3.1 Perimeter

Find the length of a rectangle if its length is twice its width and the perimeter is 48 inches.

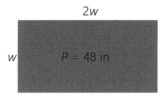

▶ $48 = 2w + 2(2w) = 6w$

▶ The length of w is $\frac{48}{6}$ = 8 inches. Therefore, the length of the rectangle is 2(8) = 16 inches

10.3.1 Perimeter

▶ Tell the students that ratios can be a useful tool for determining perimeter and dimensions of polygons. Go over the following problem with them. First, ask them if they have any ideas on how to solve it themselves. Then work through it with them on the board or via the slide.

Tell students that the perimeter of a triangle is just the sum of the sides, so you can plug the information you are given into the equation.

$22 = 7 + 2x + 3x$

$22 = 7 + 5x$

$5x = 15$

$x = 3$

The side lengths of the triangle are 7, 6, and 9. The length of the shortest side is 6 cm.

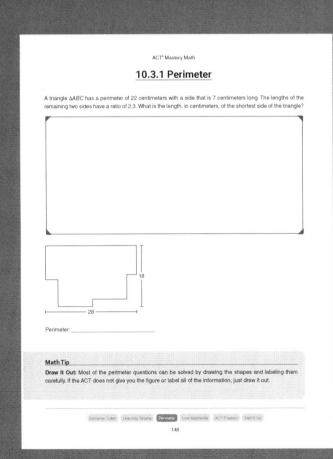

Student Page 148

10.3.1 Perimeter

▶ Remind the students that so far, we have mostly spoken about either regular or common polygons. Display the shape on the slide and label the sides.

▶ Teacher Dialogue: **How would you find the perimeter? What is it?**

Point out that there are unknown side lengths but there should be a way to find the total vertical and horizontal lengths of the polygon.

Help the students calculate the perimeter of the polygon. Show them that if all of the angles are 90°, an entire flat side is equal to the sum of all the sides parallel to it, even if they aren't on the same line. In this figure, the top side is 28 inches long. The four pieces that are parallel to it, making up the bottom of the figure, add up to also be 28 inches. It doesn't matter that you don't know the individual lengths because you are adding them all up anyway when calculating perimeter. Likewise, the three sides on the right of the figure add up to 18 inches, as do the two sides parallel to them on the left of the figure.

The perimeter should be $P = 18 + 18 + 28 + 28 = 92$ inches. Let students know that when the angles of the polygon are all 90°, the perimeter can often be found by adding twice the vertical length and twice the horizontal length, as if the polygon were simply a rectangle.

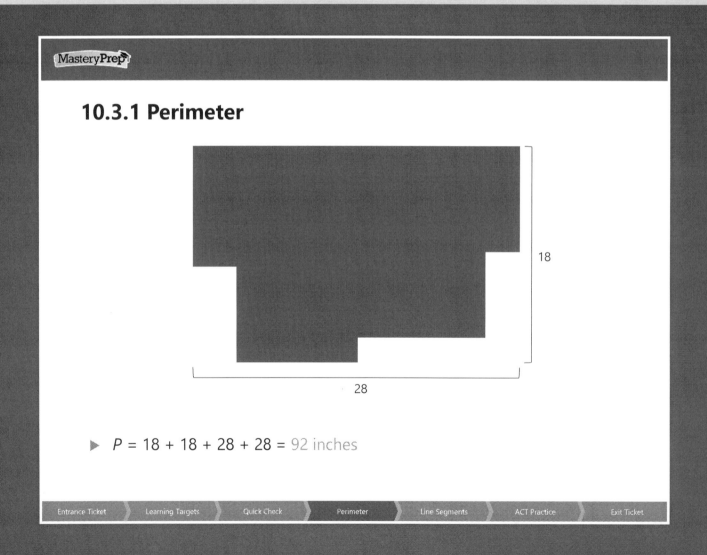

Lesson 10 – Perimeter and Line Segments

10.3.2 Line Segments

Points X and Y lie on $\overline{WZ}$, as shown below. The length of $\overline{WZ}$ is 12 units, $\overline{WY}$ is 8 units long, and $\overline{XZ}$ is 10 units long. How many units long, if it can be determined, is $\overline{XY}$?

Marie is centering a tapestry on her living room wall. As shown in the figure below, the rectangular wall is 36 feet in length, and the tapestry is 4 feet in height and 8 feet in length. The right edge of the tapestry will be x feet from the right edge of the wall, and the left edge of the tapestry will also be x feet from the left edge of the wall. What is the value of x, in feet?

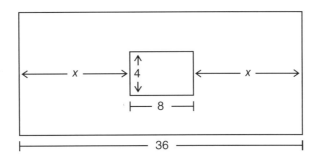

10.3.2 Line Segments

▶ Switch gears to discuss finding the lengths of line segments or portions of line segments.

▶ Pose the question on the slide to students. Before immediately working through this question, ask the students if they know how to solve it.

Draw it out. Label the line. Use addition and subtraction to calculate the overlap.

Demonstrate this concept: Draw out the line segment and label it. Then take the students through the following steps. Point out that you are provided with the lengths of $\overline{WZ}$ = 12, $\overline{WY}$ = 8, and $\overline{XZ}$ = 10. This means that $\overline{WX}$ = 12 − 10 = 2 and $\overline{YZ}$ = 12 − 8 = 4. $\overline{WZ}$ = $\overline{WX}$ + $\overline{XY}$ + $\overline{YZ}$ or 12 = 2 + $\overline{XY}$ + 4. The length of $\overline{XY}$ = 6 units.

As you find the new measurement values, it may help to draw the line segment on the board and write the measurements over the appropriate places.

10.3.2 Line Segments

Points X and Y lie on $\overline{WZ}$, as shown below. The length of $\overline{WZ}$ is 12 units, $\overline{WY}$ is 8 units long, and $\overline{XZ}$ is 10 units long. How many units long, if it can be determined, is $\overline{XY}$?

▶ $\overline{WZ}$ = 12, $\overline{WY}$ = 8, and $\overline{XZ}$ = 10. This means that $\overline{WX}$ = 12 − 10 = 2 and $\overline{YZ}$ = 12 − 8 = 4.

▶ $\overline{WZ}$ = $\overline{WX}$ + $\overline{XY}$ + $\overline{YZ}$ or 12 = 2 + $\overline{XY}$ + 4

▶ The length of $\overline{XY}$ = 6 units

Entrance Ticket | Learning Targets | Quick Check | Perimeter | Line Segments | ACT Practice | Exit Ticket

10.3.2 Line Segments

▶ Pose the question on the slide to students.

▶ Teacher Dialogue: **How might you solve this question? Is any of the information provided unnecessary?**

Work through the problem with the students on the board. Draw out the figure and explain that too much information was given; the height is not necessary for this question to be answered. Note to the students that the equation for x can be set up as $36 = x + 8 + x$ or $36 = 8 + 2x$. The value of $x = 14$. There are 14 feet of wall on either side of the tapestry.

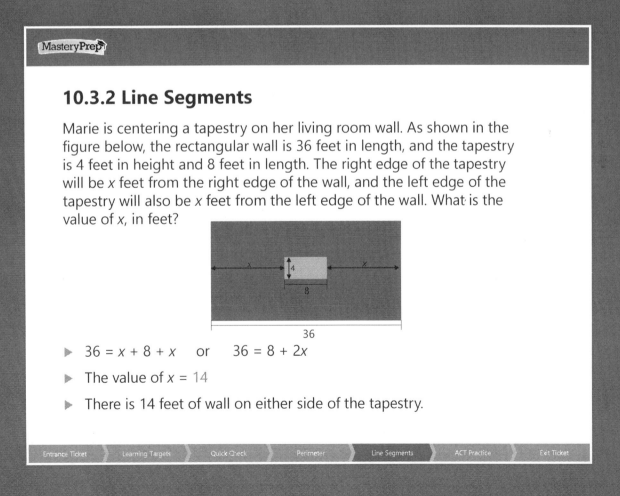

10.4 ACT Practice

▶ Have students work on questions from the ACT practice sets here. Pacing should be 3 minutes per practice set or 60 seconds per question.

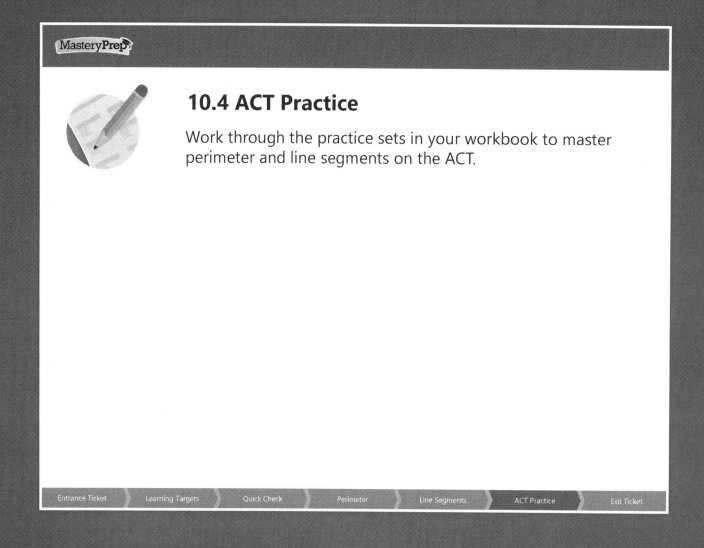

MasteryPrep

10.4 ACT Practice

Work through the practice sets in your workbook to master perimeter and line segments on the ACT.

| Entrance Ticket | Learning Targets | Quick Check | Perimeter | Line Segments | ACT Practice | Exit Ticket |

10.4.1 Set One

1. The Summersdale Community Council is planning the renovation of a park in the center of the town. The park will be a rectangular region of 85 feet by 175 feet with an area of 14,875 square feet. There will be a wooden fence along the perimeter of the park. What is the total length of the fence, in feet?

   A. 250
   B. 340
   C. 410
   D. 480
   E. 520

1. **The correct answer is E.** Add the length of the sides.

   $85 + 85 + 175 + 175 = 520$

2. The length of a rectangle is 8 inches longer than its width. If the perimeter of the rectangle is 36 inches, what is the width, in inches?

   F. 13
   G. 10
   H. 5
   J. 4
   K. 3

2. **The correct answer is H.** Set up as an equation and solve for width.

   $2(8 + w) + 2w = 36$

   $16 + 2w + 2w = 36$

   $4w = 20$

   $w = 5$

3. The figure below is composed of equilateral triangle $\triangle ABD$ and another equilateral triangle $\triangle BCD$. The length of $\overline{AD}$ is 12 inches. What is the perimeter of figure $ABCD$?

   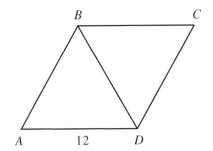

   A. 12
   B. 24
   C. 44
   D. 48
   E. 60

3. **The correct answer is D.** An equilateral triangle has equal sides. So the perimeter of $ABCD$ is

   $12 + 12 + 12 + 12 = 48.$

4. A certain square has the same perimeter as a regular pentagon (a 5-sided polygon with all sides and interior angles congruent). If 1 side of the pentagon is 72 millimeters, how many millimeters long is 1 side of this square?

   F. 45
   G. 60
   H. 75
   J. 90
   K. 135

4. **The correct answer is J.** Calculate the perimeter of the pentagon and divide by 4. 72 + 72 + 72 + 72 + 72 = 360 mm, which is the perimeter of both the pentagon and the square.

360 ÷ 4 = 90 mm

5. The polygon below, whose side lengths are given in meters, has 2 unknown sides. Each angle between adjacent sides measures 90°. What is the polygon's perimeter, in meters?

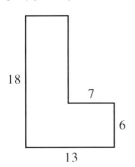

   A. 44
   B. 62
   C. 80
   D. 158
   E. 234

5. **The correct answer is B.** The length of the top side is 13 − 7 = 6. The side of the top right side is 18 − 6 = 12. The perimeter is 18 + 13 + 6 + 7 + 12 + 6 = 62.

6. Joseph is constructing a rectangular fence for his garden. A diagram of the fence is shown below. Which of the following expressions gives the perimeter of Joseph's fence?

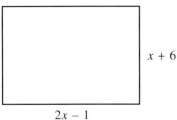

   F. $3x + 5$
   G. $3x + 10$
   H. $6x + 10$
   J. $6x + 20$
   K. $2x^2 + 11x - 6$

6. **The correct answer is H.** Add the length of the sides, combining like terms.

$2(2x - 1) + 2(x + 6)$

$4x - 2 + 2x + 12$

$6x + 10$

10.4.3 Set Three

7. Points A, B, C, and D lie on a line in the given order. Point C is the midpoint of $\overline{BD}$, $\overline{AC}$ is 10 mm long, and $\overline{AD}$ is 15 mm long. How many millimeters long is $\overline{BD}$?
   A. 5
   B. 8
   C. 10
   D. 12
   E. 15

7. The correct answer is C. Draw out the problem.

A	B	C	D

--------------------10------------------------

------------------------------15-------------------------------

$\overline{CD}$ is 5. Since C is the midpoint of $\overline{BD}$, you know $\overline{BC}$ is also 5. $\overline{BD}$ is 5 + 5 = 10.

8. Justin is centering a mosaic on his bedroom wall. As shown in the figure below, the rectangular wall is 28 feet in length, and the mosaic is 3 feet in height and 6 feet in length. The right edge of the mosaic will be y feet from the right edge of the wall, and the left edge of the mosaic will also be y feet from the left edge of the wall. What is the value of y, in feet?

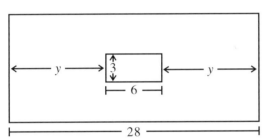

   F. 9
   G. 10
   H. 10.5
   J. 11
   K. 12.5

8. The correct answer is J. Set up an equation and solve for y.

$28 = 2y + 6$

$22 = 2y$

$11 = y$

9. For the line segment below, the ratio of the length of $\overline{XY}$ to the length of $\overline{YZ}$ is 1:6. If it can be determined, what is the ratio of the length of $\overline{XY}$ to the length of $\overline{XZ}$?

   A. 1:5
   B. 1:7
   C. 3:1
   D. 7:1
   E. Cannot be determined from the given information

9. The correct answer is B. If the ratio of $\overline{XY}$ to $\overline{YZ}$ is 1:6, the total amount of parts in $\overline{XZ}$ is 7. So the ratio of $\overline{XY}$ to $\overline{XZ}$ is 1:7.

10.4.4 Set Four

10. A triangle $\triangle ABC$ has a perimeter of 53 centimeters with a side that is 18 centimeters long. The lengths of the remaining two sides have a ratio of 3:4. What is the length, in centimeters, of the shortest side of the triangle?

F. 15
G. 18
H. 20
J. 36
K. 40

10. The correct answer is F. Set up an equation and solve.

$18 + 3x + 4x = 53$

$7x = 35$

$x = 5$

Thus, the other two sides are $(3)(5) = 15$ and $(4)(5) = 20$. The shortest side is 15.

---

11. On the line segment below, the ratio of the length of $\overline{TU}$ to the length of $\overline{UV}$ is 4:7. If it can be determined, what is the ratio of the length of $\overline{TU}$ to the length of $\overline{TV}$?

A. 1:7
B. 2:11
C. 4:11
D. 11:4
E. Cannot be determined from the given information

11. The correct answer is C. If the ratio of $\overline{TU}$ to $\overline{UV}$ is 4:7, the total amount of parts in $\overline{TV}$ is 11. So the ratio of $\overline{TU}$ to $\overline{UV}$ is 4:11.

---

12. Points X and Y lie on $\overline{WZ}$ as shown below. The length of $\overline{WZ}$ is 36 inches; $\overline{WY}$ is 16 inches long; and $\overline{XZ}$ is 28 inches long. How many inches long, if it can be determined is $\overline{XY}$?

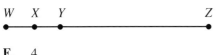

F. 4
G. 8
H. 12
J. 16
K. Cannot be determined from the given information

12. The correct answer is G. Since you are given the lengths of $\overline{WZ}$ and $\overline{XZ}$, you can find the length of $\overline{WX}$.

$\overline{WX} = 36 - 28 = 8$ inches.

Find the length of $\overline{XY}$ by subtracting the length of $\overline{WX}$ from the length of $\overline{WY}$.

$\overline{XY} = 16 - 8 = 8$ inches

10.4.5 Set Five

13. In the figure shown below, each pair of intersecting line segments meets at a right angle, and all lengths are given in millimeters. What is the perimeter, in millimeters, of the given figure?

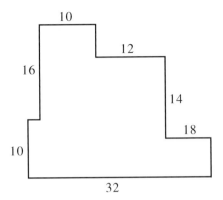

A. 80
B. 88
C. 96
D. 102
E. 116

13. The correct answer is E. The bottom length is 32, so the distance of the top lengths will also be 32. The length of the left side is 10 + 16 = 26, so the distance of the right lengths will also be 26. The perimeter is 32 + 32 + 26 + 26 = 116.

14. Quadrilateral *WXYZ* shown below is in the standard (x,y) coordinate plane. For this quadrilateral, $WZ = 7$, $YZ = 6$, $XY = \sqrt{53}$, and $WX = 8$, all in coordinate units.

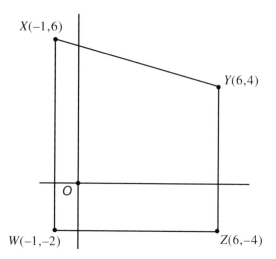

Which of the following is closest to the perimeter of quadrilateral *WXYZ*, in coordinate units?
F. 22.6
G. 25.7
H. 28.3
J. 31.4
K. 35.8

14. The correct answer is H. Add the lengths of the sides.
$$7 + 6 + 8 + \sqrt{53} = 21 + \sqrt{53} \approx 28.3$$

15. The perimeter of a parallelogram is 76 inches, and the measure of 1 side is 17 inches. What are the lengths of the 3 remaining sides?
A. 17, 17, 17
B. 17, 17, 42
C. 17, 20, 20
D. 17, 21, 21
E. Cannot be determined from the given information

15. The correct answer is D. One of the sides must be 17 inches. The remaining two can be calculated from the given information.
$$76 - 17 - 17 = 42$$
$$42 \div 2 = 21$$
The three remaining sides are 17, 21, 21.

ACT® Mastery Math

Sum It Up

Perimeter and Line Segments

Length
The measurement of the side of a figure or shape

Width
The measurement from side to side of a figure or shape

Perimeter
The measurement of the distance around a two-dimensional shape

Tips and Techniques

Draw It Out: Most perimeter questions can be solved by drawing the shapes and labeling them carefully. If the ACT does not give you the figure or label all of the information, just draw it out.

Use Ratios: A ratio can be a useful tool for determining perimeter and dimensions of polygons when there are unknown sides.

10.5 Exit Ticket

► Students complete the three questions on their exit ticket.

Students are timed 3 minutes for the three questions (60 seconds per question). There is no break between questions.

10.5 Exit Ticket Review

▶ Students work the first question.

1. **The correct answer is E.** Add the lengths of the sides. The two flat sides equal the sum of the sides opposite and parallel to them. In this case, both of the flat sides are equal to 4 + 4. This gives four sides each measuring 8. The sum of all the sides, therefore, is 8 + 8 + 8 + 8 = 32.

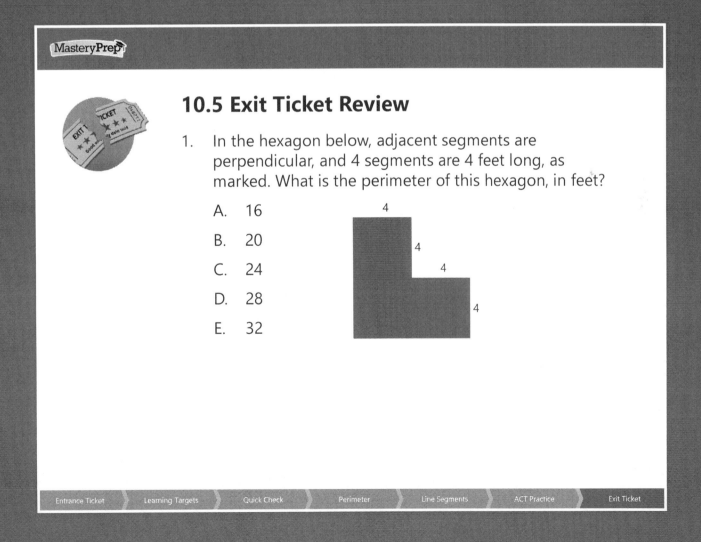

10.5 Exit Ticket Review

▶ Students work the second question.

2. **The correct answer is F.** Assume the perimeter of the larger square is 16 for the purposes of this question. Each side would then be 4 units long. The perimeter of one of the smaller squares would be 2 + 2 + 2 + 2 = 8, so the ratio of the perimeters would be 8:16, or 1:2.

10.5 Exit Ticket Review

2. A square is partitioned into 4 squares of equal area with each sharing a vertex at the center of the original square. What is the ratio of the perimeter of 1 of the smaller squares to the perimeter of the original square?

   F. 1:2

   G. 1:3

   H. 1:4

   J. 1:5

   K. 1:6

10.5 Exit Ticket Review

▶ Students work the third question.

3. **The correct answer is D.** If the triangle is reflected over the line BC, then side a becomes the height of the triangle, and the triangle now has side measurements of $b + b + c + c = 2(b + c)$.

▶ After all three questions are completed, students exchange papers. Solve the three exit items step by step on the board. Students grade using their red pens and then return papers to their classmates.

▶ After solving the three exit items, revisit the learning targets slide. Students again assess their knowledge and confidence on the same 1 to 4 scale that they used at the beginning of the lesson. Students write this number in the designated area at the start of the lesson in their workbooks, along with any comments or questions they might have.

▶ Finally, to close the lesson, have students return to the cover page of the lesson and write a caption for the picture there. The caption should be a one-sentence summary of the lesson, a main rule or tip they want to remember, or an explanation of how the picture relates to the topic. If there is additional time, students can share and compare their captions with the class.

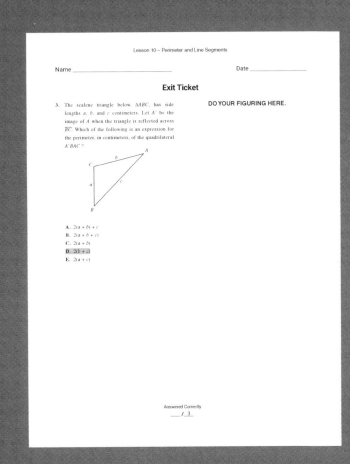

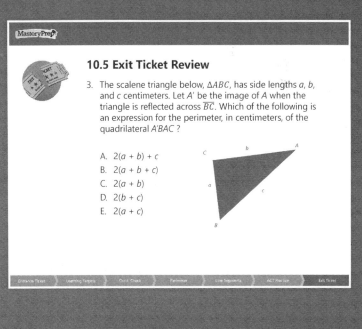

Polygon Area

This lesson will cover how to calculate the area of geometric shapes, as well as how to work backward to find the dimensions of geometric shapes when given the area.

ACT Standards:

G 303. Compute the area of rectangles when whole number dimensions are given

G 403. Compute the area and perimeter of triangles and rectangles in simple problems

G 506. Compute the area of triangles and rectangles when one or more additional simple steps are required

Student Page 157

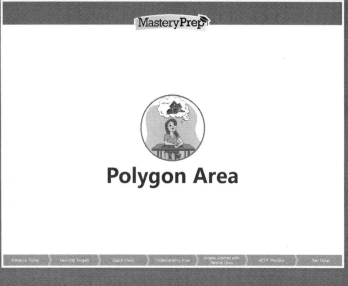

11.1 Entrance Ticket

Student Page 158

▶ Have the students solve the problem and write a paragraph about how they found the answer to the question on the slide.

Five congruent squares are put together without gaps or overlap to form a figure shaped like a plus sign. The perimeter of the figure is 72 cm. Find the area of the figure, in cm².

▶ Have students share and explain their answers.

Draw five congruent squares in the shape of a plus sign. Count the number of sides from the outside perimeter. There are 12. Because the shapes are congruent squares, you know all the sides are equal and can be represented by one variable. You also know the perimeter is 72. Set up an equation: $12x = 72$. Solve for x, $x = 6$. You now know that the side length of the squares is 6. Find the area of one square, $6 \cdot 6 = 36$. Since there are five squares, multiply the area of one square times five, $36 \cdot 5 = 180$ cm².

11.2 Learning Targets

▶ Review learning targets with your students, displayed on the slide and in their workbooks.

▶ After reviewing the learning targets, ask students to assess their knowledge and confidence level on these targets. They should rate themselves on a scale of 1 to 4, with 1 being not confident or uncertain, and 4 being completely confident or certain. They should circle this number in the designated section of their workbooks.

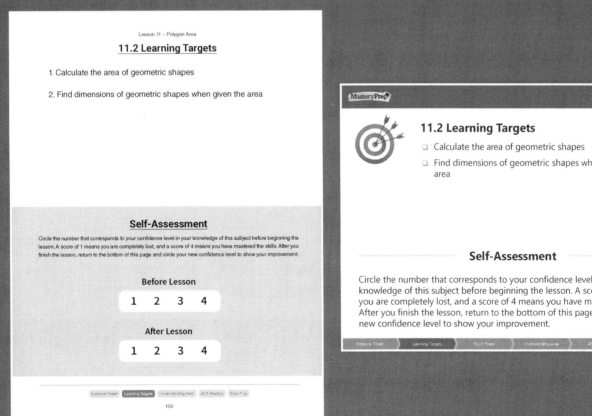

Student Page 159

11.2 Quick Check

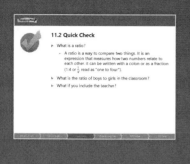

▶ Teacher Dialogue: **What is a ratio?**

A ratio is a way to compare two things. It is an expression that measures how two numbers relate to each other. It can be written with a colon or as a fraction (1:4 or $\frac{1}{4}$, read as "one to four").

▶ Teacher Dialogue: **What is the ratio of boys to girls in the classroom? What if you include the teacher?**

Answers will vary based on classroom demographic.

▶ Teacher Dialogue: **What is the area formula for a triangle?**

Triangle: $\dfrac{base \cdot height}{2}$

▶ Teacher Dialogue: **What is the area formula for a rectangle/square?**

Rectangle/square: length · width

▶ Teacher Dialogue: **What is the area formula for a parallelogram?**

If students don't know the answer, ask them how they could divide a parallelogram into shapes they do know how to find area for. (Show them how this shape could be cut into a rectangle and two triangles. If you can find the area for those pieces individually and add them up, then you can find the area for the whole shape.) Remind them that if they get stuck on the ACT because they don't remember a formula, they can try this method instead.

Parallelogram: base · height

▶ Teacher Dialogue: **What is the area formula for a trapezoid?**

If students don't know the answer, ask them how they could divide a trapezoid into shapes they do know how to find area for. (Show them how this shape could be cut up into a rectangle and two triangles. If you can find the area for those pieces individually and add them up, then you can find the area for the whole shape.) Remind them that if they get stuck on the ACT because they don't remember a formula, they can try this method instead.

Trapezoid: $\dfrac{b_1 + b_2}{2}$ · height

▶ Teacher Dialogue: **What is the phrase written on the side view mirror of cars?**

Objects in mirror are closer than they appear.

> **Objects in Mirror are Exactly as They Appear:** Questions on the ACT about area often provide pictures, which are almost always drawn to scale. This means that if one side of a figure looks equal to another, it probably is.

Sometimes you can assume a trapezoid or triangle is isosceles (etc.), even if the ACT doesn't say it is.

11.3.1 Understanding Area

▶ Tell the students they are going to turm the classroom into an epic walk-in closet fit for the stars. The next order of business is to update the flooring. Students should show their work in the space provided in their workbooks.

The class can choose how they want to update the flooring. (Heated tiles for bare feet in the morning? Solid diamond flooring? Gold plated tiles? Soft cashmere carpet?)

▶ Teacher Dialogue: **What do you need to know in order to solve for the cost of flooring?**

Answers include dimensions of room, area of room, cost of flooring per square foot, etc. Give the students the dimensions of the room. They can use the dimensions to find the area of the room. If they do not have their work from the perimeter lesson, you can give the students the dimensions of the room.

▶ Teacher Dialogue: **Solve for total cost if the cost of flooring is $15.00 per square foot.**

To find the answer, calculate the area of the room, length · width. Then multiply the area by the cost per square foot for the flooring. This will give you the price of the flooring of the classroom-turned-walk-in closet.

Make sure the students understand that they <u>multiply</u> the area by the flooring price per square foot. Explain that the cost of the flooring is for only one square foot, but they need the cost for 55* square feet (*insert your classroom area here). If they struggle to grasp this, tell them they can set it up as a proportion. (Change 55 to the area of your classroom in the example below.) Let them know x represents the cost of flooring for the whole room.

$$\frac{x}{55\text{ft}^2} = \frac{\$15}{1\text{ft}^2}$$

Your operation becomes $\dfrac{55 \cdot 15}{1} = x$

> **Draw It Out**: On the ACT, everyone is an artist! Visualizing the problem will help you figure out which math operations to use. Draw out the remodeling question.

▶ Draw a large rectangle to represent the room. Draw a tiny square to represent the square foot pricing.

▶ Teacher Dialogue: **If this small square costs $100, will the larger rectangle cost more or less than that?**

More. Knowing you need a bigger number than 100 helps you understand that you need to multiply 100 by something. This type of reasoning will be a big help on more complicated questions on the ACT.

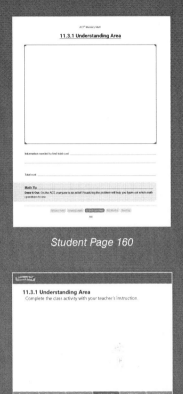

Student Page 160

Lesson 11 – Polygon Area

11.3.1 Understanding Area

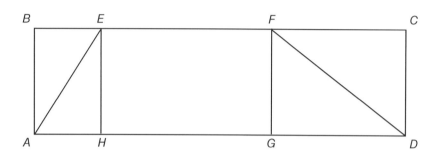

Total area of composite shape: _____

11.3.1 Understanding Area

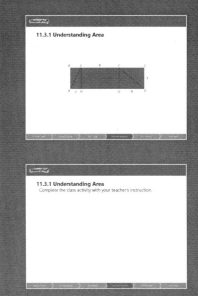

▸ Show the students the composite shape.

▸ Teacher Dialogue: **What do you need to know to find the area of this composite shape?**

Find the area of each individual shape and add them together.

▸ Give them lengths of line segments between two adjacent letters only. That is, you can give them measurements of *EF* or *HG*, but do not give them the measurements of *BC* or *AD*. Students choose which line segment they want to know the length of in order to solve the problem. See if students can find the area using the given line segment length. If they do not choose an appropriate one, let them attempt calculations before giving them the opportunity to ask for another line segment measurement.

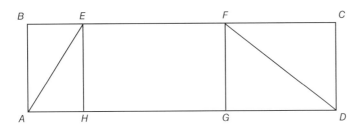

▸ Teacher Dialogue: **Find the area of rectangle *ABCD*.**

There are several ways to find the area. You can find the area of all the triangles and then the center rectangle and add them together.

The area of triangle *AEH* $\dfrac{\text{base} \cdot \text{height}}{2} = \dfrac{2 \cdot 3}{2} = 3$. Triangle *ABE* has the same measurements and, therefore, has the same area.

The area of triangle *FGD* is $\dfrac{\text{base} \cdot \text{height}}{2} = \dfrac{4 \cdot 3}{2} = 6$. Triangle *FCD* has the same measurements and, therefore, has the same area.

The area of rectangle *EFGH* is base · height = 8 · 3 = 24.

3 + 3 + 6 + 6 + 24 = 42 ft^2

You can also find the area of just rectangles. Find the area of rectangle *BEHA*, rectangle *EFGH*, and rectangle *FCDG*. Add them together.

Area of rectangle *BEHA* is base · height = 2 · 3 = 6.

Area of rectangle *FCDG* is base · height = 4 · 3 = 12.

Area of rectangle *EFGH* is base · height = 8 · 3 = 24.

6 + 12 + 24 = 42 ft^2

11.3.1 Understanding Area

▶ Teacher Dialogue: **If you are given a complicated shape on the ACT and you don't remember the formula for it, you can divide it into rectangles and triangles for easier calculations. Draw it out!**

Show how a trapezoid can be divided into a rectangle and two triangles.

Show how a parallelogram can be divided into a rectangle and two triangles.

Also remind students that objects in mirror are exactly as they appear—if you divide a trapezoid into a rectangle and two triangles and the two triangles look exactly the same, they probably are! Treat them as if they have equal measurements.

Consider this procedure when faced with complicated area problems:

Shown: What drawing, description, or measurements does the problem give you?

Shape: What properties do you already know about this shape?

Solve: Use given measurements and properties to solve for unknowns.

11.4 ACT Practice

▶ Have students work on questions from the ACT practice sets here. Pacing should be 3 minutes per practice set or 60 seconds per question.

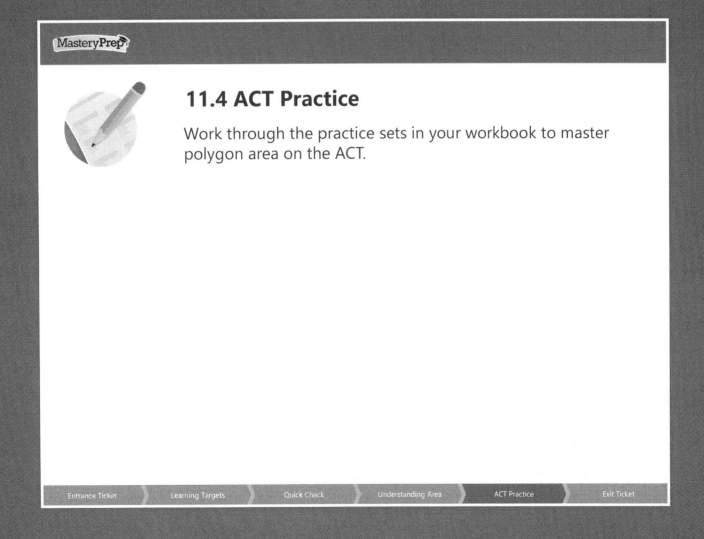

11.4.1 Set One

1. A flyer has a surface area of 88 square inches. If the length of the paper is 11 inches, what is the width, in inches?

    A.   4
    B.   8
    C.   22
    D.   77
    E.   968

1. **The correct answer is B.** Use the area formula to solve for width.

    $11w = 88$

    $w = 8$

2. The dimensions of a right triangle are shown below in feet. What is the area of the triangle, in square feet?

    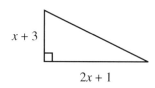

    F. $x^2 + 3$

    G. $x^2 + 9$

    H. $x^2 + \dfrac{7}{2}x + \dfrac{3}{2}$

    J. $2x^2 + 7x + 3$

    K. $6x^2$

2. **The correct answer is H.** Use the area formula to calculate the total area.

    $\dfrac{1}{2}(x + 3)(2x + 1)$

    $\dfrac{1}{2}(2x^2 + 6x + x + 3)$

    $\dfrac{1}{2}(2x^2 + 7x + 3)$

    $x^2 + \dfrac{7}{2}x + \dfrac{3}{2}$

3. In rhombus $XYZQ$ below, $\overline{XZ}$ is 10 centimeters long, and $\overline{YQ}$ is 4 centimeters long. What is the area of $XYZQ$, in square centimeters?

    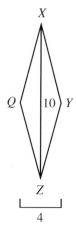

    A.   8
    B.   10
    C.   20
    D.   40
    E.   100

3. **The correct answer is C.** You can divide the shape into triangles and calculate their areas, and then add to determine the total area.

    Area of triangle XYZ: $\dfrac{1}{2}(10)(2) = 10$

    Area of triangle ZQX: $\dfrac{1}{2}(10)(2) = 10$

    $10 + 10 = 20$

11.4.2 Set Two

4. The area of $\triangle ABC$ below is 36 square centimeters. If height $\overline{BD}$ is 9 centimeters, how long is the base of $\overline{AC}$, in centimeters?

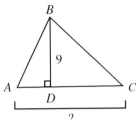

F. 2
G. 4
H. 6
J. 8
K. 10

4. **The correct answer is J.** Use the area formula to calculate the length of the base.

$$\frac{1}{2}(9)(b) = 36$$

$$\frac{1}{2}b = 4$$

$$b = 8$$

5. A farmer wants to double the area of his rectangular 6-meter-by-10-meter garden. The 10-meter length will be increased by 2 meters. By how many meters must the width increase?

A. 2
B. 4
C. 6
D. 10
E. 12

5. **The correct answer is B.** Calculate the area, double it, and then use this new area to solve for the new width. Determine how much larger this width is from the original.

$6 \cdot 10 = 60$

$60 \cdot 2 = 120$

$12w = 120$

$w = 10$, which is $10 - 6 = 4$ meters larger than the original width.

6. On the standard (x,y) plane below, 1 side of the rectangle is on the axis, and the vertices of the opposite side are on the graph of the parabola given by $y = 7 - x^2$. Let z represent any value of x, such that $0 \le z \le \sqrt{7}$. Which of the following expressions, in terms of z, represents the area of any such rectangle?

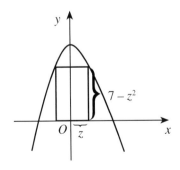

F. $-z^3 + 7z$
G. $-z^2 + 7z$
H. $-z^2 + 7z + 2$
J. $-2z^3 - 14z$
K. $-2z^3 + 14z$

6. **The correct answer is K.** Use the graph to help determine the length and width, whose product will represent the area of the rectangle.

Area = $(2z)(7 - z^2)$

Area = $14z - 2z^3$

Rearrange the terms to begin with the variable of the highest power and area = $-2z^3 + 14z$

11.4.3 Set Three

---

7. In a certain rectangle, the ratio of the lengths of 2 adjacent sides is 4 to 3. If the area of the rectangle is 192 square centimeters, what is the length, in inches, of the longer side?

  A. 6
  B. 12
  C. 16
  D. 32
  E. 36

7. **The correct answer is C.** Use the area formula to solve.

$(4x)(3x) = 192$

$12x^2 = 192$

$x^2 = 16$

$x = 4$

So the longer side is $4 \cdot 4 = 16$.

---

8. The length of a rectangle is 4 times the length of a smaller rectangle. The 2 rectangles have the same width. The area of the smaller rectangle is X square units. The area of the larger rectangle is yX square units. Which of the following is the value of y ?

  F. $\dfrac{1}{16}$

  G. $\dfrac{1}{4}$

  H. 1

  J. 4

  K. 16

8. **The correct answer is J.** Calculate the area of both rectangles and then solve for the value of y.

Smaller rectangle: $A = lw = X$

Larger rectangle: $A = 4lw = 4X$

So $y = 4$.

---

9. For trapezoid $ABCD$ shown below, $\overline{AB}$ is 7 inches, $\overline{CD}$ is 4 inches, and the perimeter is 43 inches. What is the area of the trapezoid, in square inches?

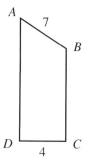

  A. 28
  B. 32
  C. 36
  D. 64
  E. 128

9. **The correct answer is D.** Use the area formula of a trapezoid to solve.

Length of AD and BC:

$43 - 7 - 4 = 32$

$A = (\dfrac{b_1 + b_2}{2}) \cdot h$

$A = (\dfrac{32}{2}) \cdot 4$

$A = 64$

11.4.4 Set Four

10. The area of the trapezoid below is 24 square meters, the altitude is 4 meters, and the length of one base is 2 meters. What is the length, x, of the other base, in meters?

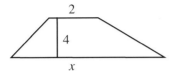

F. 3
G. 4
H. 8
J. 10
K. 12

10. The correct answer is J. Use the formula for the area of a trapezoid to solve for x.

$$A = (\frac{b_1 + b_2}{2}) \cdot h$$
$$24 = (\frac{2 + x}{2}) \cdot 4$$
$$6 = \frac{2 + x}{2}$$
$$12 = 2 + x$$
$$10 = x$$

11. In the standard (x, y) coordinate plane, if a triangle has vertices at $A(-1, 3)$, $B(2, 3)$, and $C(2, -4)$, then what is its area, in square coordinate units?

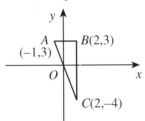

A. 3

B. 7

C. 8

D. 10

E. $10\frac{1}{2}$

11. The correct answer is E. Calculate the distance between the points and then use the area formula of a triangle to solve.

$$AB = 2 - (-1) = 3$$
$$BC = 3 - (-4) = 7$$
$$A = \frac{1}{2}(3)(7)$$
$$A = \frac{21}{2} = 10\frac{1}{2}$$

12. In the figure below, the area of the larger square is 100 square inches, and the area of the smaller square is 64 square inches. What is x, in inches?

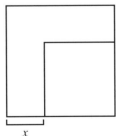

F. 2
G. 8
H. 10
J. 18
K. 36

12. The correct answer is F. If the area of the larger square is 100, then each side is 10 square inches ($10 \cdot 10 = 100$). If the area of the smaller square is 64, then each side is 8 square inches ($8 \cdot 8 = 64$). So the length of x is $10 - 8 = 2$.

13. In the figure below, A, E, F, and B are collinear, and the measurements are in inches. The area of rectangle $ABCD$ is 52 square inches. What is the area of trapezoid $CDEF$, in square inches?

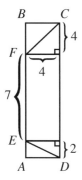

A. 26
B. 30
C. 34
D. 40
E. 80

13. The correct answer is D. Use the area formula for a trapezoid to solve.

Length of $CD = 2 + 7 + 4 = 13$

$$A = (\frac{b_1 + b_2}{2}) \cdot h$$

$$A = (\frac{13 + 7}{2}) \cdot 4$$

$$A = (\frac{20}{2}) \cdot 4$$

$$A = 40$$

---

14. In the figure below, B and C are on $\overline{AD}$, and E and F are on $\overline{DG}$. The measurements are given in meters. Both $ABFG$ and $BCEF$ are trapezoids. The area A of a trapezoid is given by $A = \frac{1}{2}h(b_1 + b_2)$, where h is the height, and b_1 and b_2 are the lengths of the parallel sides.

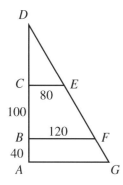

What is the area of $BCEF$, in square meters?

F. 5,600
G. 8,400
H. 10,000
J. 14,000
K. 20,000

14. The correct answer is H. Use the area formula for a trapezoid to solve.

$$A = (\frac{b_1 + b_2}{2}) \cdot h$$

$$A = (\frac{80 + 120}{2}) \cdot 100$$

$$A = (\frac{200}{2}) \cdot 100$$

$$A = 100 \cdot 100 = 10,000$$

15. Each of the 4 sides of a dog dish has the shape of a trapezoid, as shown below.

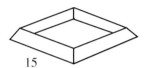

15

The length of the bottom of each side is 15 cm, and the length of the top of each side is $12\frac{1}{2}$ cm. What is the length of the median of each trapezoid, in centimeters?

A. 12

B. $12\frac{1}{2}$

C. 13

D. $13\frac{1}{4}$

E. $13\frac{3}{4}$

15. The correct answer is E. The median of a trapezoid is equal to one-half the sum of the bases. So the median of this trapezoid is

$$\frac{15 + 12.5}{2} = \frac{27.5}{2} = 13\frac{3}{4}$$

ACT® Mastery Math

Sum It Up

Polygon Area

Ratios
An expression that measures how two numbers compare to each other

Area Formulas

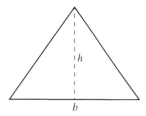

$$\text{Area} = \frac{\text{base} \cdot \text{height}}{2}$$

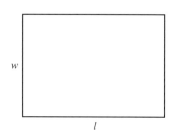

$$\text{Area} = \text{length} \cdot \text{width}$$

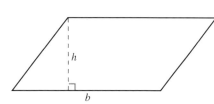

$$\text{Area} = \text{base} \cdot \text{height}$$

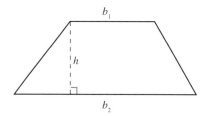

$$\text{Area} = \frac{\text{base}_1 + \text{base}_2}{2} \cdot \text{height}$$

Tips and Techniques

Draw It Out: On the ACT, everyone is an artist! Visualizing the problem will help you figure out which math operations to use.

Objects in Mirror are Exactly as They Appear: Questions on the ACT about area often provide pictures, which are almost always drawn to scale. This means that if one side of a figure looks equal to another, it probably is.

Entrance Ticket   Learning Targets   Understanding Area   ACT Practice   Sum It Up

168

11.5 Exit Ticket

▶ Students complete the three questions on their exit ticket.

Students are timed 3 minutes for the three questions (60 seconds per question). There is no break between questions.

11.5 Exit Ticket Review

▶ Students work the first question.

1. **The correct answer is B.** Use the formula for the area of the parallelogram and solve.

$A = $ base $\cdot$ height

$A = (8 + 17)(6)$

$A = (25)(6)$

$A = 150$ square meters

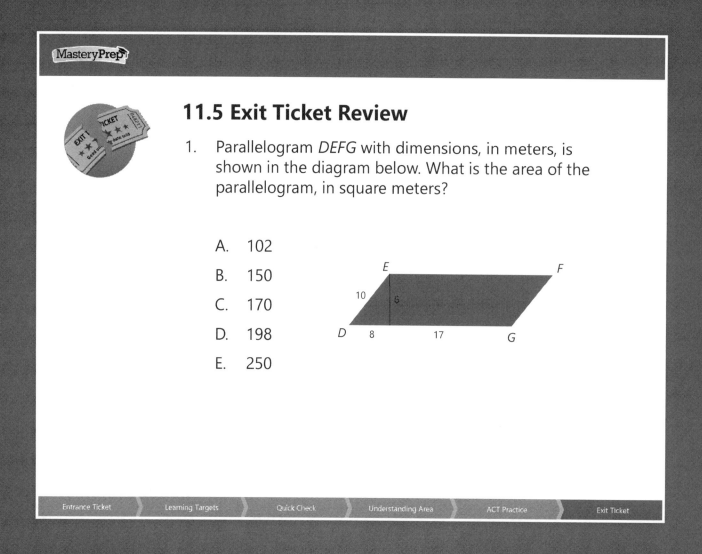

11.5 Exit Ticket Review

▶ Students work the second question.

2. **The correct answer is F.** Use the formula for the area of a triangle and solve.

$A = \dfrac{1}{2}bh$

$A = (\dfrac{1}{2})(9)(6)$

$A = 27$ square centimeters

11.5 Exit Ticket Review

2. In the rectangle below, *H* is a point on side *EF* of rectangle *DEFG*. The measurements given are in centimeters. What is the area of triangle *DHG*, in square centimeters?

F.   27

G.   30

H.   36

J.   72

K.   81

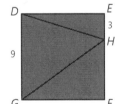

Entrance Ticket   Learning Targets   Quick Check   Understanding Area   ACT Practice   Exit Ticket

11.5 Exit Ticket Review

▶ Students work the third question.

  3. **The correct answer is E.** Let 3 represent the side of square X for the purposes of the problem. The area of the square would then be $(3)(3) = 9$. The area of the rectangle would then be $(7)(2) = 14$. Thus, the ratio of the area of the square X to the area of the rectangle Y is $9:14$.

▶ After all three questions are completed, students exchange papers. Solve the three exit items step by step on the board. Students grade using their red pens and then return papers to their classmates.

▶ After solving the three exit items, revisit the learning targets slide. Students again assess their knowledge and confidence on the same 1 to 4 scale that they used at the beginning of the lesson. Students write this number in the designated area at the start of the lesson in their workbooks, along with any comments or questions they might have.

▶ Finally, to close the lesson, have students return to the cover page of the lesson and write a caption for the picture there. The caption should be a one-sentence summary of the lesson, a main rule or tip they want to remember, or an explanation of how the picture relates to the topic. If there is additional time, students can share and compare their captions with the class.

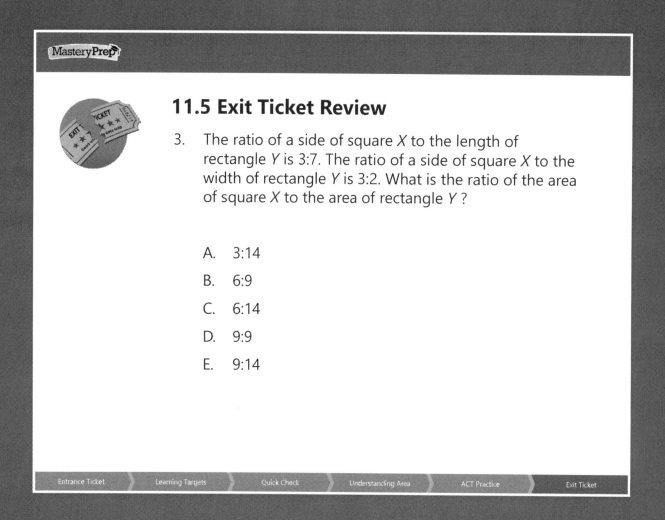

MasteryPrep

11.5 Exit Ticket Review

3. The ratio of a side of square X to the length of rectangle Y is $3:7$. The ratio of a side of square X to the width of rectangle Y is $3:2$. What is the ratio of the area of square X to the area of rectangle Y?

    A. 3:14

    B. 6:9

    C. 6:14

    D. 9:9

    E. 9:14

Entrance Ticket   Learning Targets   Quick Check   Understanding Area   ACT Practice   Exit Ticket

Circle Area and Circumferance

This lesson will cover calculations for finding area and circumference of circles. Students will learn to find these values when basic details are given but also when problems are more complex, requiring them to work backward or to take extra steps to figure out information needed that is not explicitly given.

ACT Standards:

G 507. Compute the area and circumference of circles after identifying necessary information

Student Page 169

12.1 Entrance Ticket

▶ Have students do the following:

Write a paragraph (at least five sentences) answering the following riddle:

A number of children are standing in a circle. They are evenly spaced, and the 7th child is directly opposite the 18th child. How many children are there altogether?

▶ There are 22 children standing in a circle.

Ask a few students to share their answers and their explanations.

▶ Teacher Dialogue: **How many people solved it by drawing it out? Did anyone use an equation or math operations?**

Students can solve this by drawing it out.

1. Draw a circle with a mark of 7 at one spot on the circle and a mark directly across from it labeled 18.

2. Make tallies from 7 to 18. Label them with the consecutive numbers 8, 9, 10, 11, etc. They will find that between the 7 and 18 there are 10 marks/numbers representing students. Since the children are evenly spaced, you know there are also 10 students between the 7th and 18th student on the other side of the circle.

3. Make 10 marks on the other side of the circle between 18 and 7. Label the marks with numbers.

4. You can go backward from 7 all the way to 1, then forward from 18 until you run out of marks. The number 22 will be your last mark before 1.

Students can also solve this using math operations. The difference between 7 and 18 is 11. The difference on the other side of the circle will need to be the same. 18 + 11 = 29. You know that 7 of the 29 are already the first of the standing children, so 29 − 7 will give us the total number of children, 22.

Students could also subtract 18 from 7 to give the number of students on each side of the circle (11). Since there are two sides of the circle, students multiply 11 by 2 to get the solution.

▶ Teacher Dialogue: **Which method is easier? Which makes more sense to you? Why? How did drawing it out help you solve the problem?**

▶ Teacher Dialogue: **What aspect of the circle is being measured?**

Circumference

▶ Teacher Dialogue: **What unit is it being measured in?**

Children

Student Page 170

12.2 Learning Targets

▶ Review learning targets with your students, displayed on the slide and in their workbooks.

▶ After reviewing the learning targets, ask students to assess their knowledge and confidence level on these targets. They should rate themselves on a scale of 1 to 4, with 1 being not confident or uncertain, and 4 being completely confident or certain. They should circle this number in the designated section of their workbooks.

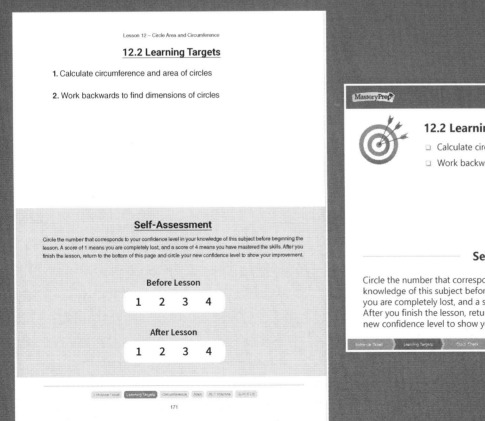

Student Page 171

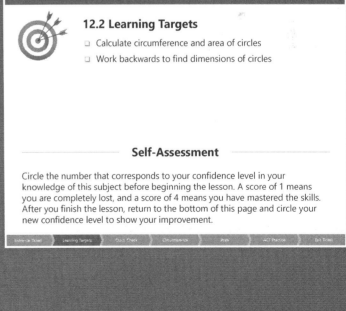

12.2 Quick Check

▶ Teacher Dialogue: **What is a ratio?**

  <u>Ratio:</u> The relationship between two different values or amounts

▶ Remind students that using ratios is a way to compare two things. It is an expression of the number of desired outcomes versus the number of other outcomes. It can be written with a colon or as a fraction (1:4 or $\frac{1}{4}$, read as *one to four*).

▶ Teacher Dialogue: **What is the ratio of boys to girls in the classroom?**

▶ Teacher Dialogue: **What if you include the teacher?**

  Answers will vary based on classroom demographic.

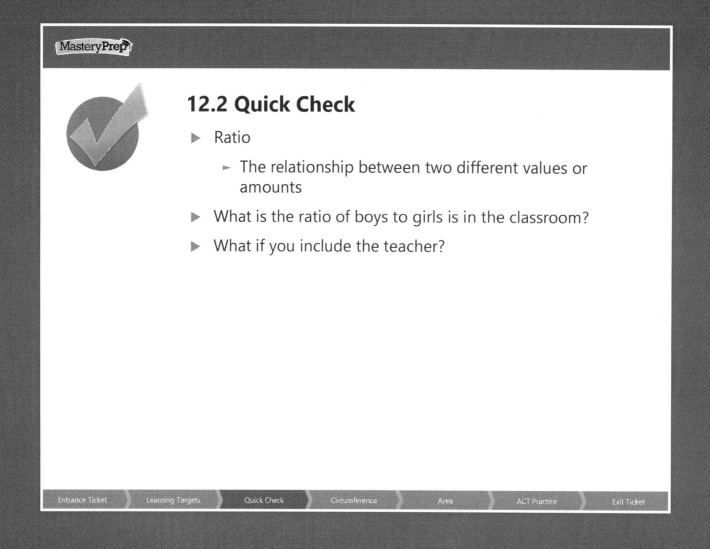

12.2 Quick Check

▶ Make sure the students are comfortable and familiar with the following definitions. See if students can give a definition before you provide it for them. After each definition is reviewed, have a student draw each concept on the board for the class.

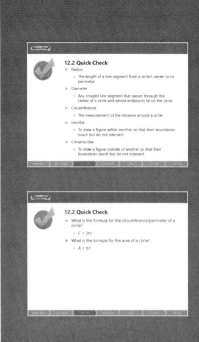

▶ Teacher Dialogue: **What is a radius?**

Radius: The length of a line segment from a circle's center to its perimeter

▶ Teacher Dialogue: **What is a diameter?**

Diameter: Any straight line segment that passes through the center of a circle and whose endpoints lie on the circle

▶ Teacher Dialogue: **How do you find the diameter if you are given the radius?**

Double the radius. The diameter is twice the length of the radius.

▶ Teacher Dialogue: **How do you find the radius if given the diameter?**

Divide the diameter by two. The radius is half the length of the diameter.

▶ Teacher Dialogue: **What is the circumference of a circle?**

Circumference: The measurement of the distance around a circle

▶ Teacher Dialogue: **What is the perimeter of a circle? What is the circumference of a circle? Is there a difference?**

There is no difference between the circumference and the perimeter of a circle. The circumference is the name for the perimeter of a circle.

▶ Teacher Dialogue: **What does it mean when a figure in math is inscribed?**

Inscribe: To draw a figure within another so that their boundaries touch but do not intersect

▶ Teacher Dialogue: **What is the difference between inscribing a shape and circumscribing a shape?**

Circumscribe: To draw a figure outside of another so that their boundaries touch but do not intersect

▶ Teacher Dialogue: **What is the formula for the circumference/perimeter of a circle?**

$C = 2\pi r$. Tell students they can remember this with the phrase "2-pi-rrrimeter."

Remember, circumference is the perimeter of a circle.

▶ Teacher Dialogue: **What is the formula for the area of a circle?**

$A = \pi r^2$. Tell students they can remember this with the phrase "pi-r-sq'area."

12.3.1 Circumference

▶ Teachers read this story aloud for the students.

In a galaxy far, far away, the Circonian martians have made a monumental discovery—a planet not unlike their own—inhabited by a strange race of creatures. There are no corners in the Circonian world, and no straight edges either. Their bodies are round, their food is round, and they live in circular dwellings. Every geographic feature on their planet is made of soft curves and spheres. However, this new planet is full of other shapes. The harsh edges and bold corners of this unknown planet worry the Circonians, who are headed to the planet to deliver a message to its strange and lanky inhabitants.

The Circonian martians board their spaceship ready for voyage to this newfound land. They enter the Milky Way galaxy near Pluto and stop there to greet their distant allies, the Icekan aliens, who live on the cold and rocky planet. Eventually the Circonians reach Saturn, a planet they are rather unfamiliar with. They mistake the rings of Saturn for roads the inhabitants of Saturn have constructed. The captain of the spaceship believes the road is a shortcut to their destination and steers the ship along its direction. Before long, the spaceship crew starts to complain. It seems like this road is never ending!

▶ Present the students with this problem.

▶ Teacher Dialogue: **The Circonian martians travel the outermost ring of Saturn three times before realizing they are going in circles! How far out of their way have they traveled before they get back on the route toward their destination?**

Ask the students what the answer is. If they can't answer it, ask them what they need to do to find the answer. What other information do you need to know? What formula do you need to know? What is the formula for circumference?

If the students say *radius*, ask them: If I gave you the radius of just the planet Saturn, would that be enough? (Answer: No, they need the radius of the ring.)

▶ Generate some discussion on what combinations of information they could use to solve the problem. Eventually, concede to give them the radius of Saturn and the measurement of the distance between the largest ring and the surface of Saturn.

The radius of Saturn is 36,184 miles. The outermost ring of Saturn is 8,000,000 miles from the surface of the planet. The formula for circumference is $2\pi r$. Have students use 3.14 for π and round to the nearest whole number.

Student Page 172

12.3.1 Circumference

▶ Give the students a few minutes to answer the question. Students should do their calculations in the space provided in their workbooks. Have students share their answers. Give the correct answer and work the problem in its entirety on the board, asking different students to walk you through each step.

Draw a circle representing the ring. The ring's radius is the radius of Saturn plus the distance of the ring from the planet. 36,184 + 8,000,000 = 8,036,184. Plug this value for r into the formula $2\pi r$. 2(3.14)(8,036,184) = 50,467,235.52. This is the circumference of the ring. Because the martians have traveled the ring three times, multiply this value by three to find the answer. 50,467,235.52 · 3 = 151,401,706.6 which rounds to about **151,000,000 miles**! It's a good thing spaceships travel fast!

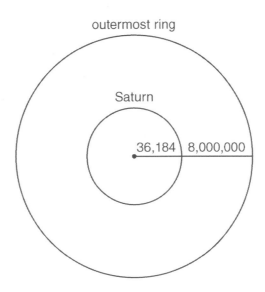

12.3.1 Circumference

Student Page 173

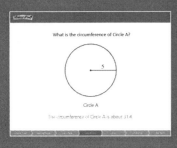

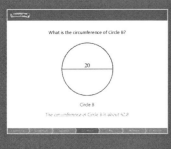

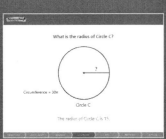

▶ Work these basic circumference problems with the students. Have them attempt the answer on their own, then write the calculations on the board while explaining the answer.

> Encourage them to draw out the problems. On the ACT, everyone is an artist! It doesn't matter how it looks. Draw out the questions to help yourself make sense of them.

> When drawings are already given on ACT problems, the figures are usually drawn to scale. That means if something looks about half the size of something else, it probably is. If two angles look equal, they probably are. If it looks like it could be a midpoint, it most likely is. Tell students to use this to their advantage when solving problems involving geometric drawings.

▶ Try these problems as a class:

▶ Teacher Dialogue: **What is the circumference of a circle with a radius of 5 cm?**

Circumference = $2\pi(5) = 10\pi$, or about 31.4

▶ Teacher Dialogue: **What is the circumference of a circle with a diameter of 20 cm?**

That radius is half the diameter. $20 \div 2 = 10$. Plug 10 in for r in the circumference formula. Circumference = $2\pi(10) = 20\pi$ or about 62.8.

▶ Teacher Dialogue: **What is the radius of a circle with a circumference of 30π?**

Students work backward using the same formula. Remember in the formula *circumference* = $2\pi r$, the *circumference* on the left of the equal sign is part of the formula. You can plug a value in there if you know it. $30\pi = 2\pi r$. Divide both sides by 2π, and you're left with $r = 15$.

> **Working Backward:** Remind students that items on both sides of the equal sign are part of the formula. This means that in the formula perimeter = $2\pi r$, perimeter is part of the formula. It's one of the variables. Remind them that if they are given the perimeter but not a radius or diameter, they plug it into the formula the same way and solve for the unknown. (Examples of this will come up during the ACT practice section.)

12.3.2 Area

▶ Continue the story of the Circonian martians.

▶ Teacher Dialogue: **The Circonian martians finally arrive in the atmosphere of the mysterious new planet. They discover that its gangly inhabitants call themselves Earthlings. The Circonians are suspicious of the Earthlings. Rather than making a grand entrance and an attempt at diplomacy, the Circonians leave behind cryptic messages in the form of crop circles all over the fields of this planet called Earth. They leave quickly, fully expecting the Earthlings to heed their stern demands!**

▶ Before showing students the slide, present the students with this problem. Refer them to the picture in their workbook and the six circles in the crop circle design.

▶ Teacher Dialogue: **The crop circles left behind by the martians are a code. They tell the Earthlings what the Circonians demand from them. The area of each circle in the design corresponds to a letter. What information do you need to know to break the code?**

Students will need diameter or radius of each circle in the design. They will also need to know the formula for the area of a circle (πr^2). Have students use 3.14 for π and round to the nearest whole number.

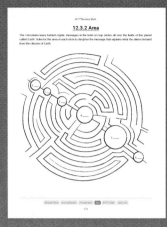

Student Page 174

Student Page 175

12.3.2 Area

► Now show them the slide. The slide reveals various diameters or radii of the circles the students will need for calculation.

► Walk the students through finding the area of the first circle and the corresponding letter for that area. Have them solve for the remaining circles on their own to break the code.

The first circle has an area of $\pi 6^2 = 113$, which corresponds to the letter D.

► Let students work on the calculations for the other circles and break the code. Walk around the room monitoring students to make sure they are on task or help them with any questions they may have.

The second circle has a diameter of 6, meaning its radius is 3. Its area is $\pi 3^2 = 28$, which corresponds to the letter O.

The third circle has a diameter of 8, meaning its radius is 4. Its area is $\pi 4^2 = 50$, which corresponds to the letter N.

The fourth circle has an area of $\pi 15^2 = 707$, which corresponds to the letter U.

The fifth circle has an area of $\pi 20^2 = 1256$, which corresponds to the letter T.

The sixth circle has a diameter of 10, meaning its radius is 5. Its area is $\pi 5^2 = 79$, which corresponds to the letter S.

► After students have finished their calculations, click to reveal the answer on the slide. You can have the students announce the answer together as a class for the big reveal.

DONUTS

► Teacher Dialogue: **The aliens only eat circle foods and don't have this delicious treat on their planet! In order to maintain peace in the universe, the Earthlings must share their donuts!**

MasteryPrep

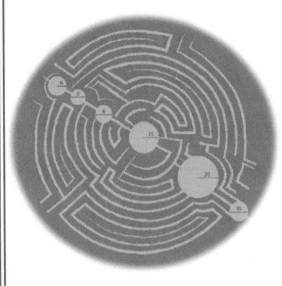

Circconian Crop Circles

▶ The Circonians leave behind cryptic messages in the form of crop circles all over the fields of this planet called Earth. Solve for the area of each circle to decipher the message that explains what the aliens demand from the citizens of Earth.

▶ The aliens demand donuts!

A = 19	J = 1	S = 79
B = 31	K = 47	T = 1,256
C= 6	L = 92	U = 707
D = 113	M = 9	V = 100
E = 2	N = 50	W = 15
F = 44	O = 28	X = 0
G = 201	P = 99	Y = 571
H = 378	Q = 314	Z = 10
I = 21	R = 8	

Entrance Ticket Learning Targets Quick Check Circumference Area ACT Practice Exit Ticket

12.4 ACT Practice

▶ Have students work on questions from the ACT practice sets here. Pacing should be 3 minutes per practice set or 60 seconds per question.

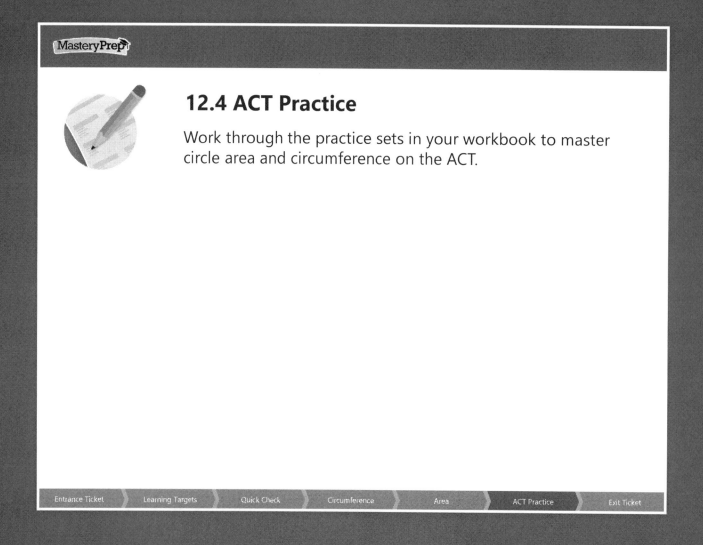

MasteryPrep

12.4 ACT Practice

Work through the practice sets in your workbook to master circle area and circumference on the ACT.

Entrance Ticket   Learning Targets   Quick Check   Circumference   Area   ACT Practice   Exit Ticket

12.4.1 Set One

1. What is the circumference, in inches, of a circle with a radius of 8 inches?

   A. 4π
   B. 8π
   C. 12π
   D. 16π
   E. 64π

1. **The correct answer is D.** To solve this problem, use the formula for the circumference of a circle, which is $2\pi r$. Plug in the given value for the radius into the formula.

Circumference = $2\pi(8)$

Circumference = 16π

2. The circle shown below has a diameter of 14 inches. What is the circumference of the circle, in inches?

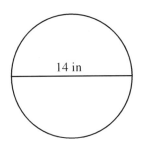

14 in

   F. 7π
   G. 14π
   H. 28π
   J. 49π
   K. 196π

2. **The correct answer is G.** To solve this problem, first find the value for the radius, then plug that into the formula for the circumference of a circle, which is $2\pi r$. You know that the radius is half of the diameter. The diameter of this circle is 14, so the radius is 7. Plug 7 into the formula for the circumference of a circle as the radius.

Circumference = $2\pi(7)$

Circumference = 14π

3. The perimeter of a circular field is 500 feet. Which of the following is closest to the radius of the field, in feet? (Note: $\pi \approx 3.14$)

   A.   10
   B.   50
   C.   80
   D. 160
   E. 250

3. **The correct answer is C.** In this problem, you are given the circumference of the circle, which is 500 feet, and asked to find the radius. Plug this information into the formula for the circumference of a circle and solve for the radius. Make sure you change π to 3.14 when solving.

Circumference = $2\pi r$

$500 = 2(3.14)r$

$500 = 6.28r$

$r = 79.6$, which rounds up to 80 feet.

4. Circles A, B, and C have radii with measures of x centimeters, $3x$ centimeters, and $6x$ centimeters, respectively. What is the ratio of the radius of Circle B to the diameter of Circle C ?

   F. 1:2
   G. 1:4
   H. 1:12
   J. 2:1
   K. 4:1

4. The correct answer is G. You already know that the radius of Circle B is 3x. To find the diameter of Circle C, multiply its radius by 2. The diameter of Circle C is 6x · 2 = 12x. Now you can find the ratio between these two values. Remember to simplify your answer.

$3x:12x$

$3:12$

$1:4$

5. The circle shown in the figure below has a diameter of 12 meters. What is the area of the circle, in square meters?

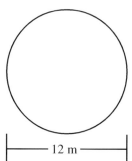

|— 12 m —|

   A. 6π
   B. 12π
   C. 24π
   D. 36π
   E. 144π

5. The correct answer is D. To solve this problem, first find the value for the radius, and then plug that into the formula for the area of a circle, which is πr^2. You know that the radius is half of the diameter. The diameter of this circle is 12 meters, so the radius is 6 meters. Plug 6 into the formula for the area of a circle as the radius.

Area = πr^2

Area = $\pi(6)^2$

Area = 36π

6. If a circle has a circumference of 108π inches, how many inches long is its radius?

   F. $\sqrt{108}$
   G. 27
   H. 54
   J. 108
   K. 216

6. The correct answer is H. In this problem, you are given the circumference of the circle, which is 108π inches, and you are asked to find the radius. Plug this information into the formula for the circumference of a circle and solve for the radius.

Circumference = $2\pi r$

$108\pi = 2\pi r$

$108 = 2r$

r = 54 feet

12.4.3 Set Three

7. If a circle has a circumference of $\frac{6}{5}\pi$ centimeters, how long is its radius, in centimeters?

A. $\frac{3}{5}$

B. $\frac{5}{6}$

C. $\frac{6}{5}$

D. $\frac{5}{3}$

E. $\sqrt{\frac{6}{5}}$

7. **The correct answer is A.** In this problem, you are given the circumference of the circle, which is $\frac{6}{5}\pi$ centimeters, and you are asked to find the radius. Plug this information into the formula for the circumference of a circle and solve for the radius.

Circumference = $2\pi r$

$\frac{6}{5}\pi = 2\pi r$

$\frac{6}{5} = 2r$

$\frac{6}{5} \cdot \frac{1}{2} = r = \frac{6}{10}$, which can be reduced to $\frac{3}{5}$

8. A circle that lies on the standard (x,y) coordinate plane has its center at $(8,-6)$ and passes through the origin. What is the area of this circle, in square coordinate units?

F. 14π
G. 20π
H. 36π
J. 64π
K. 100π

8. **The correct answer is K.** In this problem, you need to find the distance from the center to the origin because you know that the origin is a point on the circle. This distance is the radius of the circle. Find this distance by creating a right triangle with its hypotenuse being the distance from the center to the origin and its legs, measuring 8 and 6. Use the Pythagorean Theorem to find the radius.

$6^2 + 8^2 = r^2$

$36 + 64 = r^2$

$100 = r^2$

$10 = r$

Finish this problem by plugging the value that you found for the radius into the formula for the area of a circle, which is πr^2.

Area = πr^2

Area = $(\pi)(10)^2$

Area = 100π

9. Richard brought his dog to the park and tied his leash to a flagpole while he had a picnic. The dog could reach 12 feet from the flagpole in any direction. What is the approximate area of the ground, in square feet, that the dog could reach from the flagpole? (Note: $\pi \approx 3.14$)

   A. 19
   B. 38
   C. 75
   D. 113
   E. 452

9. **The correct answer is E.** In this problem, the flagpole acts as the center of the circle, and the dog's leash acts as the radius. Knowing this, you can solve for the area of the circle by plugging in 12 feet for the radius in the formula for the area of a circle. Make sure you change π to 3.14 when solving.

Area = πr^2

Area = $(3.14)(12)^2$

Area = $(3.14)(144)$ = 452.16 which can be rounded down to 452.

12.4.4 Set Four

10. The figure below shows four congruent semicircles that touch only at the corners of a square. The path from point X, along the diameters of the semicircles, back to point X is 96 inches long. How long is the path from point X, along the arcs of the semicircles, back to point X, in inches?

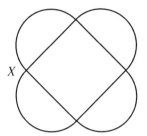

F.　24π
G.　48π
H.　96π
J.　144π
K.　288π

10. The correct answer is G. To solve this problem, you have to recognize that since the path along the 4 diameters is 96 inches long, each diameter is 96 ÷ 4 = 24 inches long. This means that the radii of the semicircles are 24 ÷ 2 = 12 inches long. To find the length of the path along the four congruent semicircles, you need to use the circumference formula. Since there are four semicircles, that means there are 2 full circles. Use the formula twice and add your results together to find the path along the perimeter of the semicircles.

Path along the arcs = 2πr + 2πr

Path along the arcs = 2π(12) + 2π(12)

Path along the arcs = 24π + 24π = 48π

11. The figure below shows a small circle with a diameter $\overline{AC}$ and a large circle with a diameter $\overline{AB}$ that is 32 inches long. Point C is the center of the large circle. What is the area, in square inches, of the small circle?

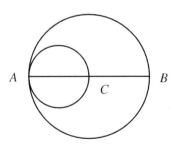

A.　8π
B.　16π
C.　32π
D.　40π
E.　64π

11. The correct answer is E. Since $\overline{AC}$ is the diameter of the small circle and C is the center of the large circle, you know that the diameter of the small circle is equal to the radius of the large circle. Therefore, the diameter of the small circle is half the diameter of the large circle. $\overline{AC}$ is half of 32, which is 16. To find the area of this circle, you first need to find the radius. The radius is half of 16, which is 8. Now you can plug this value into the formula for the area of a circle.

Area = πr²

Area = π(8)²

Area = 64π

12. The square in the figure below has a perimeter of 40 inches. The circle is inscribed in the square and is tangent to the square at the midpoints of its sides. What is the area of the circle, in square inches?

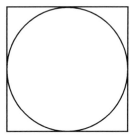

F. 4π
G. 10π
H. 16π
J. 25π
K. 100π

12. **The correct answer is J.** To solve this problem, you need to find the length of one of the sides of the square. This length will be equal to the length of the diameter of the circle. The perimeter of the square is 40, which means that each of its 4 sides is 10 inches long. Now divide the diameter by 2 to find the radius.

$10 \div 2 = 5$ inches. Use the formula for the area of a circle to find the area.

Area = πr^2

Area = $(\pi)(5)^2$

Area = 25π

12.4.5 Set Five

13. The figure below shows a circular well that has a diameter of 7 feet. What is the circumference of the well, in feet?

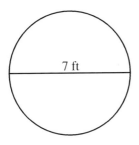

7 ft

A. $\frac{7}{2}\pi$

B. 7π

C. $\frac{49}{4}\pi$

D. 14π

E. 49π

13. The correct answer is B. To solve this problem, you need to find the value for the radius and plug that into the formula for the circumference of a circle, which is $2\pi r$. You know that the radius is half of the diameter. The diameter of this circle is 7, so the radius is $\frac{7}{2}$. Plug $\frac{7}{2}$ into the formula for the circumference of a circle as the radius.

Circumference = $2\pi(\frac{7}{2})$

Circumference = 7π

14. Rectangle *ABCD*, shown below, has side lengths of 8 inches and 10 inches. What is the area, in square inches, of the largest circle that can fit within rectangle *ABCD* ?

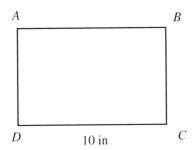

A   B

D   10 in   C

F. 8π
G. 16π
H. 20π
J. 64π
K. 100π

14. The correct answer is G. Since the smallest side of the rectangle is 8 inches, the largest the circle's diameter can be is 8 inches. Since the diameter is 8 inches, the radius is 8 ÷ 2 = 4 inches. Use the formula for the area of a circle to find the area.

Area = πr^2

Area = $(\pi)(4)^2$

Area = 16π

15. If the diameter of a circle is doubled, the area of the resulting circle is how many times the area of the original circle?

  A. 2
  B. 4
  C. 6
  D. 8
  E. 10

15. The correct answer is B. If the diameter of the circle is doubled, the radius is also doubled. If the radius is doubled, the area of the new circle is 4 times the size of the old one. Look at two circles, one with a radius of 5, and one with a radius of 10, which is 5 doubled.

Area = πr^2

Area = $(\pi)(5)^2$

Area = 25π

Area = πr^2

Area = $(\pi)(10)^2$

Area = 100π

100π is four times the size of 25π. Here's another way to look at it, in which you square 5 and multiply it separately:

Area = πr^2

Area = $(\pi)(5 \cdot 2)^2$

Area = $(\pi)(25 \cdot 4)$

Area = 100π

ACT® Mastery Math

Sum It Up

Circle Area and Circumference

Circumference of a Circle = $2\pi r$
Remember this formula by saying "Circle circumference is 2-pi-rrrimeter."

Area of a Circle = πr^2
Remember this formula by saying "Circle area is pi-r-sq'area."

Tips and Techniques

Draw It Out: It does not have to be pretty. On the ACT, everyone is an artist.

Drawn to Scale: It is usually safe to assume that figures in ACT math problems are drawn to scale. If it looks like a midpoint, it probably is! If two angles look the same size, they probably are!

Math Mirror: Items on both sides of the equal sign are part of the formula. This means that in the formula *area* $= \pi r^2$, *area* is part of the formula. It is one of the variables. If you are given the area but not a radius or diameter, you can plug the area into the formula and solve for the unknown.

12.5 Exit Ticket

▶ Students complete the three questions on their exit ticket.

Students are timed 3 minutes for the three questions (60 seconds per question). There is no break between questions.

Lesson 12 – Circle Area and Circumference

Name _____   Date _____

Exit Ticket

1. Lauren is putting in a circular window in her living room ceiling. The window will have a radius of 3 feet. Using 3.14 for π, what is the approximate perimeter, in feet, of the window? Round your answer to the nearest foot.

   DO YOUR FIGURING HERE.

   A.   6
   B.   9
   C.   18
   D.   19
   E.   28

2. What is the area, in square inches, of the largest circle that can fit within a rectangle with side lengths 4 and 18 ?

   F.   4π
   G.   16π
   H.   18π
   J.   22π
   K.   324π

3. The ratio of the radii of two circles is 3:7. What is the ratio of their circumferences?

   A.   1:1
   B.   3:7
   C.   3:14π
   D.   6π:7
   E.   9:49

   Answered Correctly
   ____ / 3

MasteryPrep

12.5 Exit Ticket

Solve the questions on your exit ticket.

Entrance Ticket | Learning Targets | Quick Check | Circumference | Area | ACT Practice | Exit Ticket

12.5 Exit Ticket Review

▶ Students work the first question.

1. **The correct answer is D.** To solve this problem, use the formula for the circumference of a circle, which is $2\pi r$. Remember that the circumference of a circle is the same as its perimeter. Plug in the given value for the radius into the formula. Make sure you change π to 3.14 when solving.

> Circumference = $2\pi(3)$
>
> Circumference = 6π
>
> Circumference = 6(3.14) = 18.84, which you can round to 19 feet.

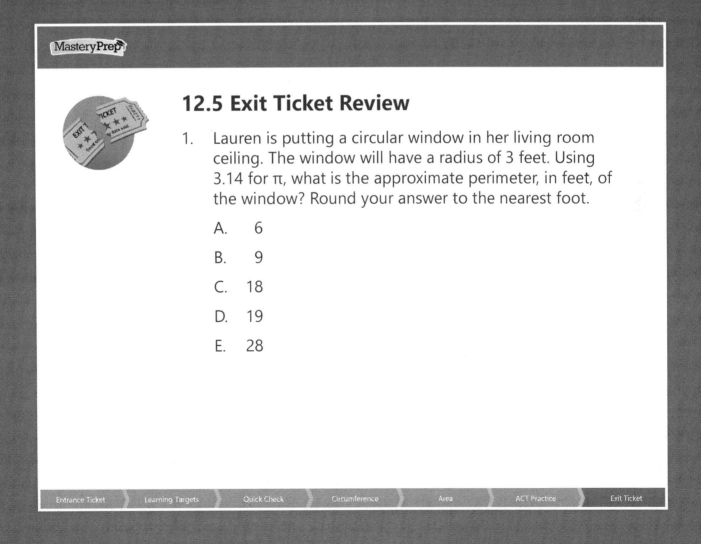

MasteryPrep

12.5 Exit Ticket Review

1. Lauren is putting a circular window in her living room ceiling. The window will have a radius of 3 feet. Using 3.14 for π, what is the approximate perimeter, in feet, of the window? Round your answer to the nearest foot.

   A. 6

   B. 9

   C. 18

   D. 19

   E. 28

Entrance Ticket | Learning Targets | Quick Check | Circumference | Area | ACT Practice | Exit Ticket

12.5 Exit Ticket Review

▶ Students work the second question.

2. **The correct answer is F.** Since the smallest side of the rectangle is 4 inches, the largest the circle's diameter can be is 4 inches. Since the diameter is 4 inches, the radius is $4 \div 2 = 2$ inches. Use the formula for the area of a circle to find the area.

$$\text{Area} = \pi r^2$$
$$\text{Area} = (\pi)(2)^2$$
$$\text{Area} = 4\pi$$

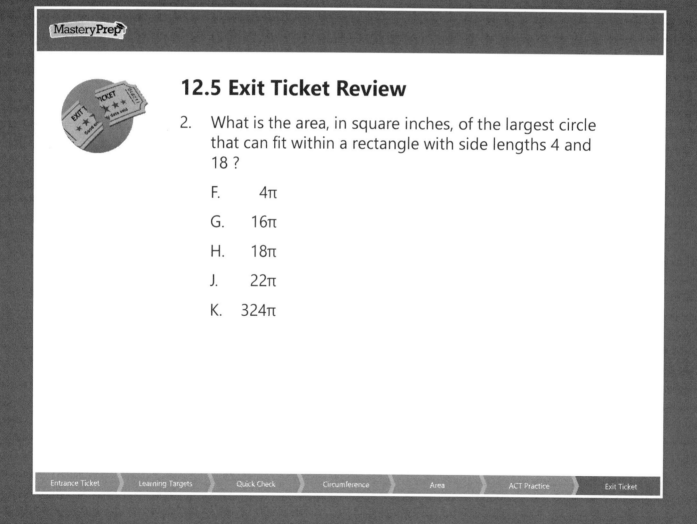

MasteryPrep

12.5 Exit Ticket Review

2. What is the area, in square inches, of the largest circle that can fit within a rectangle with side lengths 4 and 18 ?

   F. 4π

   G. 16π

   H. 18π

   J. 22π

   K. 324π

Entrance Ticket | Learning Targets | Quick Check | Circumference | Area | ACT Practice | Exit Ticket

12.5 Exit Ticket Review

▶ Students work the third question.

3. **The correct answer is B.** Since a circumference is the radius multiplied by 2π, the ratio of the radii of two circles will be equal to the ratio of the circumferences of those two circles. Look at some math to help explain this. Find the ratio of the circumferences of two circles with radii of 3 units and 7 units.

> Circumference of Circle 1: $2\pi(3) = 6\pi$
>
> Circumference of Circle 2: $2\pi(7) = 14\pi$

Now you can find the ratio of the circumference of the circle with radius 3 to the circumference of the circle with radius 7. Make sure you reduce your ratio

> $6\pi : 14\pi = 6 : 14 = 3 : 7$

▶ After all three questions are completed, students exchange papers. Solve the three exit items step by step on the board. Students grade using their red pens and then return papers to their classmates.

▶ After solving the three exit items, revisit the learning targets slide on the slide. Students again assess their knowledge and confidence on the same 1 to 4 scale that they used at the beginning of the lesson. Students write this number in the designated area at the start of the lesson in their workbooks, along with any comments or questions they might have.

▶ Finally, to close the lesson, have students return to the cover page of the lesson and write a caption for the picture there. The caption should be a one-sentence summary of the lesson, a main rule or tip they want to remember, or an explanation of how the picture relates to the topic. If there is additional time, students can share and compare their captions with the class.

Volume

This lesson will show how to calculate the volume of three-dimensional figures and how to work backward to find the dimensions of three-dimensional figures.

ACT Standards:

G 601. Use relationships involving area, perimeter, and volume of geometric figures to compute another measure (e.g., surface area for a cube of a given volume and simple geometric probability)

Student Page 183

13.1 Entrance Ticket

Student Page 184

▶ Have students answer this brain teaser and write a paragraph explaining how they found the answer.

▶ Brain teaser: If you have a 3-gallon bucket, a 4-gallon bucket, and a water source, how can you measure out exactly 2 gallons?

Remind students this needs to be an exact measurement. They can't just fill the 4-gallon bucket and pour out "about half" of it.

Fill the 3-gallon bucket with water. Pour this water into the 4-gallon bucket. There is room for 1 more gallon in the 4-gallon bucket. Fill the 3-gallon bucket again. Pour some of the water into the 4-gallon bucket until it is full. You will have poured out 1 gallon from the 3-gallon bucket into the 4-gallon bucket, leaving exactly 2 gallons in the 3-gallon bucket.

Note: Students may come up with more than one way to solve the problem.

▶ Teacher Dialogue: **A gallon is a unit of measure that describes volume. What is the volume of the larger bucket in terms of gallons?**

Four gallons

▶ Teacher Dialogue: **If the four-gallon bucket only has three gallons of water in it, what fraction of its volume is filled with water?**

$\dfrac{3}{4}$

13.2 Learning Targets

▶ Review learning targets with your students, displayed on the slide and in their workbooks.

▶ After reviewing the learning targets, ask students to assess their knowledge and confidence level on these targets. They should rate themselves on a scale of 1 to 4, with 1 being not confident or uncertain, and 4 being completely confident or certain. They should circle this number in the designated section of their workbooks.

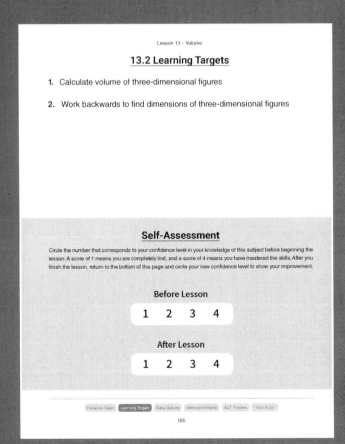

Student Page 185

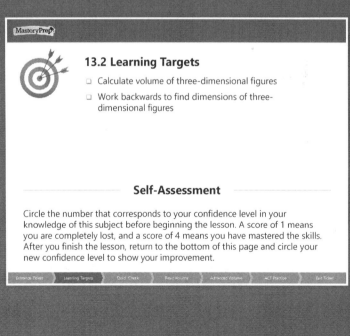

13.2 Quick Check

▶ Teacher Dialogue: **Define *radius*.**

Radius: The length of a line segment from a circle's center to its perimeter

▶ Teacher Dialogue: **Define *diameter*.**

Diameter: Any straight line segment that passes through the center of a circle and whose endpoints lie on the circle

▶ Teacher Dialogue: **Define *length*.**

Length: The measurement of the side of a figure or shape (usually the longest dimension)

Teacher Dialogue: **Define *width*.**

Width: Measurement from side to side of a figure or shape

▶ Teacher Dialogue: **Define *height*.**

Height: Measurement from top to bottom of a figure or shape

▶ Teacher Dialogue: **Define *depth*.**

Depth: Measurement of how deep something is (how far *down* or *back* it goes)

▶ Take an object in the room that is a rectangular prism. Ask the students if each side is the height, length, or width.

▶ Then rotate the shape. Ask for the height, length, width. Ask the students if rotating it changed the volume.

▶ Teacher Dialogue: **The labels are there to help us remember what side we are talking about; in terms of the actual dimensions of the shape, you can call each side whatever you want.**

13.2 Quick Check

▶ Show students the video animation on the slide. Explain that calculating volume is like measuring how much pizza is in a stack of pizzas. It is just the area of the pizza shape times the height of the stack of pizzas. All of the volume formulas are the same area formula times the height.

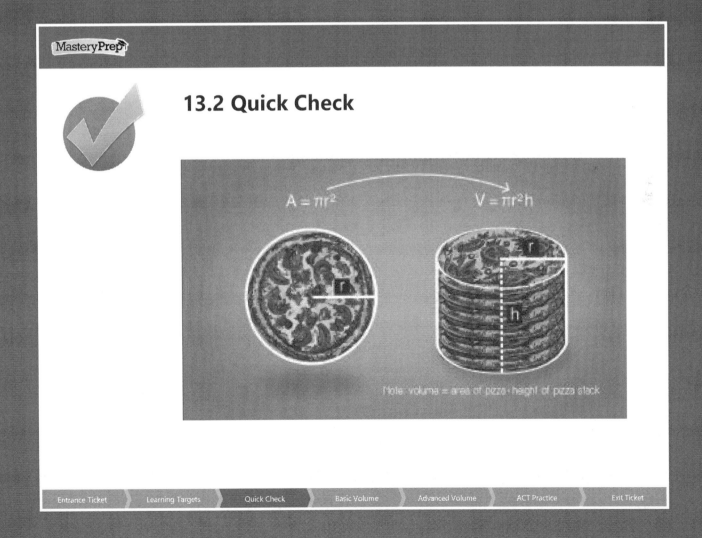

13.3.1 Basic Volume

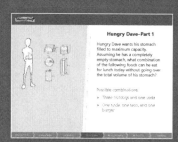

Student Page 186

▶ **Teacher Dialogue:** **Hungry Dave is a high school student just like you. Recently, he's decided he wants to try to live up to his name. He's determined to eat as much as he possibly can every day for the next month. If Hungry Dave wants his stomach filled to maximum capacity, what combination of the following foods could he eat for lunch today? Food options are tacos, burgers, oranges, hot dogs, and sodas.**

▶ At this point, do not show students the measurement values on the slide.

   Students should eventually realize that they can't answer the problem with the given information.

▶ **Teacher Dialogue:** **What do you need to know in order to solve the problem?**

   The volume of Hungry Dave's stomach and the volume of each food option

▶ **Teacher Dialogue:** **How would you solve the problem if you had more information?**

   Find the volume of each food. Add these volumes together in different combinations to see how close you can get to the volume of Hungry Dave's stomach without going over.

▶ Reveal the food and stomach measurement values on the slide.

▶ **Teacher Dialogue:** **The most basic way to find the volume of a figure is to find the area of the main shape and multiply it by how long or high the shape is. Remember the pizza stacks!**

▶ Demonstrate finding the volume of the taco for the students.

   Find the area of the triangle using the formula: area $= \dfrac{base \; \cdot \; height}{2}$.

   Area $= \dfrac{2 \cdot 3}{2} = 3$. Then multiply the area by the length of the taco. $3 \cdot 4 = 12$ in³.

   The taco is 12 in³ in volume.

13.3.1 Basic Volume

▶ Teacher Dialogue: **Which food/shape can we not use this basic method for?**

The orange/sphere

▶ Teacher Dialogue: **The formula for volume of a sphere will be provided to you on the ACT. Volume = $\frac{4}{3}\pi r^3$. What is the volume of the orange?**

Volume = $\frac{4}{3}$ (3.14)(1.5)^3 = 14.13 or about 14 in^3.

▶ Teacher Dialogue: **Find the volume for the other foods. Then come up with combinations of foods that will fit in Hungry Dave's stomach without exceeding its volume. Use 3.14 for π and round to the nearest whole number.**

▶ Have students attempt to solve the problem now that they have the needed information and you have modeled finding the volume of the taco and orange. Students should do their work in the blank space provided in their workbooks.

▶ Have students share their results with the class. Ask the students why everyone doesn't have the same answer. See who gets a combination closest to 61 without going over.

Volume of the burger: volume of a cube = length^3 = 3^3 = 27 in^3

Volume of the hotdog: volume of a rectangular prism = length · width · height. $V = 1.5 \cdot 1.5 \cdot 6 = 13.5$ = about 14 in^3

Volume of the soda: volume of a cylinder = πr^2 · height

$V = 3.14(1)^2 \cdot 6 = 18.84$ = about 19 in^3

Possible combinations:

- Three hotdogs and one soda: 3(14) + 19 = 61
- One soda, one taco, and one burger: 19 + 12 + 27 = 58

13.3.2 Advanced Volume

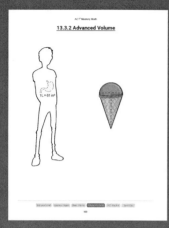

Student Page 188

Student Page 189

▶ Teacher Dialogue: **Hungry Dave is already hungry again. How many ice cream cones will fit in his stomach? (The volume of a cone = $\frac{1}{3}\pi r^2 h$. The formula for the volume of a sphere is $V = \frac{4}{3}\pi r^3$. These formulas will be provided on the ACT if a question asks for these calculations.)**

▶ Reveal the measurement values on the slide. Students solve the problem, showing their work on the blank space provided in their workbooks.

▶ Teacher Dialogue: **How would you solve this problem?**

Volume of the cone is $\frac{1}{3} \cdot 3.14(1.25)^2 \cdot 3 = 4.906$ in³. Volume of the sphere is $\frac{4}{3}\pi r^3 = \frac{4}{3}(3.14)(1.25)^3 = 8.177$. Since the scoop of ice cream is only half of a sphere, divide this value by 2. $8.177 \div 2 = 4.0885$ in³. Add the volume of the half sphere and the cone to get the full volume of the ice cream cone.

$4.0885 + 4.906 = 8.9945 =$ about 9 in³

Divide Hungry Dave's stomach capacity by the volume of the ice cream cone to see how many ice cream cones he can eat. $61 \div 9 = 6.777$. Hungry Dave can eat 6 ice cream cones.

> **Draw It Out:** Show your work and model any problems. Be an ACT artist! This will help you make fewer careless errors.

13.3.2 Advanced Volume

▶ Teacher Dialogue: **Now Hungry Dave is craving his favorite sandwich, the PB&J. But Hungry Dave is a very peculiar boy. Unlike some kids who want the crust cut off their sandwiches, Hungry Dave ONLY likes to eat the crust. What do you need to know to figure out how many sandwich crusts Hungry Dave can eat?**

Possible answers include volume of sandwich, dimensions of sandwich, dimensions of crust to be cut off, etc.

▶ Reveal the measurement values on the slide. Students solve the problem, showing their work on the blank space provided in their workbooks.

▶ Teacher Dialogue: **How would you solve this problem?**

Find the volume of the entire sandwich. Subtract the volume of the sandwich to be removed. Divide Hungry Dave's stomach capacity by the volume of the crust-only sandwich.

Find the volume of the sandwich before the middle is cut out. Remind the students that volume is the area of the main shape multiplied by the thickness or height. The square that is the bread has an area of $5 \cdot 5 = 25$. Multiply this by the thickness. $25 \cdot 1 = 25$ in³.

Find the volume of the sandwich without the crust. If 0.5 inches is removed on every side, the new dimensions of the sandwich are $4 \cdot 4$. (Show picture or draw it out for students. $5 - 0.5 - 0.5 = 4$ for both sides.) Find the volume in the same way. The area of the main shape, a square, is $4 \cdot 4 = 16$. Multiply it by the height of the sandwich. $16 \cdot 1 = 16$ in³.

Subtract the volume of the crustless sandwich from the volume of the whole sandwich to find the volume of just the crust. $25 - 16 = 9$ in³.

How many crusts can Hungry Dave eat? Divide his stomach capacity by the volume of the crust of one sandwich. $61 \div 9 = 6.777$. Hungry Dave can eat 6 sandwich crusts.

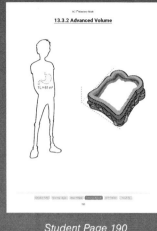

Student Page 190

Student Page 191

13.3.2 Advanced Volume

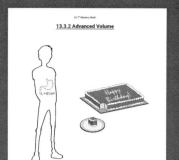

Student Page 192

Student Page 193

▶ Teacher Dialogue: **It's Hungry Dave's birthday! He wants to eat as much cake as he can possibly fit in his stomach. What do you need to know in order to find out how many pieces of cake Hungry Dave can eat?**

Answers include size of cake, volume of cakes, dimensions of cake, how many pieces of cake it is cut into, volume of pieces of cake, dimensions of pieces of cake, etc.

▶ Reveal the measurement values on the slide. Students solve the problem, showing their work in the blank space provided in their workbooks.

▶ Teacher Dialogue: **How would you solve this problem?**

First find the volume of the entire cake, which is the area of the main shape times the thickness of the cake. The area of the rectangle is 13 · 9 = 117. Multiply this by the thickness of the cake. 117 · 1.5 = 175.5 in³.

Next, find the volume of a piece of the cake. Area of the main shape times the thickness of the cake. The area of the square is 1.5 · 1.5 = 2.25. Multiply this by the thickness of the cake. 2.25 · 1.5 = 3.375 in³.

Now find out how many pieces of cake the whole cake can be divided into, and find out how many pieces of cake Hungry Dave's stomach can hold. Both of these will need to be done; order doesn't matter.

Divide Hungry Dave's stomach capacity by the volume of a piece of cake. 61 ÷ 3.375 = 18.07 = about 18 pieces of cake.

Now find what fraction of the cake 18 pieces is. Figure out how many pieces of cake make up the whole cake. Divide the volume of the entire cake by the volume of an individual piece. 175.5 ÷ 3.375 = 52 pieces.

Now set up the fraction. Dave can eat 18 out of 52 pieces of the cake or $\frac{18}{52}$ of a cake. That's about a third of an entire cake!

13.4 ACT Practice

▶ Have students work on questions from the ACT practice sets here. Pacing should be 3 minutes per practice set or 60 seconds per question.

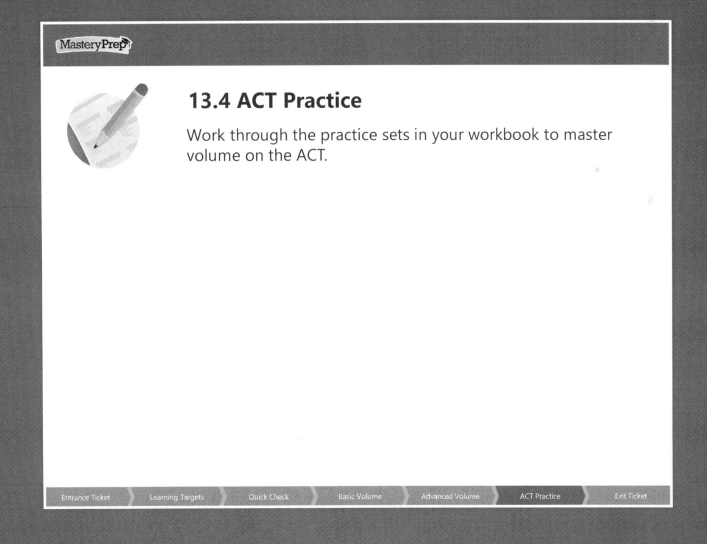

MasteryPrep

13.4 ACT Practice

Work through the practice sets in your workbook to master volume on the ACT.

Entrance Ticket | Learning Targets | Quick Check | Basic Volume | Advanced Volume | ACT Practice | Exit Ticket

13.4.1 Set One

1. A rectangular solid is 5 inches wide, 8 inches long, and 3 inches tall. What is the volume of this rectangular solid, in cubic inches?

   A. 16
   B. 43
   C. 64
   D. 65
   E. 120

1. The correct answer is E. Multiply the height, length, and width.

$V = (5)(8)(3)$

$V = (40)(3) = 120$

2. Eliza's parents are installing an above-ground swimming pool in their backyard. The pool is a right circular cylinder with a diameter of 18 feet and a height of 7 feet, as shown in the figure below.

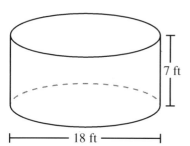

Once her parents fill the pool, it will have a depth of 6 feet. What is the volume of water, to the nearest cubic foot, that will be in the pool once it is filled?

(Note: The volume, V, of a right circular cylinder with radius r and height h is given by the formula $V = \pi r^2 h$.)

   F. 170
   G. 1,527
   H. 1,781
   J. 2,375
   K. 6,107

2. The correct answer is G. Plug in the radius (1/2 the diameter) and depth into the volume formula (use depth of the water, not height of the pool, as the question is asking for the volume of water in the pool).

$V = \pi(9)^2(6)$

$V = \pi(81)(6)$

$V = 486\pi \approx 1,527$

3. What is the height, in centimeters, of a rectangular prism that is 80 centimeters wide, 40 centimeters long, and has a volume of 160,000 centimeters?

   A. 5
   B. 20
   C. 39
   D. 40
   E. 50

3. The correct answer is E. Solve for the missing value, knowing that volume = height · width · length.

$(80)(40)(h) = 160,000$

$3,200h = 160,000$

$h = 50$

13.4.2 Set Two

4. Cube A has side lengths that are 3 times as long as Cube B. How many times larger is the volume of Cube A compared to the volume of Cube B?

    F. 2
    G. 3
    H. 6
    J. 9
    K. 27

4. **The correct answer is K.** Multiply each dimension by three to determine the change in volume.

Cube A: $V = (3l)(3w)(3h)$

$V = 27lwh$

Cube B: $V = lwh$

Since lwh represents the volume of Cube B, the volume of Cube A will be 27 times greater.

5. A large cube has edges that are twice as long as those of a small cube. If the edges of the small cube are 6 inches, how many more cubic inches is the volume of the large cube than the small cube?

    A.   8
    B. 216
    C. 432
    D. 1,512
    E. 1,728

5. **The correct answer is D.** A cube has the same height, length, and width. If the large cube has edges twice as long as the small cube, with edges of 6 inches, then the volume is represented by $(12)(12)(12) = 1,728$ cubic inches. The volume of the small cube is $(6)(6)(6) = 216$ cubic inches. $1,728 - 216 = 1,512$ cubic inches

6. There are two right circular cylinders. The large cylinder has a height 2 times the size of the height of the small cylinder and a radius 3 times the size of the small cylinder. How many times larger is the volume of the large cylinder compared to the volume of the small cylinder?

(Note: The volume, V, of a right circular cylinder with radius r and height h is given by the formula $V = \pi r^2 h$.)

    F. 2
    G. 3
    H. 5
    J. 6
    K. 18

6. **The correct answer is K.** Multiply the dimensions by the given amounts to determine the change in volume.

Large cylinder: $V = \pi(3r)^2(2h)$

$V = \pi(9r^2)(2h)$

$V = 18\pi r^2 h$

Small cylinder: $V = \pi r^2 h$

Since $\pi r^2 h$ represents the volume of the small cylinder, the volume of the large cylinder will be 18 times greater.

13.4.3 Set Three

7. A rectangular solid is 13 inches wide, 10 inches long, and 5 inches tall. What is the volume of this rectangular solid, in cubic inches?

   A. 28
   B. 63
   C. 135
   D. 195
   E. 650

7. **The correct answer is E.** Multiply the dimensions together.

$$V = (13)(10)(5)$$
$$V = (130)(5) = 650$$

8. While baking a cake, Kevin used 82.5 cubic inches of frosting to cover the top. If this frosting were spread in an even layer over the top of the rectangular cake shown below, about how many inches deep would the layer of frosting be? Round your answer to the nearest hundredth of an inch.

15 in

11 in

   F. 0.25
   G. 0.50
   H. 0.75
   J. 1.00
   K. 1.25

8. **The correct answer is G.** Solve for the missing value in the volume equation.

$$82.5 = (15)(11)(h)$$
$$82.5 = 165h$$
$$0.50 = h$$

9. There are two spheres of different sizes. The large sphere has a radius 3 times the size of the small sphere. How many times larger is the volume of the large sphere compared to the volume of the small sphere?

(Note: The volume of a sphere is $\frac{4}{3}\pi r^3$, where r represents the length of the radius of the sphere.)

   A. 81
   B. 27
   C. 9
   D. 6
   E. 3

9. **The correct answer is B.** Multiply the dimensions by the given amounts to determine the change in volume.

Large sphere: $V = \frac{4}{3}\pi(3r)^3$

$$V = \frac{4}{3}\pi(27r^3)$$

Small sphere: $V = \frac{4}{3}\pi r^3$

Since $\frac{4}{3}\pi r^3$ represents the volume of the small sphere, the volume of the large sphere will be 27 times greater.

13.4.4 Set Four

10. Martha's parents are building a concrete basketball court in her backyard so she can practice all the time. The basketball court has a length of 47 feet and a width of 50 feet, as shown below. If the court is 6 inches thick, how much concrete will they need to pour, in cubic feet?

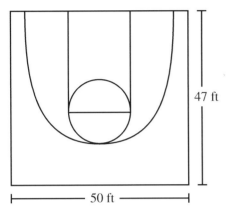

47 ft

50 ft

F. 1,175
G. 2,350
H. 4,700
J. 14,100
K. 84,600

10. The correct answer is F. Multiply the dimensions together (remember to convert 6 inches to 0.5 feet).

$(47)(50)(0.5) = V$

$(47)(25) = 1,175$

---

11. Tyler filled up his hot tub, which is a right rectangular prism, with 480 cubic feet of water. The hot tub is 12 feet long and 10 feet wide. What is the depth of the water in the hot tub? Round your answer to the nearest foot.

A. 2
B. 4
C. 22
D. 40
E. 48

11. The correct answer is B. Solve for the missing value in the volume equation.

$480 = (12)(10)(h)$

$480 = 120h$

$h = 4$

---

12. The length of the rectangular prism shown below is three times the width. The height and the width are the same. If the volume of the prism is 81 cubic centimeters, what is the length of the prism, in centimeters?

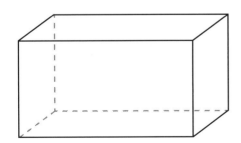

F. 3
G. 9
H. 18
J. 27
K. 49

12. The correct answer is G. Let w equal the width of the prism. The length can be represented by $3w$ and the height by w. Volume then equals $(w)(w)(3w)$.

$(w)(w)(3w) = 81$

$3w^3 = 81$

$w^3 = 27$

$w = 3$, so length is equal to $3(3) = 9$

13.4.5 Set Five

13. Your dog, Cujo, has a water bowl, shown below, that is in the shape of a right circular cylinder with a diameter of 8 inches. The bowl is filled with water to a uniform depth of 4 inches. What is the volume of the water in the water bowl, in cubic inches?

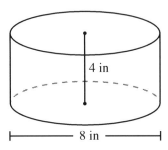

(Note: The volume, V, of a right circular cylinder with radius r and height h is given by the formula $V = \pi r^2 h$.)

A. 12π
B. 16π
C. 32π
D. 64π
E. 256π

13. **The correct answer is D.** Plug the dimensions into the volume formula for cylinders.

$V = \pi(4)^2(4)$

$V = \pi(16)(4) = 64\pi$

14. Cylinders Q and P are both right circular cylinders. The height of Cylinder Q is 3 times the height of Cylinder P, and the radius of Cylinder Q is 2 times the radius of Cylinder P. The volume of Cylinder Q is how many times the volume of Cylinder P ?

(Note: The volume, V, of a right circular cylinder with radius r and height h is given by the formula $V = \pi r^2 h$.)

F. 3
G. 4
H. 5
J. 7
K. 12

14. **The correct answer is K.** Multiply the dimensions by the given amounts to determine the change in volume.

Cylinder Q: $V = \pi(2r)^2(3h)$

$V = \pi(4r^2)(3h) = 12\pi r^2 h$

Cylinder P: $V = \pi r^2 h$

Since $\pi r^2 h$ represents the volume of Cylinder P, the volume of Cylinder Q will be 12 times greater.

15. Right triangle $\triangle ABC$, shown below, has a vertical leg 6 inches long and a hypotenuse 10 inches long. If the triangle was rotated 360° around the vertical leg to form a right circular cone, what would be the volume of this cone, in cubic inches?

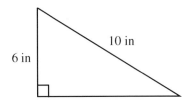

(Note: The volume, V, of a right circular cone with radius r and height h is given by the formula $V = \dfrac{1}{3}\pi r^2 h$.)

A. 32π
B. 96π
C. 128π
D. 288π
E. 384π

15. The correct answer is C. Calculate the length of the other leg of the triangle to determine the radius. Then input these values into the volume formula.

Use the Pythagorean theorem: $100 - 36 = 64$, and the square root of $64 = 8$

$$\frac{1}{3}\pi(8)^2(6) = 128\pi$$

Lesson 13 – Volume

Sum It Up

Volume

Radius
The length of a line segment from a circle's center to its perimeter

---

Diameter
Any straight line segment that passes through the center of a circle and whose endpoints lie on the circle

---

Length
The measurement of a side of a figure or shape

Width
The measurement from side to side of a figure or shape

Height
The measurement from top to bottom of a figure or shape

Depth
The measurement of how deep something is (how far down or back it goes)

Entrance Ticket   Learning Targets   Basic Volume   Advanced Volume   ACT Practice   Sum It Up

201

13.5 Exit Ticket

▶ Students complete the three questions on their exit ticket.

Students are timed 3 minutes for the three questions (60 seconds per question). There is no break between questions.

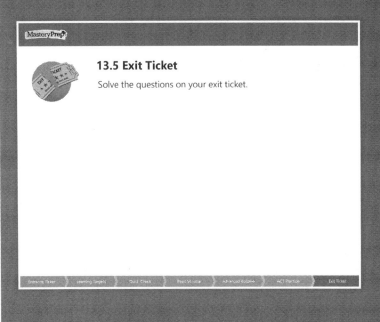

13.5 Exit Ticket Review

▸ Students work the first question.

1. **The correct answer is D**. Use the formula for the volume of a triangular prism to find the volume.

$$V = (\frac{1}{2} b \cdot h) \cdot l$$

$$V = (\frac{1}{2} (3) \cdot 4) \cdot 12$$

$$V = 6 \cdot 12 = 72 \text{ cubic inches}$$

MasteryPrep

13.5 Exit Ticket Review

1. A right triangular prism that is 12 inches long, 3 inches wide, and 4 inches tall is represented by the figure below. What is the volume of the prism, in cubic inches?

   A. 18

   B. 24

   C. 31

   D. 72

   E. 144

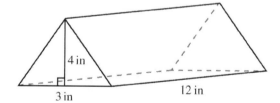

Entrance Ticket   Learning Targets   Quick Check   Basic Volume   Advanced Volume   ACT Practice   Exit Ticket

13.5 Exit Ticket Review

Students work the second question.

2. **The correct answer is J.** Multiply the dimensions of the cake together to find the total volume. Then multiply the dimensions of each piece together and divide into the total volume.

   Cake: (20)(16)(2) = 640 cubic inches

   Piece: (4)(2)(2) = 16 cubic inches

   $\frac{640}{16}$ = 40 pieces in the cake

13.5 Exit Ticket Review

2. Carl baked a cake for his sister's birthday party. The cake was 20 inches long, 16 inches wide, and 2 inches thick. He cut the entire cake into equal pieces. Each piece is 4 inches long, 2 inches wide, and 2 inches thick. How many total pieces of cake are there?

   F. 16

   G. 20

   H. 30

   J. 40

   K. 80

Entrance Ticket   Learning Targets   Quick Check   Basic Volume   Advanced Volume   ACT Practice   Exit Ticket

13.5 Exit Ticket Review

▶ Students work the third question.

> **3. The correct answer is E.** Find the volume of the cylinder and hemisphere separately, and then add them together.
>
> Cylinder: $\pi(18)^2(30) = 9{,}720\pi$
>
> Hemisphere: $\dfrac{2}{3}\pi(18)^3 = 3{,}888\pi$
>
> Total: $9{,}720\pi + 3{,}888\pi = 13{,}608\pi$

▶ After all three questions are completed, students exchange papers. Solve the three exit items step by step on the board. Students grade using their red pens and then return papers to their classmates.

▶ After solving the three exit items, revisit the learning targets slide. Students again assess their knowledge and confidence on the same 1 to 4 scale that they used at the beginning of the lesson. Students write this number in the designated area at the start of the lesson in their workbooks, along with any comments or questions they might have.

▶ Finally, to close the lesson, have students return to the cover page of the lesson and write a caption for the picture there. The caption should be a one-sentence summary of the lesson, a main rule or tip they want to remember, or an explanation of how the picture relates to the topic. If there is additional time, students can share and compare their captions with the class.

Inequalities

This lesson will cover concepts such as how to solve inequalities and how to graph and recognize inequalities on a number line.

ACT Standards:

A 405. Match simple inequalities with their graphs on the number line (e.g., $x \geq -35$)

A 503. Solve first-degree inequalities when the method does not involve reversing the inequality sign

A 504. Match compound inequalities with their graphs on the number line (e.g., $-10.5 < x \leq 20.3$)

A 602. Solve linear inequalities when the method involves reversing the inequality sign

A 603. Match linear inequalities with their graphs on the number line

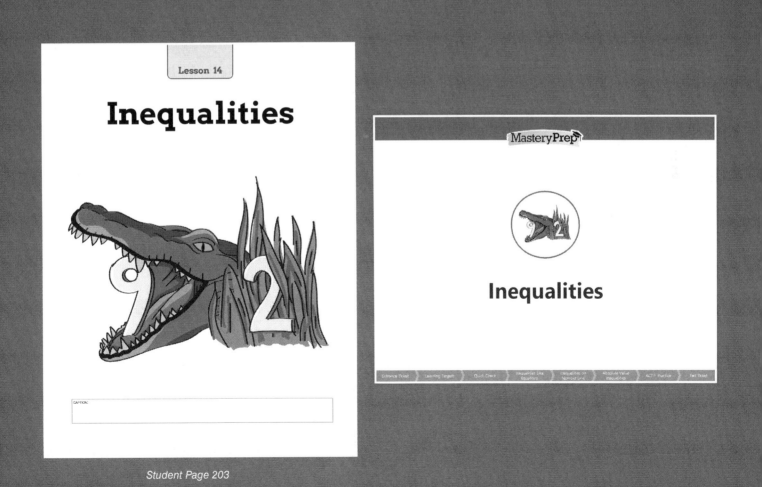

Student Page 203

14.1 Entrance Ticket

▶ Have students try the following three ACT practice questions. Students should work independently. Once the entrance ticket has been completed, review the questions with the students and have them share their answers. Give students the correct answers to the questions, as well as a step-by-step demonstration of how to solve the problems, but do not go into detailed explanation. This will serve as an introduction to the lesson content but is not intended to be the main lesson.

1. **The correct answer is D.** The arrows extend to the left of −3 and to the right of 2, meaning x is less than −3 or greater than 2, as seen in choice D. The dots on the number line are filled in, meaning x can also be equal to −3 or 2, which choice D also shows.

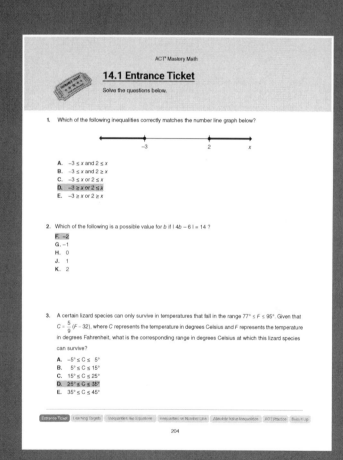

Student Page 204

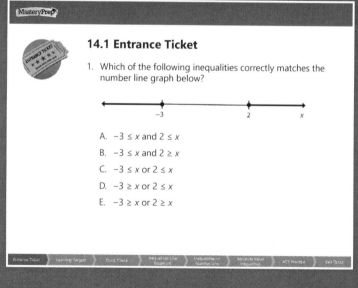

14.1 Entrance Ticket

2. **The correct answer is F.** Solve the equation by isolating b.

$|4b - 6| = 14$

$4b - 6 = 14$ $4b - 6 = -14$

$4b = 20$ $4b = -8$

$b = 5$ $b = -2$

So -2 is a possible value for b.

MasteryPrep

14.1 Entrance Ticket

2. Which of the following is a possible value for b if $|4b - 6| = 14$?

   F. -2

   G. -1

   H. 0

   J. 1

   K. 2

Entrance Ticket | Learning Targets | Quick Check | Inequalities Like Equations | Inequalities on Number Line | Absolute Value Inequalities | ACT Practice | Exit Ticket

14.1 Entrance Ticket

3. **The correct answer is D.** Convert each temperature into Celsius to find the new bounds.

$C = \dfrac{5}{9}(77 - 32)$

$C = 25$

$C = \dfrac{5}{9}(95 - 32)$

$C = 35$

$25° \le C \le 35°$

14.1 Entrance Ticket

3. A certain lizard species can only survive in temperatures that fall in the range $77° \le F \le 95°$. Given that $C = \dfrac{5}{9}(F - 32)$, where C represents the temperature in degrees Celsius and F represents the temperature in degrees Fahrenheit, what is the corresponding range in degrees Celsius at which this lizard species can survive?

   A. $-5° \le C \le 5°$

   B. $\;\;5° \le C \le 15°$

   C. $15° \le C \le 25°$

   D. $25° \le C \le 35°$

   E. $35° \le C \le 45°$

Entrance Ticket | Learning Targets | Quick Check | Inequalities Like Equations | Inequalities on Number Line | Absolute Value Inequalities | ACT Practice | Exit Ticket

14.2 Learning Targets

▶ Review learning targets with your students, displayed on the slide and in their workbooks.

▶ After reviewing the learning targets, ask students to assess their knowledge and confidence level on these targets. They should rate themselves on a scale of 1 to 4, with 1 being not confident or uncertain, and 4 being completely confident or certain. They should circle this number in the designated section of their workbooks.

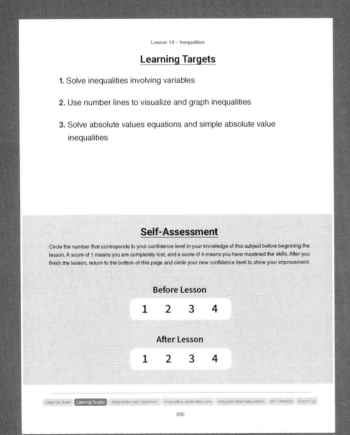

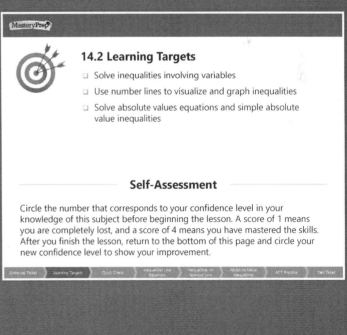

Student Page 205

14.2 Quick Check

▶ Teacher Dialogue: **What does the < sign represent?**
Less than

▶ Teacher Dialogue: **What does the > sign represent?**
Greater than

▶ Teacher Dialogue: **What does the ≤ sign represent?**
Less than or equal to

▶ Teacher Dialogue: **What does the ≥ sign represent?**
Greater than or equal to

▶ Teacher Dialogue: **What does the = sign represent?**
Equal to

▶ Teacher Dialogue: **The inequality sign is like an open alligator mouth. The alligator wants to eat the biggest number, so the open end is always by the larger number.**

▶ Teacher Dialogue: **Define absolute value.**

<u>Absolute Value:</u> The distance a number is from zero, regardless if it is positive or negative.

14.3.1 Solving Inequalities like Equations

▶ Divide the students into teams of two or three and have each team designate a writer. Have the students compete to fill in the correct signs for the following problems, which should be on the slide and in their workbooks. The writers can write their answers on the whiteboard. The team to win will be the first team to get all the correct answers.

1. 3 __ 2
2. 70 + 9 __ 80 − 2
3. 2,237 __ 2,732
4. $3 \cdot 5 - 7$ __ $2 \cdot 6 \div 3$
5. 2^3 __ $4 + 2^2$
6. $x + 1$ __ $x + 2$
7. All positive even integers __ 1
8. $\dfrac{5}{12}$ __ $\dfrac{1}{3}$
9. Number of boys in the class __ Number of girls in the class (*answer varies*)

Student Page 206

Answers:

1. >
2. >
3. <
4. >
5. =
6. <
7. >
8. >
9. Dependent on the class

14.3.1 Solving Inequalities like Equations

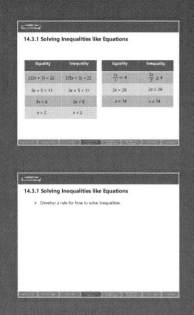

▶ Show students the following equation and inequality:

$$2(3x + 5) = 22 \qquad\qquad 2(3x + 5) < 22$$
$$3x + 5 = 11 \qquad\qquad 3x + 5 < 11$$
$$3x = 6 \qquad\qquad 3x < 6$$
$$x = 2 \qquad\qquad x < 2$$

▶ Teacher Dialogue: **What is the same and what is different about simplifying this equation and inequality?**

Everything is exactly the same, except for the equal/inequality sign.

▶ Show students the next example:

$$\frac{2x}{7} = 4 \qquad\qquad \frac{2x}{7} \geq 4$$
$$2x = 28 \qquad\qquad 2x \geq 28$$
$$x = 14 \qquad\qquad x \geq 14$$

▶ Teacher Dialogue: **What is the same and what is different about this equation and inequality?**

Everything is exactly the same, except for the equal/inequality sign.

▶ Teacher Dialogue: **Develop a rule for how to solve inequalities.**

Solve inequalities the same as regular equations, except use the inequality sign and not the equal sign.

14.3.1 Solving Inequalities like Equations

▶ Now, share with students the following examples:

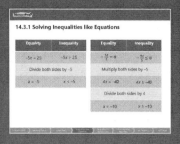

$-5x = 25$

Divide both sides by -5.

$x = -5$

$-5x > 25$

Divide both sides by -5

$x < -5$

$-\dfrac{4x}{5} = 8$

Multiply both sides by -5.

$4x = -40$

Divide both sides by 4.

$x = -10$

$-\dfrac{4x}{5} \leq 8$

Multiply both sides by -5.

$4x \geq -40$

Divide both sides by 4.

$x \geq -10$

▶ Teacher Dialogue: **What is the same and what is different about these equations and inequalities?**

The inequality sign changes direction whenever you multiply or divide by a negative number.

▶ Next, have them try to solve the following equations on their own:

$\dfrac{-x + 2}{3} = 4$

$\dfrac{-x + 2}{3} > 4$

Students should solve and come up with the following:

$\dfrac{-x + 2}{3} = 4$

$-x + 2 = 12$

$-x = 10$

$x = -10$

$\dfrac{-x + 2}{3} > 4$

$-x + 2 > 12$

$-x > 10$

$x < -10$

▶ Teacher Dialogue: **How would you update your rule with this new addition?**

Add that you must reverse the sign direction when multiplying or dividing by a negative number. Students should show their work for the question above on the lines in their workbooks. They should also write the inequalities rule (and its update) on these lines.

14.3.1 Solving Inequalities like Equations

▶ Teacher Dialogue: **What are some different words that can express inequalities?**

No more than

At least

Any words that indicate restriction of some sort

▶ Students should write these terms on the next page in their student workbook. Have students also write down the following terms to look out for. These terms appear on the slide.

1. **Equivalent**

For example, a question might ask, "What expression is equivalent to this one?"

2. **Solution Set**

For example, if the solution set was all numbers larger than 3, the answer would be written as $x > 3$ (an infinite amount of numbers).

3. **Set of All Real Numbers**

4. **Solution Statement**

5. **All Possible Values**

▶ Teacher Dialogue: **The ACT uses different words like these in its questions, and you should read carefully when trying to determine what sort of equation or inequality the question is asking about. These key words will help you decode the question.**

Read with Your Pencil: The ACT uses terminology that may confuse you. If you find any terms from class, use your pencil to circle or underline those words. Marking these familiar terms can help you focus your attention and get to the bottom of the question faster.

Student Page 207

14.3.2 Inequalities on a Number Line

▶ Have the students work in their books to practice drawing number lines and inequalities. Inform them that they should work on the following drawings individually in the space in their workbooks.

▶ Teacher Dialogue: **How would you illustrate on a number line that you are willing to work anywhere from 30 to 40 hours a week?**

Wait for students to write down their answers and then show them the correct answer on the slide.

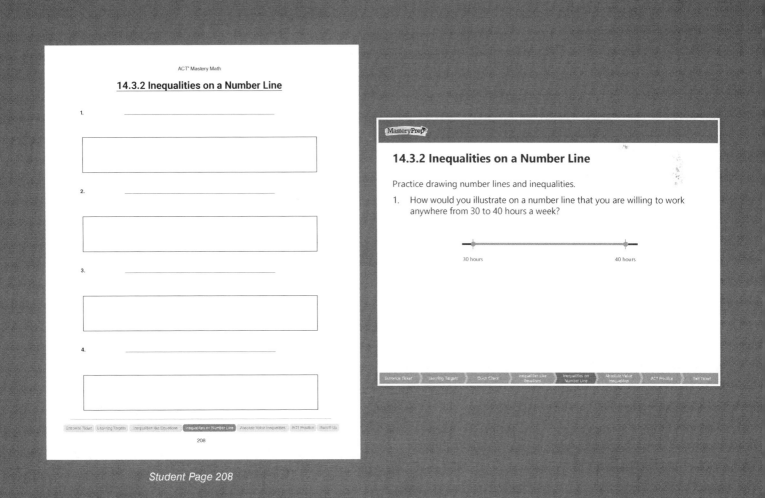

Student Page 208

14.3.2 Inequalities on a Number Line

▶ Teacher Dialogue: **How would you illustrate on a number line that you want to make at least $10 per hour at your new job?**

Wait for students to write down their answers and then show them the correct answer on the slide.

▶ Teacher Dialogue: **How would you illustrate on a number line that a person always gets at least 5 hours of sleep but never more than 9 hours of sleep?**

Wait for students to write down their answers and then show them the correct answer on the slide.

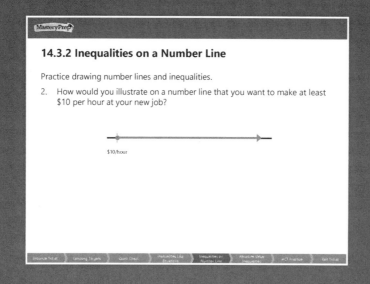

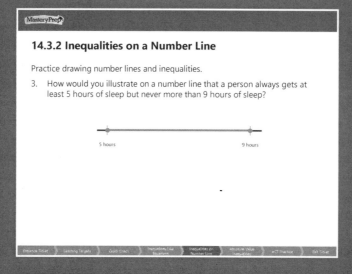

14.3.2 Inequalities on a Number Line

▶ Teacher Dialogue: **How would you illustrate on a number line that a particularly careless spender always has either more than $100 in their bank account OR more than $100 of debt at any time?**

Wait for students to write down their answers and then show them the correct answer on the slide.

▶ Teacher Dialogue: **Now, see if you can come up with an inequality that expresses each situation (in other words, an inequality that represents what you have drawn on the number line).**

1. $30 \leq x \leq 40$
2. $x \geq 10$
3. $5 \leq x \leq 9$
4. $x < -100$ or $x > 100$

▶ Teacher Dialogue: **An open dot on the number line represents > or <, without the *or equal to*. A filled-in dot includes that number and represents ≥ or ≤.**

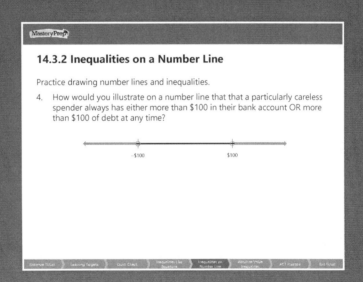

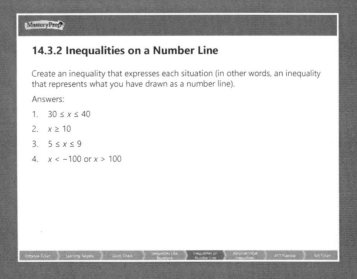

14.3.3 Absolute Value Inequalities

▸ Show the set of math calculations on the slide. The one on the left includes the absolute value symbol, *x*, and an equal sign. The one on the right shows the exact same equation but with the inequality sign instead of the equal sign. Show them, step by step, the calculations of solving for *x*.

▸ Teacher Dialogue: **What is similar about these two calculations and what is different?**

Everything but the inequality sign is the same.

▸ Show students the next set of equations on the slide and allow the students to solve for *x* independently before revealing the bullet points with the answers. Students should write their calculations in the first two side-by-side rectangles in the workbook.

$|x + 7| = 15$

$x + 7 = 15$ and $x + 7 = -15$

Solve for *x*.

$x = 15 - 7$ and $x = -15 - 7$

$x = 8$ or $x = -22$

$|x + 7| > 15$

$x + 7 > 15$ and $x + 7 < -15$

Solve for *x*.

$x > 15 - 7$ and $x < -15 - 7$

$x > 8$ or $x < -22$

▸ Show students the next set of equations on the slide and allow the students to solve for *x* independently before revealing the correct answers on the slide. Students should write their calculations using the next two side-by-side rectangles in the workbook.

$|x - 15| = 32$	$|x - 15| > 32$
$x - 15 = 32$ and $x - 15 = -32$	$x - 15 > 32$ and $x - 15 < -32$
Solve for *x*.	Solve for *x*.
$x = 32 + 15$ and $x = -32 + 15$	$x > 32 + 15$ and $x < -32 + 15$
$x = 47$ or $x = -17$	$x > 47$ or $x < -17$

Student Page 209

14.3.3 Absolute Value Inequalities

Equation	Inequality
$|x - 3| = 9$	$|x - 3| > 9$
$x - 3 = 9$ and $x - 3 = -9$	$x - 3 > 9$ and $x - 3 < -9$
Solve for *x*.	Solve for *x*.
$x = 9 + 3$ and $x = -9 + 3$	$x > 9 + 3$ and $x < -9 + 3$
$x = 12$ or $x = -6$	$x > 12$ or $x < -6$

Equation	Inequality
$|x + 7| = 15$	$|x + 7| > 15$
$x + 7 = 15$ and $x + 7 = -15$	$x + 7 > 15$ and $x + 7 < -15$
Solve for *x*.	Solve for *x*.
$x = 15 - 7$ and $x = -15 - 7$	$x > 15 - 7$ and $x < -15 - 7$
$x = 8$ or $x = -22$	$x > 8$ or $x < -22$

Equation	Inequality
$|x - 15| = 32$	$|x - 15| > 32$
$x - 15 = 32$ and $x - 15 = -32$	$x - 15 > 32$ and $x - 15 < -32$
Solve for *x*.	Solve for *x*.
$x = 32 + 15$ and $x = -32 + 15$	$x > 32 + 15$ and $x < -32 + 15$
$x = 47$ or $x = -17$	$x > 47$ or $x < -17$

14.3.3 Absolute Value Inequalities

► Teacher Dialogue: **Let's develop a rule on how to solve absolute value inequalities.**

Remind students that inequality signs reverse when you divide by a negative number. It also reverses when we are doing the negative calculation in absolute values. Negatives always make the inequality sign flip!

► Explain that "making a rule" should consist of a statement on how they will solve this type of question. After a rule is agreed upon, have students write the rule in the space provided in the workbook.

Possible and suggested answer: Solve it the same as regular equations except use of the inequality sign reverses for the negative personality calculation.

► Answers to the three examples just covered are listed in the workbook. See if students can determine a more concise way to write the answers.

► Teacher Dialogue: **Is there another way to write the answer to our first example $x > 12$ and $x < -6$ that only uses x once?**

$x < 12$ and $x > -6$ can also be written as $-6 < x < 12$

► Have them change the next two answer sets to this compound format. Make sure they know that ACT answer options are written both ways.

$x > -22$ and $x < 8$ becomes $-22 < x < 8$

$x < 47$ and $x > -17$ becomes $-17 < x < 47$

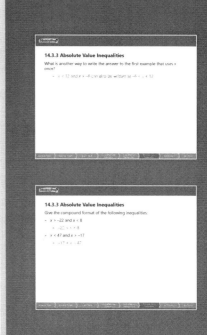

14.4 ACT Practice

▶ Have students work on questions from the ACT practice sets here. Pacing should be 3 minutes per practice set or 60 seconds per question.

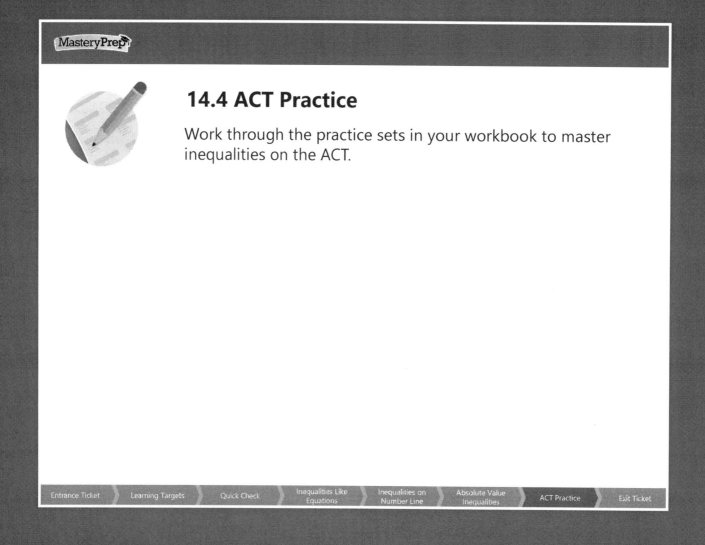

14.4.1 Set One

1. Which of the following is equivalent to the inequality $-8 + 6p \leq 4 - 3p$?

   A. $p \leq \dfrac{1}{3}$

   B. $p \leq \dfrac{4}{3}$

   C. $p \geq \dfrac{3}{4}$

   D. $p \geq 3$

   E. $p \leq 12$

1. **The correct answer is B.** Solve for p as you would an equation.

   $-8 + 6p \leq 4 - 3p$

   $9p \leq 12$

   $p \leq \dfrac{4}{3}$

2. Given numbers r and q, where $0 < r < q$, which of the following inequalities must be true for all values of r and q ?

   F. $r + 2 > q + 2$

   G. $\dfrac{r}{q} > 1$

   H. $\dfrac{1}{q} > \dfrac{1}{r}$

   J. $r^3 > q^3$

   K. $-r > -q$

2. **The correct answer is K.** If r is less than q, then by multiplying the entire inequality by -1, the inequality sign will reverse direction, so $-r > -q$.

3. At a grocery store, muffins sell for $4.00 per package, and cookies sell for $6.25 per package. These bakery items are only sold in packages. Dwayne wants to buy at least one package of muffins and one package of cookies for a party, and he must spend exactly $58.00. What is the maximum number of packages of cookies that he can buy?

   A. 4
   B. 5
   C. 7
   D. 8
   E. 9

3. **The correct answer is D.** If you want to buy one package of muffins, you will be left with $58.00 - $4.00 = $54.00. If you then spent the remaining money on cookies, you would be left with $\dfrac{\$54.00}{\$6.25} = 8.64$. Since this isn't a whole number (and you must spend exactly $58.00), keep testing out new numbers. If you want to buy two packages of muffins, you will be left with $58.00 - $8.00 = $50.00. If you spent the remaining money on cookies, you would be left with $\dfrac{\$50.00}{\$6.25} = 8$ packages of cookies. So, 8 is the maximum number of cookies you can buy.

14.4.2 Set Two

4. The inequality $-\dfrac{3x}{5} + 2 > 8$ is equivalent to which of the following inequalities?

F. $x < -\dfrac{18}{5}$

G. $x < -\dfrac{10}{3}$

H. $x < -10$

J. $x > -10$

K. $x > 10$

4. **The correct answer is H.** Solve for x as you would an equation, remembering to switch the direction of the inequality sign whenever you divide/multiply by a negative number.

$$\dfrac{-3x}{5} + 2 > 8$$

$$\dfrac{-3x}{5} > 6$$

$$-3x > 30$$

$$x < -10$$

---

5. To win the school art competition, the finalists must receive over 50% of the votes cast by their peers. If 330 students vote and x represents the minimum number of votes a finalist needs to win the competition, which of the following expressions is true?

A. $x < 165$
B. $x = 165$
C. $x > 165$
D. $x < 166$
E. $x > 166$

5. **The correct answer is C.** The finalist needs over 50% of 330 votes to win, or over 165 votes. This is represented by the expression $x > 165$.

---

6. For the system of inequalities given below, which of the following defines the solution set?

$$x \le 8$$
$$6 + 3x \ge 0$$

F. $x \ge -2$
G. $x \le 8$
H. $-18 \le x \le 8$
J. $-2 \le x \le 8$
K. $2 \le x \le 8$

6. **The correct answer is J.** Solve for x in the second equation and then use the two inequalities to determine the solution set.

$6 + 3x \ge 0$

$3x \ge -6$

$x \ge -2$

If $x \le 8$ and $x \ge -2$, then $-2 \le x \le 8$.

14.4.3 Set Three

7. The real number line graph, shown below, is represented by which of the following inequalities?

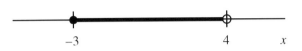

A. $-3 \leq x \leq 3$
B. $-3 \leq x < 4$
C. $0 \leq x < 4$
D. $3 \leq x \leq 4$
E. $4 < x \leq -3$

7. **The correct answer is B.** The circle around −3 is closed, so the inequality is inclusive of −3. The circle around 4 is open, so the inequality is not inclusive of 4. The region between these two values is filled in, so the inequality is represented by $-3 \leq x < 4$.

8. The number line graph pictured below is represented by which of the following inequalities?

F. $-2 \leq x$ and $5 \leq x$
G. $-2 \leq x$ and $5 \geq x$
H. $-2 \leq x$ or $5 \leq x$
J. $-2 \geq x$ or $5 \geq x$
K. $-2 \geq x$ or $5 \leq x$

8. **The correct answer is K.** The two circles are closed, so the inequality is inclusive of −2 and 5. The lines extend outward, below −2 and above 5, so the graph can be represented by the inequalities $-2 \geq x$ or $5 \leq x$.

9. The solution set for the inequality $2x - 7 \geq 3$ is represented by which of the following graphs?

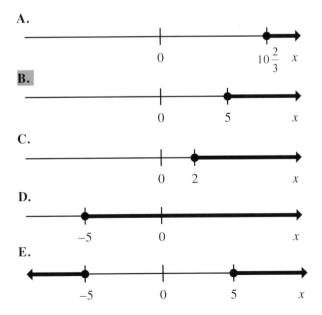

9. **The correct answer is B.** Solve for x and then determine which of the graphs matches the inequality.

$2x - 7 \geq 3$

$2x \geq 10$

$x \geq 5$

14.4.4 Set Four

---

10. Which of the following is a possible value for y if $|3y - 3| = 6$?

F. -2
G. -1
H. 0
J. 1
K. 2

10. **The correct answer is G.** Solve the equation by isolating y.

$|3y - 3| = 6$

$3y - 3 = 6$	or	$3y - 3 = -6$
$3y = 9$	or	$3y = -3$
$y = 3$	or	$y = -1$

---

11. What is the smallest positive integer y such that $|3 - y| > 6$?

A. 2
B. 6
C. 7
D. 9
E. 10

11. **The correct answer is E.** Solve the equation by isolating y.

$|3 - y| > 6$

$3 - y > 6$	or	$3 - y < -6$
$3 - 6 > y$	or	$3 + 6 < y$
$-3 > y$	or	$9 < y$

So the smallest *positive* integer that y could be is 10.

---

12. Which of the following is the solution set for $|a - 5| > 2$?

F. $a < -2$ or $a > 2$
G. $a < 3$ or $a > 7$
H. $a > 3$ and $a < 7$
J. $a > -2$ and $a < 2$
K. $a > -5$ and $a < 5$

12. **The correct answer is G.** Solve the inequality by isolating a.

$|a - 5| > 2$

$a - 5 > 2$	or	$a - 5 < -2$
$a > 7$	or	$a < 3$

14.4.5 Set Five

13. Mr. Sanders produced a progress report for each of the students in his history class. It included the student's scores on homework, quizzes, tests, and projects, as well as class averages on each of these assignments. The progress report for Sara Ortiz is given below.

Student: Ortiz, Sara			
Assignment	Possible Points	Student Score	Class Average
Homework #1	100	100	90
Homework #2	100	92	91
Homework #3	100	98	95
Homework #4	100		
Quiz #1	100	97	89
Quiz #2	100	89	83
Quiz #3	100	93	85
Test #1	100	90	82
Test #2	100	96	92
Project #1	100	100	90
Project #2	100		

If Sara wants an average of at least 95 on her homework, the solution to which of the following inequalities will tell her the score, represented by x, she must achieve on homework #4 ?

A. $\dfrac{100+92+98+x}{4} \geq 95$

B. $\dfrac{x-\left(100+92+98\right)}{4} \geq 95$

C. $\dfrac{100+92+98+x}{3} \geq 95$

D. $\dfrac{100+92+98+x}{2} \geq 95$

E. $\dfrac{\dfrac{100+92+98}{3}+x}{2} \geq 95$

13. The correct answer is A. Write an equation to solve for the missing value of the average of Sara's homework assignments, with x as the missing value, if she wants an average of greater than or equal to 95. Remember that to find an average, add up all the values and then divide that sum by the total number of values. In this case you already know the average, 95, but you do not know all of the test score values. Set up the equation to find an average using x for the unknown test score. Use greater than or equal to 95 to show that the unknown test score needs to be a value that produces an average of at least 95.

$$\frac{100 + 92 + 98 + x}{4} \geq 95$$

14. Which of the following represents the greatest integer m that satisfies the inequality $8 > \dfrac{m}{4} + 3$?

F. 19
G. 20
H. 21
J. 22
K. 24

14. The correct answer is F. Solve for m and then pick the greatest integer that fits that inequality.

$$8 > \dfrac{m}{4} + 3$$

$$5 > \dfrac{m}{4}$$

$$20 > m$$

The greatest integer that satisfies the inequality is 19, since m is less than 20.

15. The solution set for the system of inequalities represented below is illustrated by which of the following graphs?

$$2x - 3 > 2$$
$$-3x > -12$$

A.

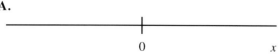

0   x

B.

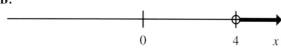

0   4 x

C.

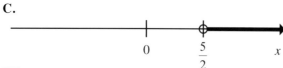

0      $\dfrac{5}{2}$ x

D.

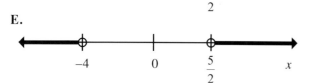

0      $\dfrac{5}{2}$ 4 x

E.

−4   0 $\dfrac{5}{2}$ x

15. The correct answer is D. Solve for x in both inequalities and then select the graph that corresponds to the solution set.

$$2x - 3 > 2$$

$$2x > 5$$

$$x > \dfrac{5}{2}$$

$$-3x > -12$$

$$x < 4$$

$$\dfrac{5}{2} < x < 4$$

ACT® Mastery Math

Sum It Up

Inequalities

<
less than

>
greater than

≤
less than or equal to

≥
greater than or equal to

=
equal to

Closed (filled-in) Circle
Inequality that includes the circled number; use the ≤ or ≥ sign

Open Circle
Inequality that does not include the circled number; use the < or > sign

Entrance Ticket   Learning Targets   Inequalities like Equations   Inequalities on Number Line   Absolute Value Inequalities   ACT Practice   Sum It Up

216

Student Page 216

391

14.5 Exit Ticket

► Students complete the three questions on their exit ticket.

Students are timed 3 minutes for the three questions (60 seconds per question). There is no break between questions.

Lesson 14 – Inequalities

Name _____   Date _____

Exit Ticket

1. Which of the following is the solution set for
   $|y - 4| > 7$?

   A. $y < -7$ or $y > 7$
   B. $y < -3$ or $y > 11$
   C. $y > -4$ and $y < 4$
   D. $y > -3$ and $y < 11$
   E. $y > -7$ and $y < 7$

   DO YOUR FIGURING HERE.

2. Given integers h and k, where $k > 7$ and
   $3h + k = 14$, which of the following represents the
   solution set for h ?

   F. $h \geq 7$
   G. $h \geq 0$
   H. $h \geq 2$
   J. $h \leq 0$
   K. $h \leq 2$

3. The solution set for $x^2 < 16$ is represented by
   which of the following graphs?

   A.
   B.
   C.
   D.
   E.

   Answered Correctly
   ____ / 3

14.5 Exit Ticket Review

▶ Students work the first question.

1. **The correct answer is B.** Solve the inequality by isolating y.

$|y - 4| > 7$

$y - 4 > 7$ or $y - 4 < -7$

$y > 11$ or $y < -3$

14.5 Exit Ticket Review

1. Which of the following is the solution set for $|y - 4| > 7$?

    A. $y < -7$ or $y > 7$

    B. $y < -3$ or $y > 11$

    C. $y > -4$ and $y < 4$

    D. $y > -3$ and $y < 11$

    E. $y > -7$ and $y < 7$

Entrance Ticket | Learning Targets | Quick Check | Inequalities Like Equations | Inequalities on Number Line | Absolute Value Inequalities | ACT Practice | Exit Ticket

14.5 Exit Ticket Review

▶ Students work the second question.

2. **The correct answer is K.** Use the guess and check method to solve this problem. Start with choice H since it is in the middle. Plug 2 in for h and see what value you get for k.

$3h + k = 14$

$3(2) + k = 14$

$6 + k = 14$

$k = 8$, which is greater than 7, so 2 is a value that satisfies the equation.

Now you can try values greater than and less than 2 to figure out whether the answer is choice H or choice K. Try 4.

$3h + k = 14$

$3(4) + k = 14$

$12 + k = 14$

$k = 2$, which is less than 7 so values greater than 2 do not satisfy this equation. This means the answer must be choice K.

14.5 Exit Ticket Review

2. Given integers h and k, where $k > 7$ and $3h + k = 14$, which of the following represents the solution set for h?

   F. $h \geq 7$

   G. $h \geq 0$

   H. $h \geq 2$

   J. $h \leq 0$

   K. $h \leq 2$

14.5 Exit Ticket Review

▶ Students work the third question.

3. **The correct answer is C.** First solve for x.

   $x^2 = 16$

   $x^2 - 16 = 0$

   $(x + 4)(x - 4) = 0$

   $x = -4, 4$

   Now you know the two points to mark on the number line for x, so you can narrow down your answer choices to either C or E. All you need to do is find out if the values for x are between -4 and 4, or outside of -4 and 4. Plug a value between -4 and 4, such as 0, into the inequality to see if it makes the statement true. If it does not , try a value greater than 4 or less than -4, such as 5 or -5.

   $x^2 < 16$

   $0^2 < 16$

   The number 0 works, so you know the values between -4 and 4 are part of the solution set so choice C is the correct answer.

▶ After all three questions are completed, students exchange papers. Solve the three exit items step by step on the board. Students grade using their red pens and then return papers to their classmates.

▶ After solving the three exit items, revisit the learning targets slide. Students again assess their knowledge and confidence on the same 1 to 4 scale that they used at the beginning of the lesson. Students write this number in the designated area at the start of the lesson in their workbooks, along with any comments or questions they might have.

▶ Finally, to close the lesson, have students return to the cover page of the lesson and write a caption for the picture there. The caption should be a one-sentence summary of the lesson, a main rule or tip they want to remember, or an explanation of how the picture relates to the topic. If there is additional time, students can share and compare their captions with the class.

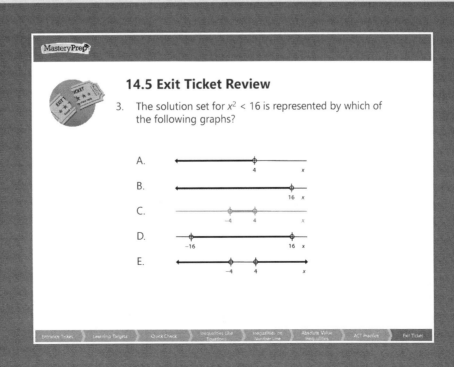

Exponents and Roots

This lesson will cover the use of exponents, including how to use them to calculate solutions to equations and how to use them in conjunction with variables to simplify expressions through multiplication and division.

ACT Standards:

A 509. Work with squares and square roots of numbers

A 510. Work with cubes and cube roots of numbers

A 511. Work with scientific notation (no questions below deal with scientific notation)

A 512. Work problems involving positive integer exponents

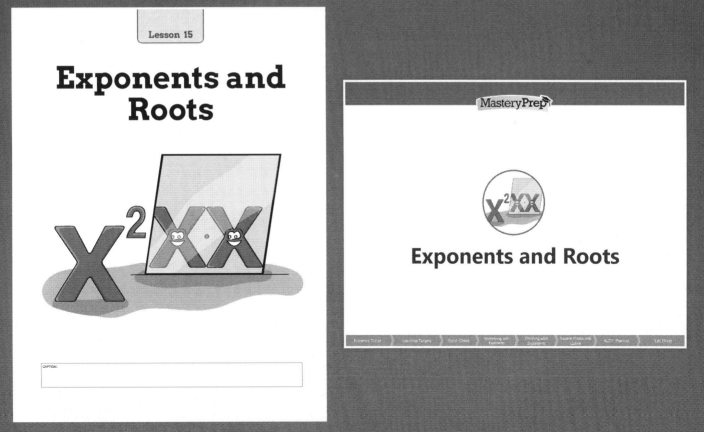

Student Page 217

15.1 Entrance Ticket

▶ Have students try the following three ACT practice questions. Students should work independently. Once the entrance ticket has been completed, review the questions with the students and have them share their answers. Give students the correct answers to the questions, as well as a step-by-step demonstration of how to solve the problems, but do not go into detailed explanation. This will serve as an introduction to the lesson content but is not intended to be the main lesson.

1. **The correct answer is E.** Solve and combine like terms.

$(3x^2y)^2 (4x^3y^2)^2$

$(9x^4y^2)(16x^6y^4)$

$144x^{10}y^6$

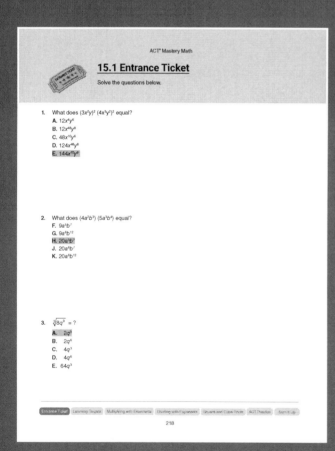

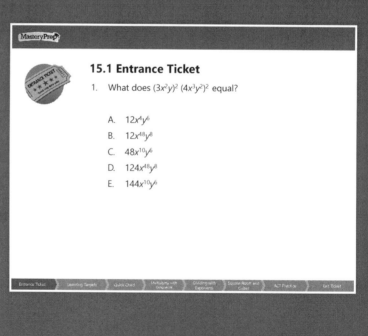

Student Page 218

15.1 Entrance Ticket

2. **The correct answer is H.** Solve and combine like terms.

$(4a^2b^3)(5a^3b^4)$

$20a^5b^7$

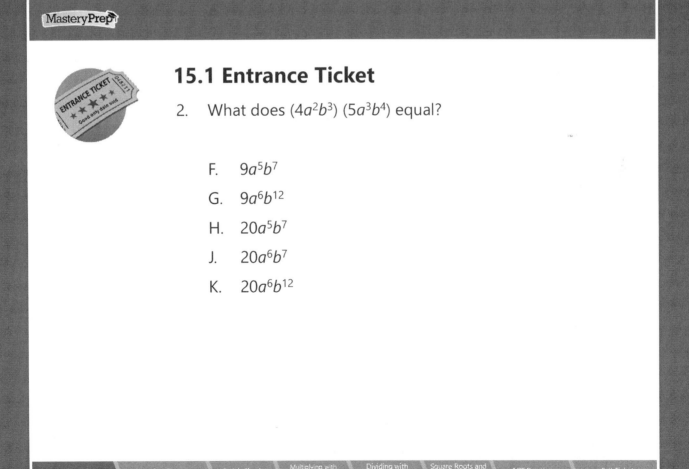

15.1 Entrance Ticket

3. **The correct answer is A.** Simplify the expression.

$$\sqrt[3]{8q^9} = \sqrt[3]{8} \cdot q^{\frac{9}{3}}$$

$$2q^3$$

15.1 Entrance Ticket

3. $\sqrt[3]{8q^9} = ?$

    A. $2q^3$

    B. $2q^6$

    C. $4q^3$

    D. $4q^6$

    E. $64q^3$

| Entrance Ticket | Learning Targets | Quick Check | Multiplying with Exponents | Dividing with Exponents | Square Roots and Cubes | ACT Practice | Exit Ticket |

15.2 Learning Targets

► Review learning targets with your students, displayed on the slide and in their workbooks.

► After reviewing the learning targets, ask students to assess their knowledge and confidence level on these targets. They should rate themselves on a scale of 1 to 4, with 1 being not confident or uncertain, and 4 being completely confident or certain. They should circle this number in the designated section of their workbooks.

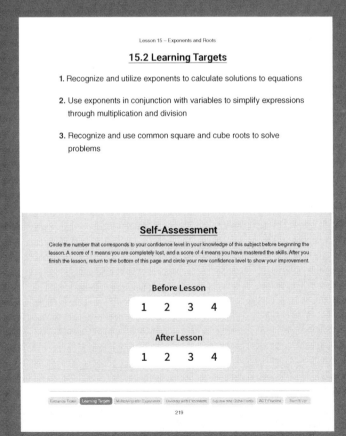

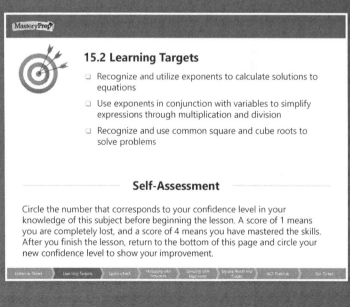

Student Page 219

15.2 Quick Check

▶ Teacher Dialogue: **What is the exponent in 2^4? What is the base?**

The exponent is 4; the base is 2.

▶ Teacher Dialogue: **Simplify 2^4.**

$2 \cdot 2 \cdot 2 \cdot 2 = 16$.

▶ Teacher Dialogue: **What is the exponent in $3x^2$? What is the base? What is the coefficient?**

The exponent is 2, the base is x, and the coefficient is 3.

▶ Teacher Dialogue: **Define *exponent*.**

<u>Exponent:</u> The power to which a number or term is raised

▶ Teacher Dialogue: **Define *base*.**

<u>Base</u>: The number at the "bottom" of an exponent, which is multiplied by itself the number of times indicated in the exponent

▶ Teacher Dialogue: **Define *squared*.**

<u>Squared:</u> A term that is raised to the second power

▶ Teacher Dialogue: **Define *cubed*.**

<u>Cubed:</u> A term that is raised to the third power

▶ Teacher Dialogue: **Define *negative exponent*.**

<u>Negative exponent:</u> An expression with an exponent that is negative

▶ Teacher Dialogue: **Define *square root*.**

<u>Square Root:</u> A value that, when used in a product two times, gives the radicand

▶ Teacher Dialogue: **Define *perfect square*.**

<u>Perfect Square:</u> An integer that can be divided into two factors that are the same integer; the result of multiplying an integer by itself

▶ Teacher Dialogue: **Define *cube root*.**

<u>Cube Root:</u> A value that, when used in a product three times, yields a given number

▶ Teacher Dialogue: **Define *perfect cube*.**

<u>Perfect Cube:</u> An integer that can be divided into three factors that are the same integer

15.3.1 Multiplying with Exponents

▸ Teacher Dialogue: **How would you write out the expression 2^5?**

$2 \cdot 2 \cdot 2 \cdot 2 \cdot 2$

▸ Teacher Dialogue: **How would you write out the expression $(2^5)(2^3)$?**

$2 \cdot 2 \cdot 2 \cdot 2 \cdot 2 \cdot 2 \cdot 2 \cdot 2$

▸ Teacher Dialogue: **How many twos is that?**

Eight

▸ Teacher Dialogue: **Rewrite 2^{5+3} using only one exponent. What does this look like written out?**

$2^8; 2 \cdot 2 \cdot 2 \cdot 2 \cdot 2 \cdot 2 \cdot 2 \cdot 2$

▸ Teacher Dialogue: **What do you notice about the second expression (2^5) (2^3), the third (2^{5+3}) and the last one (2^8) on the slide?**

They are equal. In other words: $(2^5)(2^3) = 2^{5+3} = 2^8$

They are all written out as $2 \cdot 2 \cdot 2 \cdot 2 \cdot 2 \cdot 2 \cdot 2 \cdot 2$

▸ Have students generate a rule for multiplying variables with exponents. Lead the discussion toward the general rule and then have students write the rule down in the designated portion of their workbooks:

When multiplying terms with exponents that share a common base, <u>add the exponents.</u>

Student Page 220

15.3.1 Multiplying with Exponents

▶ Show students three additional examples on the slide. Have students complete the practice questions individually, working through the problems in their workbooks.

Lesson 15 – Exponents and Roots

15.3.1 Multiplying with Exponents

1. $2^4 5^2 \cdot 2^2 5^3$

2. $(xy^7) \cdot (x^3y)$

3. $(d^2f^8g^3) \cdot (dg^2)$

Entrance Ticket | Learning Targets | Multiplying with Exponents | Dividing with Exponents | Square and Cube Roots | ACT Practice | Sum It Up

221

MasteryPrep

15.3.1 Multiplying with Exponents

1. $2^4\, 5^2 \cdot 2^2\, 5^3$
   $2^6 5^5$

2. $(xy^7) \cdot (x^3y)$
   x^4y^8

3. $(d^2f^8g^3) \cdot (dg^2)$
   $d^3f^8g^5$

Entrance Ticket | Learning Targets | Quick Check | Multiplying with Exponents | Dividing with Exponents | Square Roots and Cubes | ACT Practice | Exit Ticket

Student Page 221

15.3.1 Multiplying with Exponents

▶ Review the questions as a class. Pick one student to come up and solve each problem on the board, and then ask the class to provide feedback on the student's work. Once the class has agreed on the correct answer, move on to the next problem.

1.

$2^4 5^2 \cdot 2^2 5^3$

$2^{4+2} \cdot 5^{2+3}$

$2^6 5^5$

2.

$(xy^7) \cdot (x^3y)$

$x^{1+3} \cdot y^{7+1}$

$x^4 y^8$

3.

$(d^2 f^8 g^3) \cdot (dg^2)$

$d^{2+1} \cdot f^8 \cdot g^{3+2}$

$d^3 f^8 g^5$

15.3.1 Multiplying with Exponents

Student Page 222

▶ Next, show students the following expression:

$$(a^3)^3$$

▶ Allow a minute for students to work through their attempts to rewrite the expression using more than two exponents. The target answer is:

$$a^3a^3a^3$$

▶ Teacher Dialogue:　**How did you arrive at your answer?**

Multiply what is in the parentheses by itself three times because of the exponent outside of the parentheses (which indicates how many times the expression needs to be multiplied by itself).

▶ Instruct the class to rewrite the expression without using any exponents. The target answer is:

$$a \cdot a \cdot a \cdot a \cdot a \cdot a \cdot a \cdot a \cdot a$$

▶ Teacher Dialogue:　**How would you write this with a single exponent?**

$$a^9$$

▶ Teacher Dialogue:　**How did you arrive at your answer?**

Add the exponents when multiplying expressions with the same base.

▶ Teacher Dialogue:　**Did you notice anything interesting about the exponential relationship between $(a^3)^3$ and a^9?**

▶ Have the students come up with a rule.

▶ Then have students write the following rule in the designated space in their workbooks:

When an expression with exponents is inside parentheses and there is an exponent outside the parentheses, the exponents <u>are multiplied together.</u>

Ex: $(a^3)^3 = a^{3 \cdot 3} = a^9$

15.3.1 Multiplying with Exponents

▶ Show students three additional examples on the slide. Have students complete the practice questions individually, working through the problems in their workbooks.

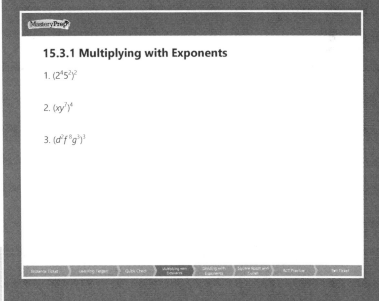

Student Page 223

15.3.1 Multiplying with Exponents

► Review the questions as a class. Pick one student to come up and solve each problem on the board, and then ask the class to provide feedback on the student's work. Once the class has agreed on the correct answer, move on to the next problem.

1.

$(2^4 5^2)^2$

$2^{4 \cdot 2} \cdot 5^{2 \cdot 2}$

$2^8 5^4$

2.

$(xy^7)^4$

$x^{1 \cdot 4} \cdot y^{7 \cdot 4}$

$x^4 y^{28}$

3.

$(d^2 f^8 g^3)^3$

$d^{2 \cdot 3} \cdot f^{8 \cdot 3} \cdot g^{3 \cdot 3}$

$d^6 f^{24} g^9$

Process of Elimination: It is essential to **eliminate wrong answers** after each step of the problem-solving process. The ACT almost always includes a few answers that will be too small or too large once you've completed a few steps. If you don't have to complete every step of the process to get the right answer choice, you will save valuable time.

15.3.2 Dividing with Exponents and Negative Exponents

▸ Show students the following expression:

▸ $$\frac{x^5 y^6}{x^3 y^3}$$

▸ Have the class rewrite the numerator and denominator using no exponents. The students should come up with:

$$\frac{xxxxxyyyyyy}{xxxyyy}$$

▸ Have the class reduce the fraction.

Students should recognize that the x and y variables that repeat on the top and bottom of the fraction cancel out, and that they can cross them out in order to reduce the fraction.

The target answer is:

$$\frac{xxyyy}{1}$$

$$x^2 y^3$$

Be sure to explain that when terms are canceled, they are actually replaced by the number 1. This does not need to be written out UNLESS all such terms with that base are canceled out, as seen in the denominator of this problem.

If students need help with this concept, remind them that $\frac{5}{5} = 1$, $\frac{13}{13} = 1$, etc.

▸ Teacher Dialogue: **Do you notice anything interesting about the reduced version, as compared to the original?**

The exponents were subtracted.

$$\frac{x^5 y^6}{x^3 y^3}$$

$$x^{5-3} y^{6-3}$$

$$x^2 y^3$$

▸ Guide the discussion toward a rule for dividing variables with exponents. Have the class write this rule in the designated space in their workbooks:

When dividing two terms with exponents that share a base, <u>subtract the exponents.</u>

Student Page 224

15.3.2 Dividing with Exponents and Negative Exponents

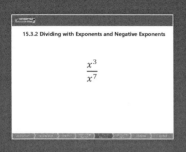

▶ Show students the following expression:

▶ $\dfrac{x^3}{x^7}$

▶ Have the class simplify the fraction.

▶ $\dfrac{x^3}{x^7}$

x^{3-7}

x^{-4}

▶ Teacher Dialogue: **What does a negative exponent mean?**

Write various student guesses on the board.

▶ Have the students rewrite $\dfrac{x^3}{x^7}$ with no exponents and then reduce.

▶ $\dfrac{xxx}{xxxxxxx}$

$\dfrac{1}{xxxx}$

$\dfrac{1}{x^4}$

▶ Guide the discussion toward a rule for dividing variables with exponents. Have the class write this rule in the designated space in their workbooks:

Negative exponents can also be written as <u>the reciprocal of the term, with a positive exponent.</u>

Ex:

$x^{-4} = \dfrac{1}{x^4}$

15.3.2 Dividing with Exponents and Negative Exponents

▶ Show students five additional examples on the slide. Have students complete the practice questions individually, working through the problems in their workbooks.

Lesson 15 – Exponents and Roots

15.3.2 Dividing with Exponents and Negative Exponents

1. $2^4 5^2 \div 2^2 5^3$

2. $(xy^7) \div (x^3 y)$

3. $(d^2 f^8 g^3) \div (dg^2)$

4. $\dfrac{x^{10}}{x^4} \div \dfrac{y^4}{y}$

5. $6x^3 yz^2 \div 3xy^2 z$

Student Page 225

MasteryPrep

15.3.2 Dividing with Exponents and Negative Exponents

1. $2^4 5^2 \div 2^2 5^3$

2. $(xy^7) \div (x^3 y)$

3. $(d^2 f^8 g^3) \div (dg^2)$

4. $\dfrac{x^{10}}{x^4} \div \dfrac{y^4}{y}$

5. $6x^3 yz^2 \div 3xy^2 z$

15.3.2 Dividing with Exponents and Negative Exponents

► Review the questions as a class. Pick one student to come up and solve each problem on the board and then ask the class to provide feedback on the student's work. Once the class has agreed on the correct answer, move on to the next problem.

1. $2^4 5^2 \div 2^2 5^3$

$2^{4-2} 5^{2-3}$

$2^2 5^{-1}$

$4 \cdot \dfrac{1}{5^1}$

$4 \cdot \dfrac{1}{5}$

$\dfrac{4}{5}$

2. $(xy^7) \div (x^3 y)$

$x^{1-3} y^{7-1}$

$x^{-2} y^6$

$\dfrac{y^6}{x^2}$

3. $(d^2 f^8 g^3) \div (dg^2)$

$d^{2-1} f^8 g^{3-2}$

$df^8 g$

4. $\dfrac{x^{10}}{x^4} \div \dfrac{y^4}{y}$

$x^{10-4} \div y^{4-1}$

$\dfrac{x^6}{y^3}$

5. $6x^3 yz^2 \div 3xy^2 z$

$\dfrac{6}{3} x^{3-1} y^{1-2} z^{2-1}$

$2x^2 y^{-1} z$

$\dfrac{2x^2 z}{y}$

15.3.3 Square and Cube Roots

▶ On the slide, show a square with one side labeled 7 km. Ask a student to suggest a crop a farmer might plant. Tell students that this is a square field and a farmer wants to know how much area he can use to plant his crop.

▶ Ask another student for a method to determine the field's area, calculated in km^2.

   Multiply two sides together to get 49 km^2

   Be sure students square the units as well.

▶ In the first square in their workbooks, students write both the area and the side measurement.

▶ Teacher Dialogue: **Multiplying a number by itself is called** *squaring* **the number because multiplying the side of a geometric square by itself gives the area of the square.**

▶ Show the next slide with 144 km^2 inside a square. Ask the class to determine the length of each side of the square. Call on students to either state or display their answer and explain how they solved the problem.

   Each side is 12 km

▶ Students write both the side measurement and the area in the next square in their workbooks. Explain that those who got the correct answer took the square root of the area to get the side length of the square.

▶ Repeat the process above with a few more side lengths and areas, listed on the slides. Students solve these problems in their workbooks. Review answers with the class.

   If area is 36 km^2, side length is 6 km.

Student Page 226

15.3.3 Square and Cube Roots

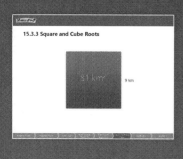

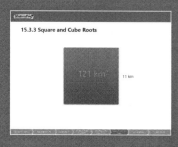

If a side length is 9 km, the area is 81 km².

If the area is 64 km², the side length is 8 km.

If a side length is 11 km, the area is 121 km².

If the area is 100 km², the side length is 10 km.

15.3.3 Square and Cube Roots

▸ Show the next slide. For one minute, students discuss in pairs whether the number $\sqrt{54}$ can be factored.

▸ For one minute, pairs discuss and prepare to offer a factored version of $\sqrt{54}$. After time is up, lead a discussion with the class toward the correct answer.

$$\sqrt{54} = \sqrt{(9 \cdot 6)} = \sqrt{9} \cdot \sqrt{6} = 3\sqrt{6}$$

▸ Students copy these calculations in the space provided in their workbooks.

▸ Teacher Dialogue: **A radicand may be broken down into its factors, and any factor that is a perfect square may be simplified and factored *out* of the radicand.**

▸ Show the cube with the side labeled 2 m. Ask students to volunteer a practical use for such a cube (ex: furniture, storage bin), then tell students that the cube's owner needs to determine its volume (how much it holds or how much space it takes up). Students write the measurements on the cube in their workbooks and calculate the volume.

$2 \cdot 2 \cdot 2 = 8 \text{ m}^3$

Be sure students cube the units as well.

▸ Teacher Dialogue: **Multiplying a number by itself three times is called *cubing* the number because multiplying a side of a geometric square by itself three times gives the volume of the cube.**

▸ Show the next slide of the cube, labeled 64 m³ inside. The same pairs as earlier together determine the length of each side of the cube. Students write the measurements and show their calculations in their workbooks.

Side length is 4 m

▸ Explain to the students that those who got the correct answer took the cube root of the area to get the side length.

> **Perfect Squares:** The square root of **any** real number can be determined by using a calculator, but you will move more quickly on the test if you know the perfect squares of numbers from 1 to 12.

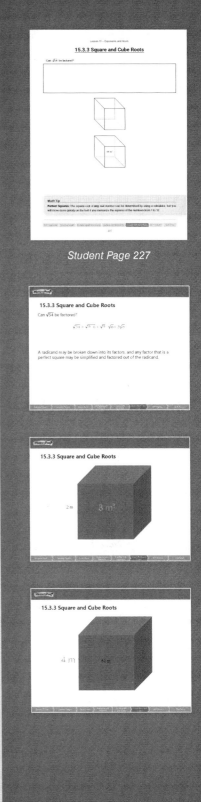

Student Page 227

15.4 ACT Practice

▶ Show students three additional examples on the slide. Have students complete the practice questions individually, working through the problems in their workbooks.

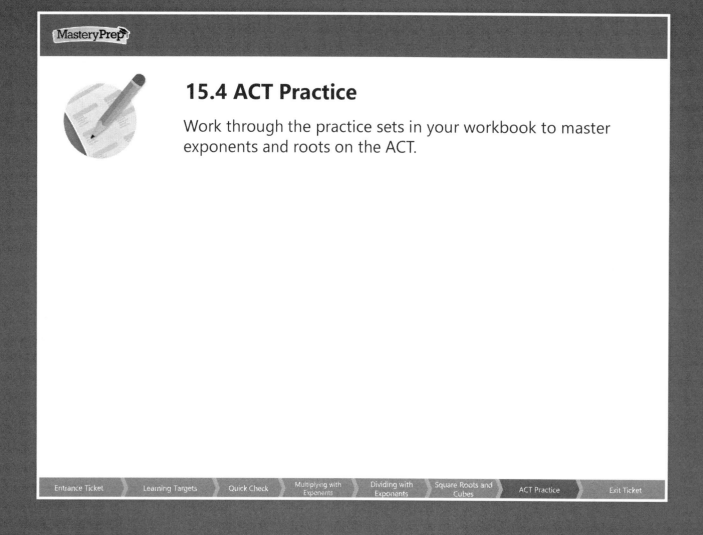

15.4.1 Set One

1. Which of the following expressions is equivalent to $-5a^3(9a^2 - 3a^4)$?
   A. $-45a^6 - 15a^{12}$
   B. $-45a^6 + 15a^{12}$
   C. $-45a^5 - 15a^7$
   D. $-45a^5 + 15a^7$
   E. $-30a$

1. **The correct answer is D.** Simplify the expression.

   $-5a^3(9a^2 - 3a^4)$

   $-45a^5 + 15a^7$

2. The expression $(5xy^3)(2x^2y)$ is equivalent to:
   F. $7x^2y^4$
   G. $7x^3y^3$
   H. $10x^2y^3$
   J. $10x^2y^4$
   K. $10x^3y^4$

2. **The correct answer is K.** Simplify the expression by combining like terms.

   $(5xy^3)(2x^2y)$

   $10x^3y^4$

3. The expression $(x^8)^{16}$ is equivalent to:
   A. x^{-8}
   B. x^2
   C. x^8
   D. x^{24}
   E. x^{128}

3. **The correct answer is E.** Simplify the expression.

   $(x^8)^{16}$

   x^{128}

15.4.2 Set Two

4. What is $4x^3 \cdot 6x^5$?
 F. $10x^2$
 G. $10x^8$
 H. $10x^{15}$
 J. $24x^8$
 K. $24x^{15}$

4. The correct answer is J. Simplify the expression.

$4x^3 \cdot 6x^5$

$24x^8$

5. The expression $(7m^2n)(6mn^3)$ is equivalent to:
 A. $13m^2n^3$
 B. $13m^3n^4$
 C. $42mn$
 D. $42m^2n^3$
 E. $42m^3n^4$

5. The correct answer is E. Simplify the expression and combine like terms.

$(7m^2n)(6mn^3)$

$42m^3n^4$

6. The expression $3a^2b^3 \cdot 5a^3b^2 \cdot 4b^2$ is equal to:
 F. $12a^5b^7$
 G. $12a^6b^{12}$
 H. $60a^5b^7$
 J. $60a^6b^{12}$
 K. $60a^6b^7$

6. The correct answer is H. Simplify the expression and combine like terms.

$3a^2b^3 \cdot 5a^3b^2 \cdot 4b^2$

$60a^5b^7$

15.4.3 Set Three

7. If $x \neq 0$, then $\dfrac{x^9}{x^3}$ equals:
   A. 1
   B. 3
   C. x^2
   D. x^3
   E. x^6

7. **The correct answer is E.** Simplify the expression.

   $$\dfrac{x^9}{x^3} = x^6$$

8. What does $3a^3 \cdot 6a^5$ equal?
   F. $9a^2$
   G. $9a^8$
   H. $9a^{15}$
   J. $18a^8$
   K. $18a^{15}$

8. **The correct answer is J.** Simplify the expression.

   $3a^3 \cdot 6a^5$

   $18a^8$

9. Calculate $\dfrac{3^2 - 1^3}{4^2 - 1^3}$.
   A. $\dfrac{1}{2}$

   B. $\dfrac{8}{15}$

   C. $\dfrac{9}{16}$

   D. $\dfrac{10}{17}$

   E. $\dfrac{2}{3}$

9. **The correct answer is B.** Simplify the expression and solve.

   $$\dfrac{3^2 - 1^3}{4^2 - 1^3} = \dfrac{9 - 1}{16 - 1} = \dfrac{8}{15}$$

15.4.4 Set Four

10. Simplify $\sqrt{24} - \sqrt{54}$.

   F. $-\sqrt{6}$

   G. -6

   H. 6

   J. $6\sqrt{6}$

   K. $\sqrt{78}$

10. The correct answer is F. Simplify the expression.

$$\sqrt{4} \cdot \sqrt{6} - \sqrt{9} \cdot \sqrt{6}$$

$$2\sqrt{6} - 3\sqrt{6}$$

$$-\sqrt{6}$$

---

11. Given $\dfrac{2\sqrt{11}}{11} = \dfrac{2\sqrt{11}}{p\sqrt{11}}$, what is the value p?

   F. 1

   G. $\sqrt{11}$

   H. 11

   J. 22

   K. 121

11. The correct answer is G. Solve by isolating p.

$$\frac{2\sqrt{11}}{11} = \frac{2\sqrt{11}}{p\sqrt{11}}$$

$$2p \cdot 11 = 22\sqrt{11}$$

$$22p = 22\sqrt{11}$$

$$p = \sqrt{11}$$

---

12. If x is a real number, what is $\sqrt[3]{x^{27}}$ equivalent to?

   F. x^{-9}

   G. $x^{\frac{1}{9}}$

   H. $|x^9|$

   J. x^9

   K. x^{24}

12. The correct answer is J. Simplify the expression.

$$\sqrt[3]{x^{27}} = x^{\frac{27}{3}}$$

$$x^9$$

15.4.5 Set Five

13. Find y in terms of x for $\sqrt{y} - \sqrt{x} = 8\sqrt{x}$, where both y and x are positive real numbers.
 A. $81x$
 B. $64x$
 C. $9x$
 D. $8x$
 E. $3x$

13. The correct answer is A. Solve by isolating y.

$$\sqrt{y} - \sqrt{x} = 8\sqrt{x}$$

$$\sqrt{y} = 9\sqrt{x}$$

Square both parts of the equation.

$$y = 81x$$

14. If $a \neq 0$, then $(a^{-4})^3 = ?$
 F. $\dfrac{1}{a^{12}}$
 G. $\dfrac{1}{a}$
 H. a^7
 J. a^{12}
 K. a^{64}

14. The correct answer is F. Simplify the expression.

$$(a^{-4})^3$$

$$a^{-12}$$

$$\frac{1}{a^{12}}$$

15. If a and b both $\neq 0$, then $\left(\dfrac{a^{-3}}{b}\right)(a^3b^3)$ is equivalent to:
 A. $a^{-9}b^3$
 B. $a^{-9}b^2$
 C. $a^{-9}b^{-2}$
 D. b^3
 E. b^2

15. The correct answer is E. Simplify the expression.

$$\left(\frac{a^{-3}}{b}\right)(a^3b^3)$$

$$\frac{a^3b^3}{a^3b}$$

$$a^{3-3}b^{3-1}$$

$$a^0b^2$$

$$b^2$$

Lesson 15 – Exponents and Roots

Sum It Up

Exponents and Roots

Exponent
The power to which a number or term is raised
Ex: 3 in the expression x^3

Base
The number or variable at the "bottom" of an exponent, which is multiplied by itself the number of times indicated by the exponent
Ex: x in the expression x^3

Coefficient
The number before the base and exponent
Ex: 7 in the expression $7x^3$

Squared
A term that is raised to the second power
Ex: "five squared" is written 5^2 and "x squared" is written x^2

Cubed
A term that is raised to the third power
Ex: "five cubed" is written 5^3 and "x cubed" is written x^3

Negative Exponent
An expression with an exponent that is negative
Ex: 5^{-3} and x^{-3}

Rules for Operations with Exponents

When **multiplying** terms with exponents that have the same base, **add** the exponents.

Ex: $3x^3 \cdot 2x^4 = 6x^{3+4} = 6x^7$

When **raising an expression** with exponents to another power, **multiply** the exponents.

Ex: $(y^3)^5 = y^{3 \cdot 5} = y^{15}$

When **dividing** terms with exponents that have the same base, **subtract** the exponents.

Ex: $\dfrac{a^9}{a^4} = a^{9-4} = a^5$

Entrance Ticket | Learning Targets | Multiplying with Exponents | Dividing with Exponents | Square and Cube Roots | ACT Practice | Sum It Up

15.5 Exit Ticket

▶ Students complete the three questions on their exit ticket.

Students are timed 3 minutes for the three questions (60 seconds per question). There is no break between questions.

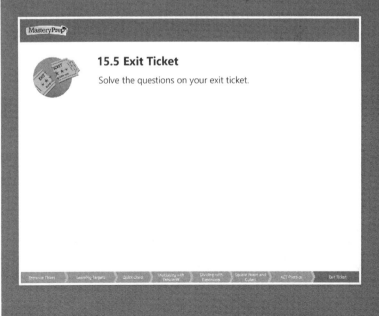

15.5 Exit Ticket Review

▶ Students work the first question.

1. **The correct answer is A.** Add the exponents. $2 + 2 + 2 + 2 = 8$, so the answer is a^8.

15.5 Exit Ticket Review

1. If a is a real number, then $a^2 \cdot a^2 \cdot a^2 \cdot a^2$ is equal to:

    A. a^8

    B. a^{16}

    C. $4a^2$

    D. $2a^4$

    E. $(4a)^2$

Entrance Ticket | Learning Targets | Quick Check | Multiplying with Exponents | Dividing with Exponents | Square Roots and Cubes | ACT Practice | Exit Ticket

15.5 Exit Ticket Review

▶ Students work the second question.

2. **The correct answer is J.** First, find the value of a by taking the square root of both sides of the equation.

$a^2 = 16$

$a = 4$

Now, plug 4 in for a in the expression.

$a^3 + \sqrt{a}$

$(4)^3 + \sqrt{4}$

$64 + 2 = 66$

15.5 Exit Ticket Review

2. If a is positive and $a^2 = 16$, what is $a^3 + \sqrt{a}$?

   F.   4

   G. 10

   H. 14

   J.   66

   K. 68

Entrance Ticket | Learning Targets | Quick Check | Multiplying with Exponents | Dividing with Exponents | Square Roots and Cubes | ACT Practice | Exit Ticket

15.5 Exit Ticket Review

► Students work the third question.

3. **The correct answer is A.** Simplify the expression.

$$\frac{x^4 y^3 z^2}{4x^2 y^5 z^3}$$

$$\frac{x^2}{4y^2 z}$$

► After all three questions are completed, students exchange papers. Solve the three exit items step by step on the board. Students grade using their red pens and then return papers to their classmates.

► After solving the three exit items, revisit the learning targets slide. Students again assess their knowledge and confidence on the same 1 to 4 scale that they used at the beginning of the lesson. Students write this number in the designated area at the start of the lesson in their workbooks, along with any comments or questions they might have.

► Finally, to close the lesson, have students return to the cover page of the lesson and write a caption for the picture there. The caption should be a one-sentence summary of the lesson, a main rule or tip they want to remember, or an explanation of how the picture relates to the topic. If there is additional time, students can share and compare their captions with the class.

Angle Properties

This lesson will cover advanced angle properties. Students will learn to use properties of angles and parallel lines to find angle measurements in complicated figures and shapes.

ACT Standards:

G 301. Exhibit some knowledge of the angles associated with parallel lines

G 401. Use properties of parallel lines to find the measure of an angle

G 402. Exhibit knowledge of basic angle properties and special sums of angle measures (e.g., 90°, 180°, and 360°)

G 501. Use several angle properties to find an unknown angle measure

G 705. Solve multistep geometry problems that involve integrating concepts, planning, and/or visualization

Student Page 235

16.1 Entrance Ticket

▶ Have students try the following three ACT practice questions. Students should work independently. Once the entrance ticket has been completed, review the questions with the students and have them share their answers. Give students the correct answers to the questions, as well as a step-by-step demonstration of how to solve the problems, but do not go into detailed explanation. This will serve as an introduction to the lesson content but is not intended to be the main lesson.

1. **The correct answer is B.** A trapezoid has one pair of parallel sides (a kite does not), so choice A can be eliminated. A kite's diagonals, sides, and angles are not necessarily all congruent, eliminating choices C, D, and E. However, a kite's diagonals are always perpendicular, so choice B is the correct answer.

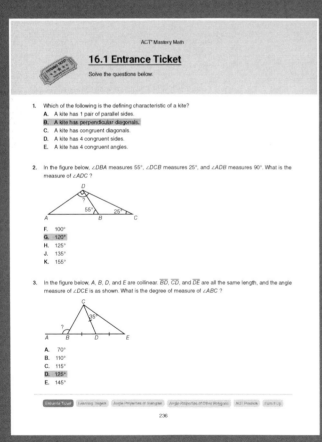

Student Page 236

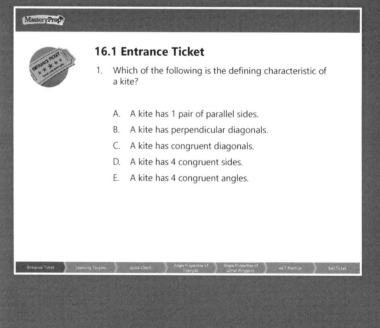

16.1 Entrance Ticket

2. **The correct answer is G.** Use the properties of triangles to calculate the missing angle. The sum of the interior angles of a triangle is 180°.

    ∠DAB = 180° − 90° − 55° = 35°

    ∠ADC = 180° − 35° − 25° = 120°

3. **The correct answer is D.** Use the properties of isosceles triangles to calculate the missing angle. ∠CED is also equal to 35°, so ∠CDE = 180° − 35° − 35° = 110°. ∠CDB is thus equal to 180° − 110° = 70°. ∠DBC and ∠DCB are equal, and so are each equal to $\frac{110°}{2}$ = 55°. ∠ABC is thus equal to 180° − 55° = 125°.

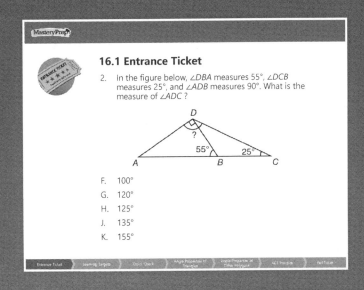

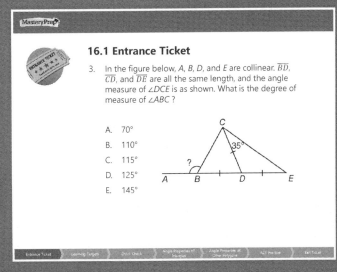

16.2 Learning Targets

▶ Review learning targets with your students, displayed on the slide and in their workbooks.

▶ After reviewing the learning targets, ask students to assess their knowledge and confidence level on these targets. They should rate themselves on a scale of 1 to 4, with 1 being not confident or uncertain, and 4 being completely confident or certain. They should circle this number in the designated section of their workbooks.

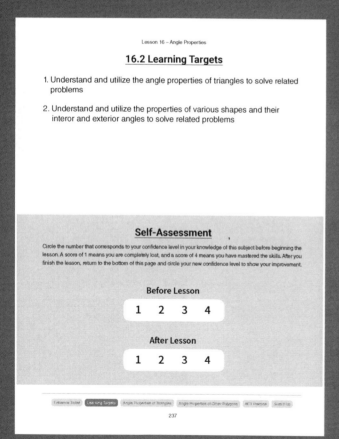

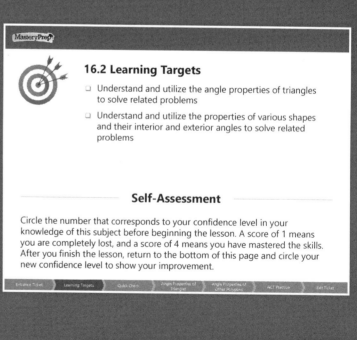

Student Page 237

16.2 Quick Check

▶ Show students the following shapes on the slides and ask for volunteers to name what they represent. Then show students the correct label and definition.

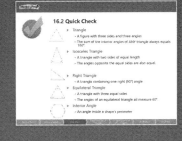

Triangle: A figure with three sides and three angles

The sum of the interior angles of ANY triangle always equals 180°.

Isosceles Triangle: A triangle with two sides of equal length

The angles opposite the equal sides are also equal.

Right Triangle: A triangle containing one right (90°) angle

Equilateral Triangle: A triangle with three equal sides

The angles of an equilateral triangle all measure 60°.

Interior Angles: An angle inside a shape's perimeter

Exterior Angles: An angle outside a shape's perimeter

Congruency (Angles and Sides): Identical in size, measure, or length

Quadrilateral: A four-sided polygon with four angles

Types include: trapezoids, parallelograms, rectangles, squares, rhombuses, etc.

Trapezoid: A quadrilateral with only one pair of parallel sides

Isosceles Trapezoid: A special case of a trapezoid in which the base angles and two sides are equal

Parallelogram: A quadrilateral whose opposite sides are parallel

Rhombus: A parallelogram with equal sides

Diagonal: A line joining two opposite corners of a quadrilateral

Pentagon: A figure with five sides and five angles

Hexagon: A figure with six sides and six angles

16.3.1 Angle Properties of Triangles

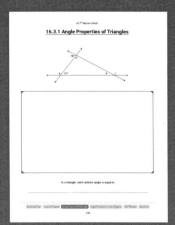

Student Page 238

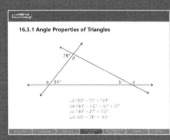

▶ Show the figure on the slide, also in the student workbook.

▶ Teacher Dialogue: **What is the value of ∠d ?**

▶ Have students pair up based on where they are seated and take 30 seconds to discuss the answer with their partners. Students should use the box below the figure to show their work. After the time is up, call on a student to provide their answer and describe how they arrived at it.

$180° − 78° = 102°$

This can be calculated this because the two angles are supplementary.

▶ Have students write this down next their calculations in their workbooks.

▶ Instruct students, in their pairs, to take 90 seconds and calculate the values of ∠a, ∠b, and ∠c, writing them down on the figure in their workbooks.

▶ Come back together as a class to review and discuss the answers. Call on one pair per angle, soliciting feedback from the class until the correct answer is agreed upon. Make sure to ask the pair that states the correct answer to explain how they arrived at it and have students write down the correct answers in their workbooks.

∠a: $180° − 51° = 129°$

Can be calculated because the two angles are supplementary

∠b: $180° − 102° − 51° = 27°$

Can be calculated because the total angles in a triangle add up to 180° (sum of the interior angles rule)

∠c: $180° − 27° = 153°$

Can be calculated because the two angles are supplementary

▶ Teacher Dialogue: **Do you notice anything interesting about the measures of exterior angles c and a, other than that they are supplementary to 51° and ∠b ?**

Each exterior angle is equal to the sum of the two interior angles farthest away.

Ex: ∠c = ∠d + measure of the angle supplementary to ∠a

$∠c = 102° + (180° − 129°) = 102° + 51° = 153°$

▶ Show students the rule on the slide and have them copy it into their workbooks in the space at the bottom of the page.

In a triangle, each exterior angle is equal to the sum of the two interior angles farthest away.

16.3.1 Angle Properties of Triangles

▶ Show the figure on the slide, also in the student workbook.

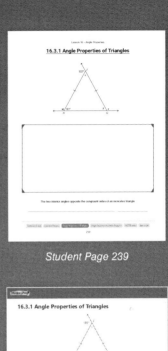

Student Page 239

▶ Teacher Dialogue: **What do the dashes here represent?**

The dashes mean that the two lines are congruent.

▶ Teacher Dialogue: **What is the measure of ∠y ?**

▶ Give students 30 seconds to discuss possible answers with their partners, along with the justification for their answer. Allow a representative from each pair to offer their guess, writing each unique guess on the board. Reveal the answer and have one of the pairs that guessed correctly explain how they arrived at their answer.

△GHJ is isosceles, so ∠y = 61°

▶ Tell students to work with their partners and try to propose a possible math rule for the interior angles of an isosceles triangle. Give students 2 minutes to observe, discuss, and propose a rule for interior angles of an isosceles triangle.

▶ Show them the rule on the slide and have them copy it into their workbooks in the space at the bottom of the page.

The two interior angles opposite the congruent sides of an isosceles triangle are also congruent.

▶ Teacher Dialogue: **What is the measure of ∠v ?**

Students should recognize that it is supplementary to the angle measuring 122° so:

∠v = 180° − 122°

∠v = 58°

▶ Give students 1 minute to individually fill in the remaining missing angles in △GHJ: ∠w and ∠x. Review and discuss the correct answers as a class. Call on a volunteer to offer an answer for each angle measure, along with an explanation.

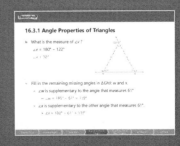

∠w is supplementary to the angle that measures 61°, so = 180° − 61° = 119°

∠x is supplementary to the other angle that measures 61° (since this is an isosceles triangle, these two angles are equal), so = 180° − 61° = 119°

16.3.2 Angle Properties of Other Polygons

▸ Display the shapes on the slide, also in student workbooks.

▸ Ask the class to identify the name of each shape. Have them label each shape in their workbooks.

   square, rhombus, rectangle, trapezoid, and parallelogram.

▸ Teacher Dialogue: **What is the sum of the interior angles in each shape?**

   360°

▸ Have students write the rule down in the designated section of their workbooks.

   The sum of the interior angles of any quadrilateral is 360°.

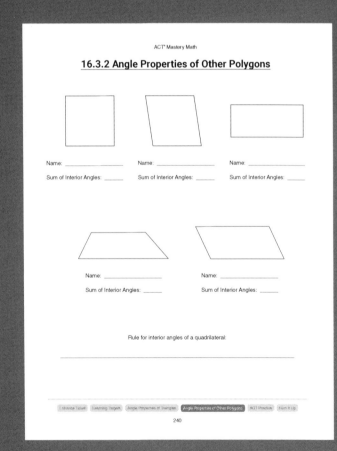

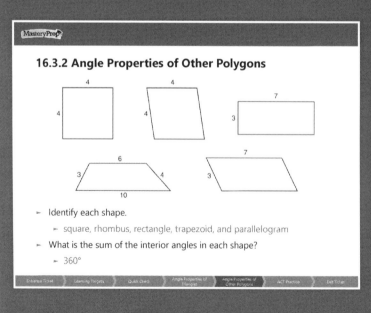

Student Page 240

16.3.2 Angle Properties of Other Polygons

▸ Show the figures on the next slide (parallelogram, rhombus, and trapezoid) and instruct students to draw them in to the boxes provided in the workbook.

▸ Have students work individually to label the missing three interior angle measures in the rhombus, parallelogram, and trapezoid. Give students 2-3 minutes to work on the problems.

▸ Point out the 83° angle in the image on the slide. Since the lines in this figure are parallel, any angles that are next to one another will add up to 180°.

▸ After this explanation, call on students to provide their answers to the interior angle measures of the first two diagrams.

Rhombus

The obtuse angle = 180° − 83° = 97°

The interior angles are thus 83°, 83°, 97°, and 97°

Parallelogram

The acute angle = 180° − 124° = 56°

The interior angles are thus 124°, 124°, 56°, and 56°

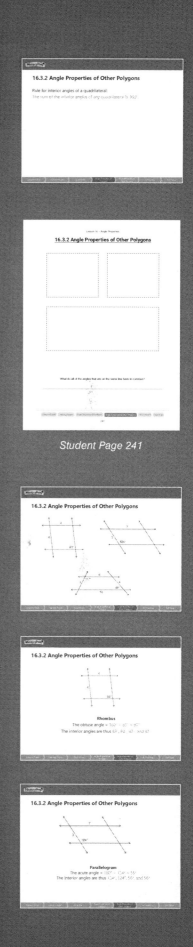

Student Page 241

435

16.3.2 Angle Properties of Other Polygons

▶ Explain to students that lines 3 and 4 in the trapezoid are NOT parallel, so the scenario here will be slightly different. Since the top and bottom lines are parallel, however, the adjacent angles along the sides are supplementary.

Trapezoid

The angle sharing a side with the 48° angle = 180° − 48° = 132°

The angle sharing a side with the 117° angle = 180° − 117° = 63°

The interior angles are thus 48°, 132°, 117°, and 63°

Reinforce to the class that in each figure, the rules governing parallel lines with a transversal apply.

▶ Teacher Dialogue: **Do you notice anything interesting about the angles that share a side in every figure?**

The sum of the angles = 180°

▶ Have students write this in the designated section of their workbooks.

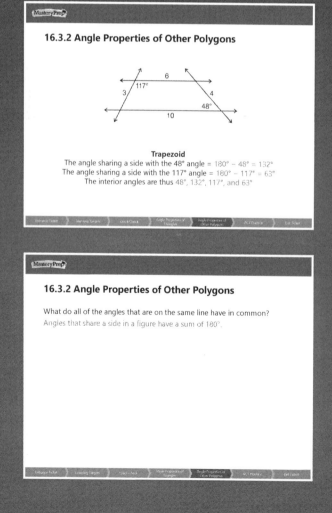

16.3.2 Angle Properties of Other Polygons

▶ Display the next slide showing diagonal lines drawn on the interior of each of the five original shapes (additional blank versions of the shapes also in the workbooks). Show students the following questions on the slide, which will also be written in their workbooks.

▶ Refer students the questions listed in the workbook. Give students 5 minutes to discuss the questions with their pairs, making educated guesses for each. Come back together as a class, and ask volunteers to answer each question. Ask the class for feedback until the correct answer is determined. Then have students write down the correct answers in their workbooks as they are reviewed.

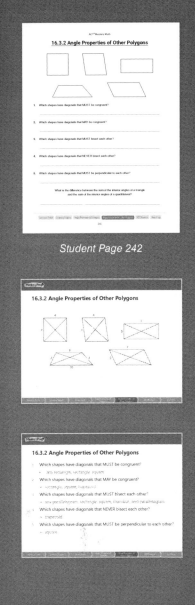

Student Page 242

1. Which shapes have diagonals that MUST be congruent?

   any rectangle: rectangle, square

2. Which shapes have diagonals that MAY be congruent?

   rectangle, square, trapezoid

3. Which shapes have diagonals that MUST bisect each other?

   any parallelogram: rectangle, square, rhombus and parallelogram

4. Which shapes have diagonals that NEVER bisect each other?

   trapezoid

5. Which shapes have diagonals that MUST be perpendicular to each other?

   square

The purpose of this exercise is to get students to think critically about the shapes and what each manipulation implies as far as measurements go. Students often get confused and overwhelmed when given a web of intersecting lines and many angles to calculate on the ACT. The point is to guide them into recognizing shapes within those lines and using common sense to think about what the lines and angles throughout them could measure.

▶ Teacher Dialogue: **What is the difference between the sum of the interior angles of a triangle and the sum of the interior angles of a quadrilateral?**

The interior angles of a triangle add up to 180°, while the interior angles of a quadrilateral add up to 360°.

▶ Have students write this down in the relevant section of their workbooks.

▶ Teacher Dialogue: **Based on this, what do you think the sum of all angles of a five-sided shape, or pentagon, is?**

The interior angles of a pentagon add up to 540°

▶ Have students write this in the designated portion of their workbooks.

16.3.2 Angle Properties of Other Polygons

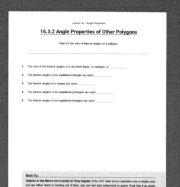

Student Page 243

▶ Teacher Dialogue: **Can you come up with a rule about the sum of interior angles of a polygon?**

▶ Lead a discussion and call on a few different students to offer their answers. Once the target answer is found, have students write it down in the designated section of their workbooks:

Each time a side is added to a shape, the sum of the interior angles increases by 180°.

▶ Refer students to the question on the workbook page. Give students 1–2 minutes to work on the problems individually, writing down the answers in their workbooks.

▶ Come back together as a class and call on a student to provide an answer and explanation for each question.

1. The sum of the interior angles of a six-sided figure, or hexagon, is…
    540° + 180° = 720°.

2. The interior angles of an equilateral triangle are each…
    180 ÷ 3 = 60°.

3. The interior angles of a square are each…
    360 ÷ 4 = 90°.

4. The interior angles of an equilateral pentagon are each…
    540 ÷ 5 = 108°.

5. The interior angles of an equilateral hexagon are each…
    720 ÷ 6 = 120°.

Objects in the Mirror Are Exactly as They Appear: If the ACT asks students to calculate a lot of angles and they are either stuck or running out of time, students can use their judgment to make a guess. They should trust that if an angle looks small, it is almost always less than 90°, and if an angle looks big, it is almost always more than 90°. Students should eliminate, mark, and move.

16.4 ACT Practice

▶ Have students work on questions from the ACT practice sets here. Pacing should be 3 minutes per practice set or 60 seconds per question.

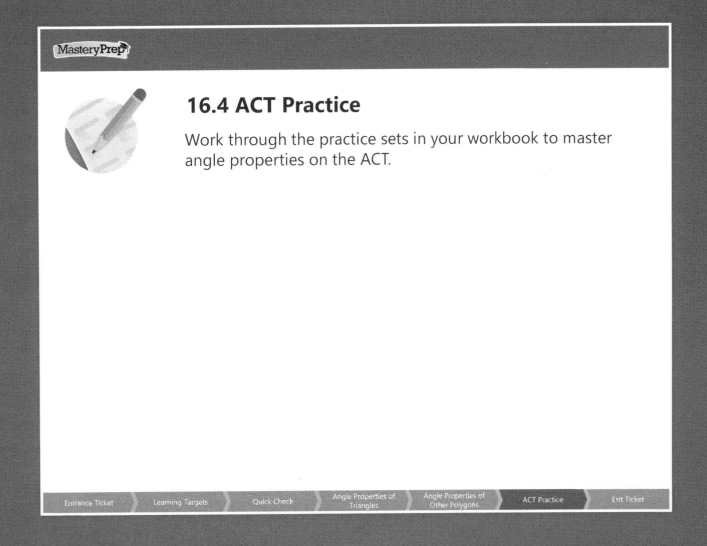

MasteryPrep

16.4 ACT Practice

Work through the practice sets in your workbook to master angle properties on the ACT.

Entrance Ticket Learning Targets Quick Check Angle Properties of Triangles Angle Properties of Other Polygons ACT Practice Exit Ticket

16.4.1 Set One

1. In △QRS, shown below, $\overline{SQ} \cong \overline{SR}$, and the measure of ∠S is 136°. What is the measure of ∠Q ?

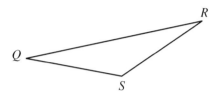

A. 11°
B. 22°
C. 44°
D. 54°
E. 68°

1. The correct answer is B. Use the properties of isosceles triangles to calculate the measure of ∠Q.

180° − 136° = 44°. ∠Q is half of 44°, which is 22°.

---

2. In the figure below, $\overline{AB}$ is congruent to $\overline{BC}$, and $\overline{AD}$ intersects $\overline{BE}$ at C. What is the measure of ∠B ?

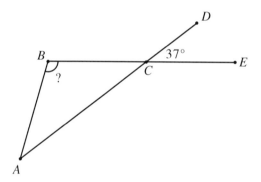

F. 23°
G. 37°
H. 74°
J. 106°
K. 143°

2. The correct answer is J. Use the properties of isosceles triangles to solve. ∠BCA is congruent to ∠DCE by vertical angles. ∠BAC is congruent to ∠BCA, so both are 37°. The measure of ∠B is then given by 180 − 37 − 37 = 106°.

---

3. In △QRS, ∠R and ∠S are congruent, and the measure of ∠Q is 128°. What is the measure of ∠S ?

A. 21°
B. 26°
C. 52°
D. 64°
E. 128°

3. The correct answer is B. Use the properties of isosceles triangles to calculate the measure of ∠S.

180° − 128° = 52°. ∠S is half of 52°, which is 26°.

16.4.2 Set Two

4. For $\triangle ABC$ below, points D and E are on the sides of the triangle. If $\overline{AB}$ is parallel to $\overline{ED}$, what is the measure of $\angle EDB$?

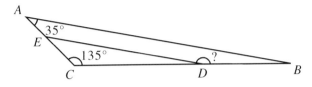

F. $85°$
G. $100°$
H. $135°$
J. $145°$
K. $170°$

4. **The correct answer is K.** Use the properties of parallel lines to solve. Since $\angle EAB$ is $35°$, $\angle DEC$ is also $35°$. The measure of $\angle EDC$ is equal to $180° − 135° − 35° = 10°$. Since $\angle EDB$ is supplementary, it is $180° − 10° = 170°$.

5. Shown below are the triangle $\triangle BCD$ and the collinear points A, B, and D. The measure of $\angle C$ is $73°$, the measure of $\angle ABC$ is $(12z)°$, and the measure of $\angle DBC$ is $(6z)°$. What is the measure of $\angle D$?

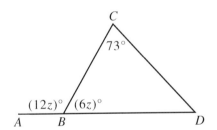

A. $21°$
B. $47°$
C. $60°$
D. $120°$
E. $133°$

5. **The correct answer is B.** Solve for z. Use this value to find the measure of $\angle D$.

$12z + 6z = 180$

$z = 10$

$6z = 60$

$\angle D = 180° − 60° − 73° = 47°$.

6. In $\triangle ABC$, $\angle A$ measures exactly $88°$, and $\angle B$ measures greater than $51°$. Which of the following best describes the measure of $\angle C$?

F. Less than $41°$
G. Greater than $41°$
H. Equal to $37°$
J. Equal to $139°$
K. Equal to $41°$

6. **The correct answer is F.** Since the interior angles of a triangle sum to $180°$, $\angle C$ measures, at most, $180° − 88° − 51° = 41°$. So, $\angle C$ must be less than $41°$.

16.4.3 Set Three

7. The blueprint of Jonathan's rectangular farm divided into 6 triangular sections is shown below. The 2 triangles that do not share an edge with the rectangle are congruent ($\triangle ABE \cong \triangle CBD$) and will hold a different crop than the other 4 triangles. The blueprint includes the measures of $\angle ABE$, $\angle CBD$, and $\angle BCD$. What is the measure of $\angle AEB$?

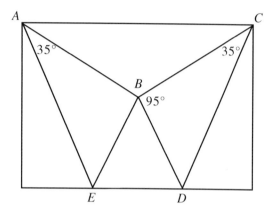

A. 35°
B. 50°
C. 95°
D. 130°
E. 145°

7. **The correct answer is B.** Since the triangles are congruent, the measure of $\angle AEB$ is equal to the measure of $\angle CDB$, which is equal to $180° - 35° - 95° = 50°$.

8. The figure below is made from a trapezoid, $ABCD$, with congruent sides, $\overline{AB}$ and $\overline{DC}$, and an equilateral triangle, $\triangle CDE$. What is the the measure of $\angle ADE$?

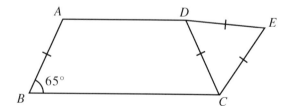

F. 235°
G. 185°
H. 175°
J. 125°
K. 115°

8. **The correct answer is H.** First, calculate the measure of $\angle ADC$.

$$\angle ADC = \frac{360° - 65° - 65°}{2} = 115°$$

Since triangle CDE is equilateral, $\angle EDC$ is 60°. $\angle ADE$ is thus equivalent to:

$115° + 60° = 175°$

Student Page 246

9. In the figure below, the measures of 5 angles of hexagon *ABCDE* are given. What is the measure of ∠E ?

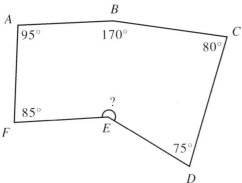

A. 95°
B. 170°
C. 180°
D. 215°
E. 235°

9. **The correct answer is D.** The sum of the interior angles of a hexagon is equal to 720°, so the measure of ∠E is equal to:

720° − 170° − 80° − 75° − 85° − 95° = 215°

Shown below is the right triangle $\triangle ABC$ within the rectangle $ABCD$ with the given dimensions.

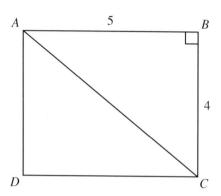

10. Which of the following statements is true regarding the measures of the interior angles of $ABCD$?

(Note: $m\angle ABC$ represents the degree measure of $\angle ABC$.)

F. $m\angle ACB = m\angle ABC$
G. $m\angle ACB = m\angle ACD$
H. $m\angle ACD + m\angle BAC = 90°$
J. $m\angle ACB + m\angle BAC + m\angle ABC = 360°$
K. $m\angle ACB + m\angle BAC + m\angle ACD + m\angle DAC = 180°$

10. The correct answer is K. $\angle D$ and $\angle B$ are both 90°. Since $\angle A$ and $\angle C$ are also both 90°, they add up to 180°. $\angle A$ is equal to $m\angle BAC + m\angle DAC$ and $\angle C$ is equal to $m\angle ACB + m\angle ACD$, so choice E is correct.

11. Pictured below are trapezoids $ABCD$ and $EFGH$ with $\angle A \cong \angle E$, $\angle B \cong \angle F$, $\angle C \cong \angle G$, and $ABCD \cong EFGH$, with $\overline{AB} \parallel \overline{CD}$ and $\overline{EF} \parallel \overline{GH}$. The measure of $\angle B$ is 95°. The measure of $\angle E$ is 65°. What is the measure of $\angle H$?

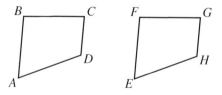

A. 95°
B. 115°
C. 130°
D. 150°
E. The answer cannot be determined from the given information.

11. The correct answer is B. Adjacent angles in a trapezoid are supplementary, so the measure of $\angle H$ is equal to 180° − 65° = 115°.

12. In the parallelogram *ABCD* below, the measure of ∠*DAB* is 72°, and the measure of ∠*BDC* is 28°. What is the measure of ∠*ADB* ?

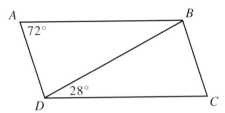

    F. 28°
    G. 70°
    H. 72°
    J. 80°
    K. 90°

12. The correct answer is J. The sum of the interior angles of a parallelogram is 360°. Since the shape has two sets of equal angles, the sum of the measures of angles *A* and *D* is 180° degrees. Thus, the measure of ∠*ADB* = 180° − 28° − 72° = 80°.

16.4.5 Set Five

13. In $\triangle QRT$ below, $\overline{RT}$ is perpendicular to $\overline{QT}$, points R, S, and T are collinear, and $\overline{QS}$ bisects $\angle TQR$. If the measure of $\angle SRQ$ is 30°, what is the measure of $\angle RSQ$?

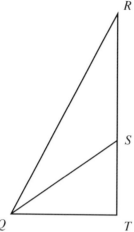

A. 60°
B. 115°
C. 120°
D. 135°
E. 150°

13. The correct answer is C. The measure of $\angle R$ is given as 30°, and since the two legs are perpendicular, the measure of $\angle T$ is 90°. The measure of $\angle Q$ is thus 180° − 30° − 90° = 60°, and since $\overline{QS}$ bisects $\angle Q$, the measure of $\angle RQS$ is half of 60, or 30°. The measure of $\angle RSQ$ is equal to 180° − 30° − 30° = 120°.

---

14. In $\triangle ABC$, $\angle B$ measures exactly 101° and $\angle C$ measures less than 34°. Which of the following best describes the measure of $\angle A$?

F. Less than 45°
G. Greater than 45°
H. Equal to 34°
J. Equal to 45°
K. Equal to 135°

14. The correct answer is G. The measure of $\angle A$ is at least 180° − 101° − 34° = 45°, so it must be greater than 45°.

15. In the figure below, 2 nonadjacent sides of a regular hexagon (6 congruent sides and 6 congruent angles) are extended until they meet at a point Z. What is the measure of ∠Z ?

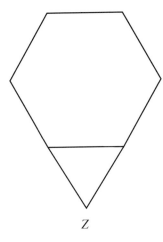

Z

A. 15°
B. 30°
C. 60°
D. 120°
E. Cannot be determined from the given information

15. The correct answer is C. The measure of each interior angle of the hexagon is equal to $\frac{720°}{6}$ = 120°. The triangle formed below is equilateral, so each angle is equal. Use the laws of supplementary angles to calculate the measure of one angle of the triangle, which is equivalent to ∠Z: 180° − 120° = 60°.

ACT® Mastery Math

Sum It Up

Angle Properties

Angle
A figure formed by two rays that connect at the vertex

Degrees
The measurement of an angle, denoted by the ° symbol

Parallel Lines
Two lines in a plane that never intersect or touch

Perpendicular Lines
Two lines in a plane that intersect at a 90° angle

Transversal Line
A line that passes through two lines in a plane

Obtuse Angle
An angle greater than 90° but less than 180°

Acute Angle
An angle that is less than 90°

Supplementary Angles
Two angles whose measures add up to 180°

Complementary Angles
Two angles whose measures add up to 90°

Vertical/Opposite Angles
The angles opposite one another when two lines in a plane cross; they are always equal

Corresponding Angles
Angles in the same position when a transversal cuts across parallel lines; they are always equal

Congruency
Equal in length or measure
Congruent angles have the same measure, and congruent lines have the same length. Congruent polygons have congruent angles and lines.

Tips and Techniques

Objects in Mirror Are Exactly as They Appear: Use the picture to help you arrive at your answer, especially if you are stuck.

Entrance Ticket   Learning Targets   Angle Properties of Triangles   Angle Properties of Other Polygons   ACT Practice   Sum It Up

252

16.5 Exit Ticket

► Students complete the three questions on their exit ticket.

Students are timed 3 minutes for the three questions (60 seconds per question). There is no break between questions.

16.5 Exit Ticket Review

▶ Students work the first question.

1. **The correct answer is E.** Because of the properties of angles made by a transversal crossing parallel lines, ∠TRQ is the same as ∠RTS, or 15°. This means the measure of ∠QTS is 22 + 15 or 37°. Because this is an isosceles trapezoid, the two base angles are equal and the sum of all the angles is 360°. The sum of the two top angles, therefore, is 360 − 2(37) = 286. Divide this by two to find the measure of one of the top angles: 286 ÷ 2 = 143°. The measure of ∠TRS is equal to 143 − 15 = 128°.

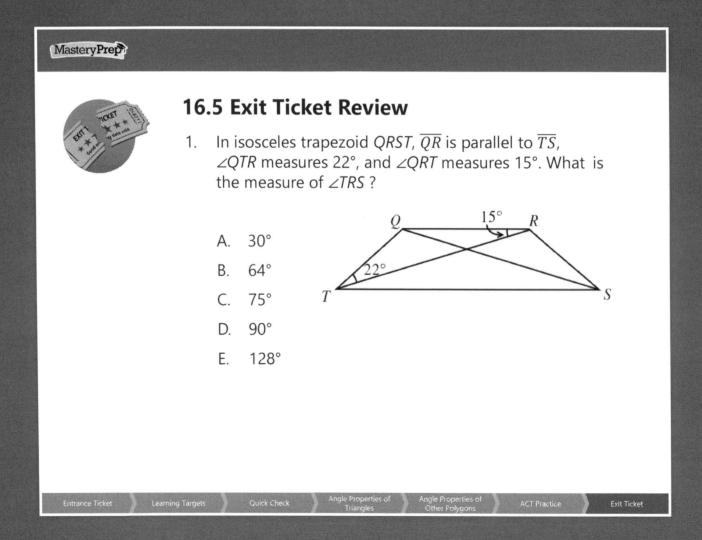

MasteryPrep

16.5 Exit Ticket Review

1. In isosceles trapezoid QRST, $\overline{QR}$ is parallel to $\overline{TS}$, ∠QTR measures 22°, and ∠QRT measures 15°. What is the measure of ∠TRS ?

    A. 30°

    B. 64°

    C. 75°

    D. 90°

    E. 128°

Entrance Ticket | Learning Targets | Quick Check | Angle Properties of Triangles | Angle Properties of Other Polygons | ACT Practice | Exit Ticket

16.5 Exit Ticket Review

► Students work the second question.

2. **The correct answer is G.** The values of two of the angles in the triangle given are 180° − 67° = 113° and 180° − 123° = 57°. Since the angles of a triangle add up to 180°, the measure of ∠y is given by 180° − 113° − 57° = 10°.

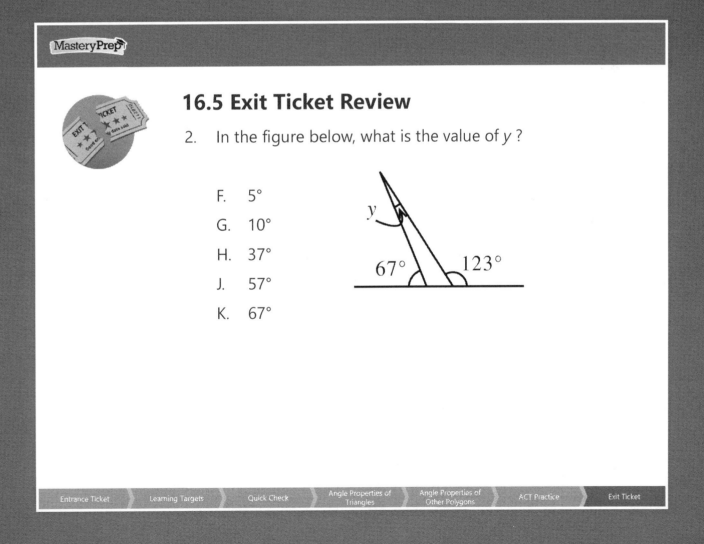

MasteryPrep

16.5 Exit Ticket Review

2. In the figure below, what is the value of *y* ?

F. 5°

G. 10°

H. 37°

J. 57°

K. 67°

Entrance Ticket   Learning Targets   Quick Check   Angle Properties of Triangles   Angle Properties of Other Polygons   ACT Practice   Exit Ticket

451

16.5 Exit Ticket Review

▶ Students work the third question.

    3. The correct answer is A. The measure of ∠A is at most 180° − 89° − 25° = 66°, so its measure must be less than 66°.

▶ After all three questions are completed, students exchange papers. Solve the three exit items step by step on the board. Students grade using their red pens and then return papers to their classmates.

▶ After solving the three exit items, revisit the learning targets slide. Students again assess their knowledge and confidence on the same 1 to 4 scale that they used at the beginning of the lesson. Students write this number in the designated area at the start of the lesson in their workbooks, along with any comments or questions they might have.

▶ Finally, to close the lesson, have students return to the cover page of the lesson and write a caption for the picture there. The caption should be a one-sentence summary of the lesson, a main rule or tip they want to remember, or an explanation of how the picture relates to the topic. If there is additional time, students can share and compare their captions with the class.

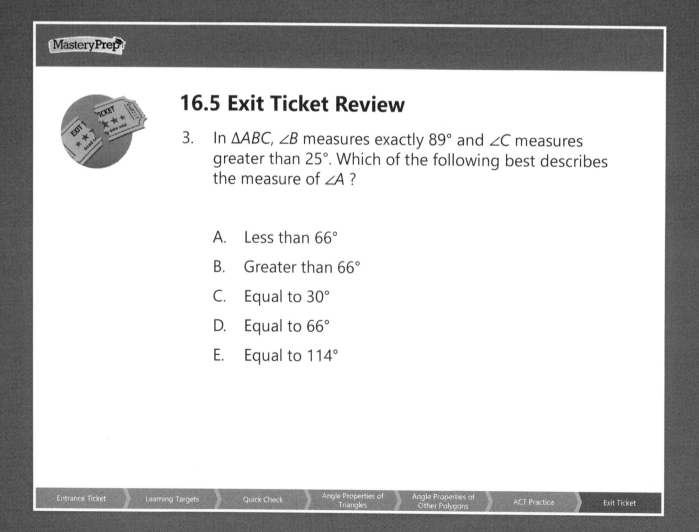

MasteryPrep

16.5 Exit Ticket Review

3.   In △ABC, ∠B measures exactly 89° and ∠C measures greater than 25°. Which of the following best describes the measure of ∠A ?

    A.   Less than 66°

    B.   Greater than 66°

    C.   Equal to 30°

    D.   Equal to 66°

    E.   Equal to 114°

Entrance Ticket | Learning Targets | Quick Check | Angle Properties of Triangles | Angle Properties of Other Polygons | ACT Practice | Exit Ticket